Workshop on Translation Quality Estimation and Automatic Post-Editing 2018

Held at AMTA 2018

Boston, Massachusetts, USA
21 March 2018

ISBN: 978-1-5108-6729-1

Printed from e-media with permission by:

Curran Associates, Inc.
57 Morehouse Lane
Red Hook, NY 12571

Some format issues inherent in the e-media version may also appear in this print version.

Copyright© (2018) by the Association for Computational Linguistics
All rights reserved.

Printed by Curran Associates, Inc. (2018)

For permission requests, please contact the Association for Computational Linguistics
at the address below.

Association for Computational Linguistics
209 N. Eighth Street
Stroudsburg, Pennsylvania 18360

Phone: 1-570-476-8006
Fax: 1-570-476-0860

acl@aclweb.org

Additional copies of this publication are available from:

Curran Associates, Inc.
57 Morehouse Lane
Red Hook, NY 12571 USA
Phone: 845-758-0400
Fax: 845-758-2633
Email: curran@proceedings.com
Web: www.proceedings.com

Contents

The 13th Conference of
The Association for Machine Translation
in the Americas
www.conference.amtaweb.org

WORKSHOP PROCEEDINGS
March 21, 2018

Translation Quality Estimation and Automatic Post-Editing

Organizers: Ramón Astudillo (Unbabel, INESC-ID)
João Graça (Unbabel)
André Martins (Unbabel, University of Lisbon)

INTRODUCTION

The goal of quality estimation is to evaluate a translation system's quality without access to reference translations (Blatz et al., 2004; Specia et al., 2013). This has many potential usages: informing an end user about the reliability of translated content; deciding if a translation is ready for publishing or if it requires human post-editing; highlighting the words that need to be changed. Quality estimation systems are particularly appealing for crowd-sourced and professional translation services, due to their potential to dramatically reduce post-editing times and to save labor costs (Specia, 2011). The increasing interest in this problem from an industrial angle comes as no surprise (Turchi et al., 2014; de Souza et al., 2015; Martins et al., 2016, 2017; Kozlova et al., 2016). A related task is that of automatic post-editing (Simard et al. (2007), Junczys-Dowmunt and Grundkiewicz (2016)), which aims to automatically correct the output of machine translation. Recent work (Martins, 2017, Kim et al., 2017, Hokamp, 2017) has shown that the tasks of quality estimation and automatic post-editing benefit from being trained or stacked together.

In this workshop, we will bring together researchers and industry practitioners interested in the tasks of quality estimation (word, sentence, or document level) and automatic post-editing, both from a research perspective and with the goal of applying these systems in industrial settings for routing, for improving translation quality, or for making human post-editors more efficient. Special emphasis will be given to the case of neural machine translation and the new open problems that it poses for quality estimation and automatic post-editing.

The workshop will consist of one full day of technical presentations, including a tentative number of 6 invited talks and 1 contributed talk, followed by a 30-minutes panel discussion. There will be a poster session featuring the papers accepted for publication in the workshop proceedings.

The workshop organizers,

André Martins (Unbabel and University of Lisbon)
andre.martins@unbabel.com

Ramon Astudillo (Unbabel and INESC-ID Lisboa)
ramon@unbabel.com

João Graça (Unbabel)
joao@unbabel.com

PROGRAM

9:00 — Welcome

9:15 - 10:00 — Nicola Ueffing: "Automatic Post-Editing and Machine Translation Quality Estimation at eBay"

10:00 - 10:30 — Rebecca Knowles: "Lightweight Word-Level Confidence Estimation for Neural Interactive Translation Prediction"

10:30 - 11:00 — Coffee Break

11:00 - 11:45 — João Graça: "Unbabel: How to combine AI with the crowd to scale professional-quality translation"

11:45 - 12:30 — Maxim Khalilov: "Machine translation at Booking.com: what's next?"

12:30 - 14:00 — Lunch break

14:00 - 14:45 — Marcin Junczys-Dowmunt: "Are we experiencing the Golden Age of Automatic Post-Editing?"

14:45 - 15:30 — Marcello Federico: "Challenges in Adaptive Neural Machine Translation"

15:30 - 16:00 — Coffee Break

16:00 - 16:20 — Eleftherios Avramidis: "Fine-grained evaluation of Quality Estimation for Machine translation based on a linguistically-motivated Test Suite"

16:20 - 16:40 — Rebecca Knowles: "A Comparison of Machine Translation Paradigms for Use in Black-Box Fuzzy-Match Repair"

16:45 - 17:30 — Discussion Panel (Nicola Ueffing, Maxim Khalilov, Marcello Federico, Marcin Junczys-Dowmunt, Alon Lavie)

INVITED SPEAKERS

Nicola Ueffing (eBay)

Title: Automatic Post-Editing and Machine Translation Quality Estimation at eBay

Abstract: This presentation will give an overview of Automatic Post-Editing and Quality Estimation research and development for e-commerce data at eBay. I will highlight two projects: (1) Application of Automatic Post-Editing and Machine Translation for Natural Language Generation for e-commerce browse pages, where the structured data describing the products is automatically "translated" into natural language; and (2) Quality Estimation for Machine Translation of eBay item titles, which compares general models and models which are specifically trained for three different categories in the inventory of eBay's marketplace platform for prediction of post-edition effort.

Bio: Nicola joined eBay's machine translation research team in May 2016. Her focus is on machine translation, both for e-commerce content and for natural language generation, and quality estimation. Prior to working for eBay, Nicola was a language modeling research scientist at Nuance Communications, leading the research and development for dictation products like Dragon NaturallySpeaking. Nicola received a PhD in computer science from RWTH Aachen University, specializing in confidence estimation for machine translation. She then joined the Interactive Language Technologies team at the National Research Council Canada as PostDoc research associate. Her research interests include machine translation as well as most other areas of computational natural language processing.

Maxim Khalilov (Booking)

Title: Machine translation at Booking.com: what's next?

Abstract: For many years, machine translation (MT) was primarily focused on the post-editing scenario, in which MT serves as a productivity increase element of a professional translation pipeline. However, in e-commerce the most desirable application of MT is direct publishing of MTed content that dictates different requirements to MT and the MT quality evaluation model.
In this talk, Maxim Khalilov will discuss the Booking.com approach to MT and its evaluation. He will also cover some scenarios in which e-commerce can benefit from advancements in quality estimation and automatic post-editing.

Bio: Maxim Khalilov is a product owner - data science at Booking.com responsible for business aspects of scaled content product development. Prior to his current role, Maxim was a CTO at bmmt GmbH, an innovative German language service provider, an R&D manager at TAUS and a post-doctoral researcher at the University of Amsterdam. Maxim has a Ph.D. from Polytechnic University of Catalonia (Barcelona, 2009), an MBA from IE Business School (Madrid, 2016) and is the author of more than 30 scientific publications.

Marcello Federico (MMT Srl/FBK Trento, Italy)

Title: Challenges in Adaptive Neural Machine Translation

Abstract: Neural machine translation represents today the state of the art in terms of performance. However, its deployment in a real-life and dynamic scenario, where multiple users work on different tasks, presents some important trade-offs and challenges. In my talk, I will describe the development and deployment of adaptive neural machine translation within the ModernMT EU project, from phrase-based to neural machine translation. Besides discussing the technological solutions adopted in ModernMT, I will connect them to the underlying research efforts conducted at FBK in the recent years, including online-learning, automatic post-editing, and translation quality estimation.

Bio: Founder and CEO of MMT Srl, Trento, Italy. Research director (on leave) and Affiliated Fellow at Fondazione Bruno Kessler, Trento, Italy. Lecturer at the ICT International Doctoral School of the University of Trento. Co-founder and scientific advisor of MateCat Srl. Research interests: machine translation, natural language processing, machine learning and artificial intelligence.

João Graça (Unbabel)

Title: Unbabel: How to combine AI with the crowd to scale professional-quality translation

Abstract: Unbabel is accelerating the shift towards a world without language barriers by enabling trustworthy, seamless and scalable translations between companies and their customers. In this talk we will show how we combine different Machine Learning techniques together with a crowd of non-professional translators and achieve professional-quality translations in an unprecedented speed and scale. We will also show how quality estimation is used in different steps of the pipeline.

Bio: João Graça is currently the CTO of Unbabel. He was previously the data scientist and natural language processing expert at Dezine and Flashgroup. João did his PhD in Natural Language Processing and Machine Learning at Instituto Superior Técnico together with the University of Pennsylvania with Professors Fernando Pereira, Ben Taskar and Luísa Coheur. He is the author of several papers in the area, his main research topics are machine learning with side information, unsupervised learning and machine translation. João is one of the co-founders of the Lisbon Machine Learning Summer School (LxMLS).

Marcin Junczys-Dowmunt (Microsoft Research)

Title: Are we experiencing the Golden Age of Automatic Post-Editing?

Abstract: In this talk I will describe the rise of neural methods in Automatic Post-Editing and why I believe that we might have reached a "Golden Age" of (neural) post-editing methods. This will be mostly based on the example of the recent WMT shared tasks on Automatic Post-Editing and my own contributions to that task. I will contrast current architectures with historic solution and will argue that only now --- with the on-set of neural sequence-to-sequence methods --- automatic post-editing has matured enough to have the potential for practical applications. However, there is a risk that this Golden Age might be very short lived and future results might be much less encouraging than the last two WMT shared task on APE might imply.

Bio: Marcin has been working in the Machine Translation team at Microsoft AI and Research -- Redmond as a Principal NLP Scientist since January 2018. Before joining Microsoft he was an Assistant Professor at the Adam Mickiewicz University in Poznan, Poland, and a visiting researcher in the MT group at the University of Edinburgh. He also collaborated for many years with the World Intellectual Property Organization and the United Nations, helping with the development of their in-house statistical and neural machine translation systems. His main research interests are neural machine translation, automatic post-editing and grammatical error correction. Most of his open-source activity is being eaten up by his NMT pet-project Marian (http://github.com/marian-nmt/marian).

Automatic Post-Editing and Machine Translation Quality Estimation at eBay
Nicola Ueffing
eBay MTScience Team
2018-03-21, AMTA Workshop

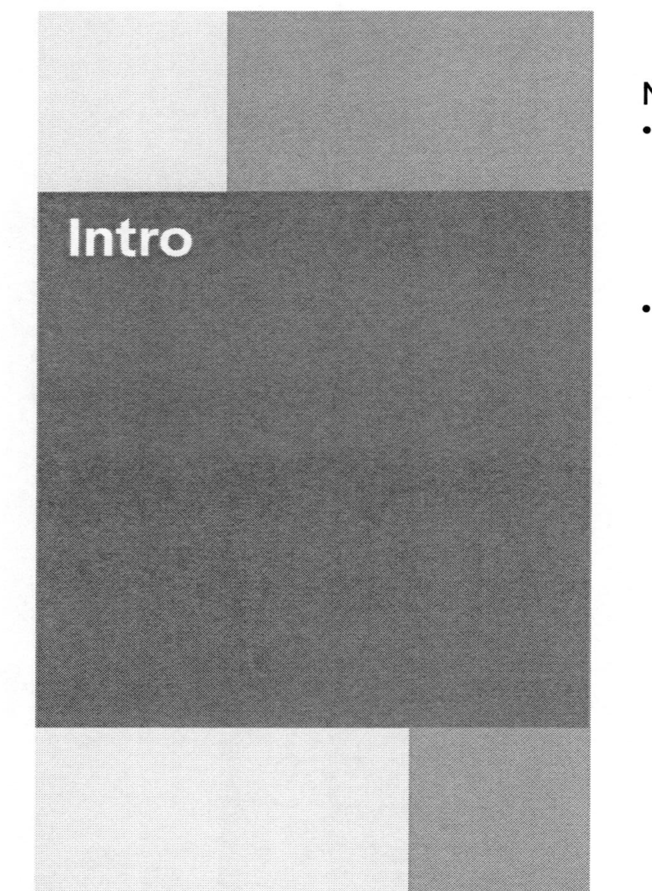

Nicola Ueffing
- Research scientist on eBay's machine translation research team since May 2016
  - machine translation for e-commerce content and for natural language generation (incl. APE)
  - A bit of quality estimation
- Prior to eBay:
  - research scientist at Nuance Communications (e.g. Dragon NaturallySpeaking)
  - PostDoc at Interactive Language Technologies team, National Research Council Canada
  - PhD in computer science from RWTH Aachen University: confidence estimation for machine translation

Overview

Proceedings for AMTA 2018 Workshop: Translation Quality Estimation and Automatic Post-Editing

Why MT at
eBay?

A Truly Global
Marketplace
170M
active buyers
57%
of business is
international
190
Markets
1.1B
live listings
Q4 2017

Applications of MT technology

Machine Translation
- Enable cross-border trade
- Translate
  - Search queries
  - Item titles
  - Item descriptions

Browse Pages: Title Generation
- Translate name-value pairs describing items into natural language

Proceedings for AMTA 2018 Workshop: Translation Quality Estimation and Automatic Post-Editing

Automatic
Post-Editing
for Browse
Page Titles
ebay

How to explore the many items on eBay?

Browse Pages

Idea:
Create permanent "browse" pages for all items & products within a category that share a certain set of name-value pairs, e.g.
- In category "Light Bulbs"
- "Wattage" = "9W"
- "Bulb Shape Code" = "E27"

Users can then navigate to
- Related/refined browse pages
- Hot offers
- Individual products

=> Also beneficial for Search Engines

How to explore so many items?

Browse Pages

Proceedings for AMTA 2018 Workshop: Translation Quality Estimation and Automatic Post-Editing

Why automatic title generation?

eBay is present
- in dozens of countries
- with thousands of categories
- with hundreds of thousands of name-value pairs
  (products aspects aka slots)

→Millions of potential browse pages (and titles)
  required!

Browse Pages

Proceedings for AMTA 2018 Workshop: Translation Quality Estimation and Automatic Post-Editing

Step 1:
rule-based title generation

Browse Pages

First approach we implemented for German:
Rule-based approach
1. Use hand-written heuristics / shallow parsers to classify each slot
2. Order slots based on slot classes
3. Realize each slot separately based on slot class
   - Use dedicated heuristics for certain combinations, e.g. Category + Product Type
4. Concatenate realizations

Proceedings for AMTA 2018 Workshop: Translation Quality Estimation and Automatic Post-Editing

Step 2:
APE

Browse Pages

For German, we have
- Millions of browse page titles in a slightly artificial language
  (our output from rule-based system)
- Parallel titles in a "natural" language (human curated titles)

=> train an APE system on those

e.g. translate
Kaukasische Wohnraum-Teppiche für Patchwork
into
Kaukasische Wohnraum-Teppiche mit Patchwork-Muster

Proceedings for AMTA 2018 Workshop: Translation Quality Estimation and Automatic Post-Editing

APE
Pros & Cons

Browse Pages

Pro
+ Straight forward
+ Large improvements in quality
+ Easy to integrate

Con
- Can only fix data that's there (can't reconstruct missing slots, slot names or context, ...)
- Sometimes learns artifacts from data (esp. when noisy)
- Will learn curation rules present when titles were created

Proceedings for AMTA 2018 Workshop: Translation Quality Estimation and Automatic Post-Editing

APE Evaluation Results

Browse Pages

corpus	curated titles: #tokens
train	3.8M
dev	8.8k
test	8.8k

Evaluation on test

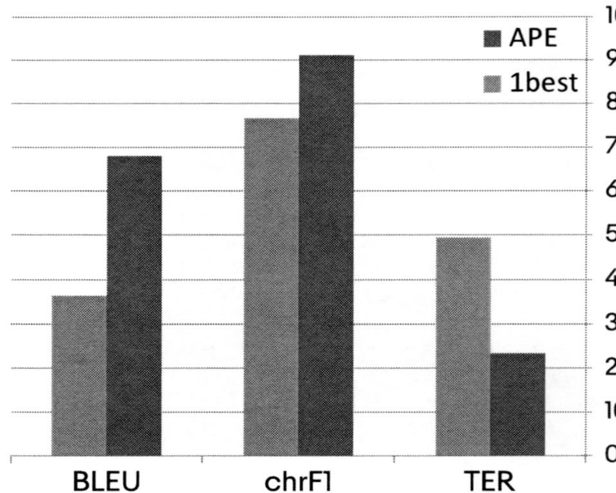

Proceedings for AMTA 2018 Workshop: Translation Quality Estimation and Automatic Post-Editing

MTQE for
e-commerce
content
ebay

eBay item titles

Intro

Item Titles
- Relatively free word order
- +adequacy
- -fluency

Categories (e-commerce), e.g.
- Cellphones & Smart Phones
- Women's Clothing
- Car Parts & Accessories
- Cycling
- Fishing
- Skin Care
- Jewelry
- …

Proceedings for AMTA 2018 Workshop: Translation Quality Estimation and Automatic Post-Editing

eBay item titles

Intro

Examples:

- For Samsung Galaxy S5 i9600 S V TPU Crystal Clear Soft Case Ultra Thin Cover NEw
- 0.3mm Thin Crystal Clear Soft Silicone Fitted Case Skin Cover For iPhone 6 4.7"
- Universal 12000mAh Backup External Battery USB Power Bank Charger for Cell Phone
- Luxury Slim Aluminum Alloy Metal Bumper Frame Case/Cover For Apple iPhone 5 5S
- Luxury Ultra thin Metal Aluminum Bumper Case PC Cover For Samsung Galaxy Note 3
- 50000mAh Portable Super Solar Charger Dual USB External Battery Power Bank DX
- Sausage boiler broth boiler butcher's boiler boiler pot boiler insert
- Rasta wig with dreadlocks Rasta Hat Rasta braids
- CUTE HELLO KITTY Stuffed Plush 12" so CUUUUUUUTE!!!!(FREE SHIPPING in USA)

Proceedings for AMTA 2018 Workshop: Translation Quality Estimation and Automatic Post-Editing

eBay item titles

Data

Data

- English-Portuguese
- Phrase-based Statistical MT
- Based on post-edition effort (HTER)
- Approx. 11k translated segments which are post-edited
- 223 different e-commerce categories

Proceedings for AMTA 2018 Workshop: Translation Quality Estimation and Automatic Post-Editing

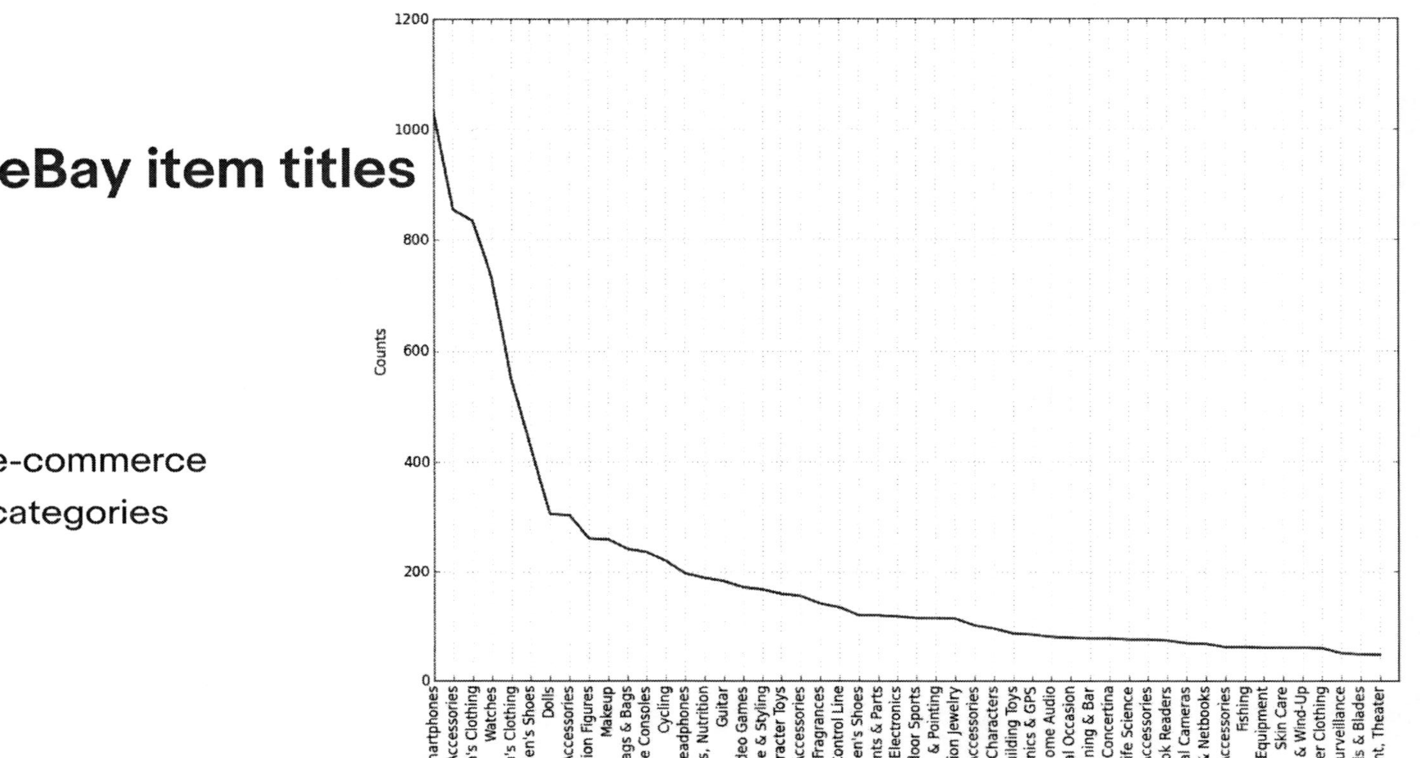

Proceedings for AMTA 2018 Workshop: Translation Quality Estimation and Automatic Post-Editing

eBay item titles

Post-edition effort per
category

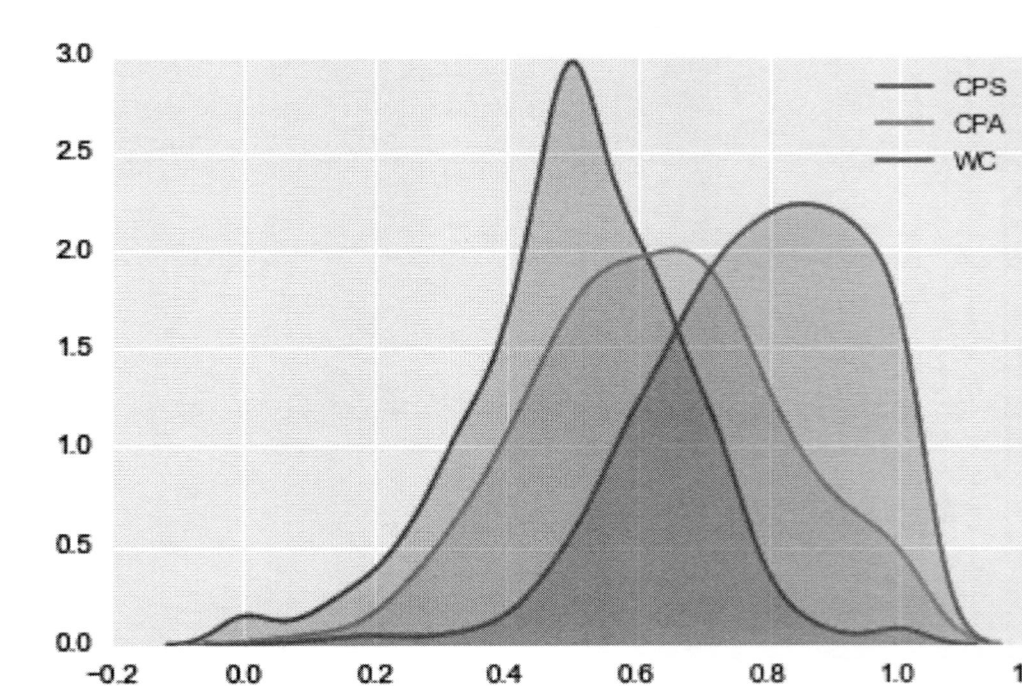

Proceedings for AMTA 2018 Workshop: Translation Quality Estimation and Automatic Post-Editing

Quality Estimation

Features

79 QuEst features:
- Black-box
- Complexity
- Adequacy
- Fluency

Item title embeddings
- Adequacy
- Concatenation of source and translation embeddings
- From paragraph2vec

NER-based
- Adequacy
- Numbers and ratio of NER tags found in source and translation

Proceedings for AMTA 2018 Workshop: Translation Quality Estimation and Automatic Post-Editing

Quality Estimation

Learning algorithms

Extremely Randomized Trees

- Ensemble of decision trees
- Random forests
  - Build on random samples from training data
  - Choose best split for random subset of features
- Extremely randomized: additionally choose best threshold from random set of thresholds

AdaBoost

- Sequence of weak learners (very small decision trees)
- Fit them on original dataset
- Then fit additional copies of classifier on same data, but adjust weights of incorrectly classified instances s.t. subsequent classifiers focus more on difficult cases
- Final prediction: weighted majority vote of all iterations
- Time consuming

Both:

- Non-linear
- Provides feature importances

Proceedings for AMTA 2018 Workshop: Translation Quality Estimation and Automatic Post-Editing

Quality Estimation

Experimental setup

- regression
- HTER labels clipped in [0, 1]
- 75/25 train/test splits
- Model selection
  - Randomized search with 5-fold cross validation (100 iterations)
  - Optimized for mean absolute error
- Evaluation
  - mean absolute error (MAE) ↓
  - Pearson's correlation ↑

Proceedings for AMTA 2018 Workshop: Translation Quality Estimation and Automatic Post-Editing

Quality Estimation

Experimental results I

Cellphones & Accessories

	Extremely Randomized Trees		AdaBoost	
	MAE↓	Pearson↑	MAE↓	Pearson↑
Baseline: Mean	15.4	0	15.4	0
QuEst79	14.3	47.3	13.6	50.3
QuEst79 + embeddings	14.3	47.6	13.8	46.4
QuEst79 + NER	**13.8**	**50.4**	**13.1**	**56.0**
QuEst79 + NER + embeddings	**13.8**	49.9	13.5	51.9

Proceedings for AMTA 2018 Workshop: Translation Quality Estimation and Automatic Post-Editing

Quality Estimation

Cellphones & Smartphones

	Extremely Randomized Trees		AdaBoost	
	MAE↓	Pearson↑	MAE↓	Pearson↑
Baseline: Mean	12.9	0	12.9	0
QuEst79	12.4	39.6	11.7	45.6
QuEst79 + embeddings	12.5	38.7	12.2	41.6
QuEst79 + NER	**12.2**	**44.2**	**11.1**	**53.5**
QuEst79 + NER + embeddings	12.3	43.4	11.8	49.3

Experimental results II

Quality Estimation

Women's Clothing

	Extremely Randomized Trees		AdaBoost	
	MAE↓	Pearson↑	MAE↓	Pearson↑
Baseline: Mean	13.0	0	13.0	0
QuEst79	**12.8**	**13.2**	13.1	6.8
QuEst79 + embeddings	12.9	10.0	**12.6**	**11.3**
QuEst79 + NER	12.8	12.2	12.9	10.8
QuEst79 + NER + embeddings	12.9	7.2	12.7	4.1

Experimental results III

- Fewer named entities than other 2 categories
- More generic description of items
- ⇒ NER not very helpful
- Many bad translations

Proceedings for AMTA 2018 Workshop: Translation Quality Estimation and Automatic Post-Editing

Quality Estimation

Analysis

- Quality prediction in the tails of the test set distribution is problematic
- Tails equals to
  - Good translations (HTER close to 0)
  - Bad translations (HTER close to 1)

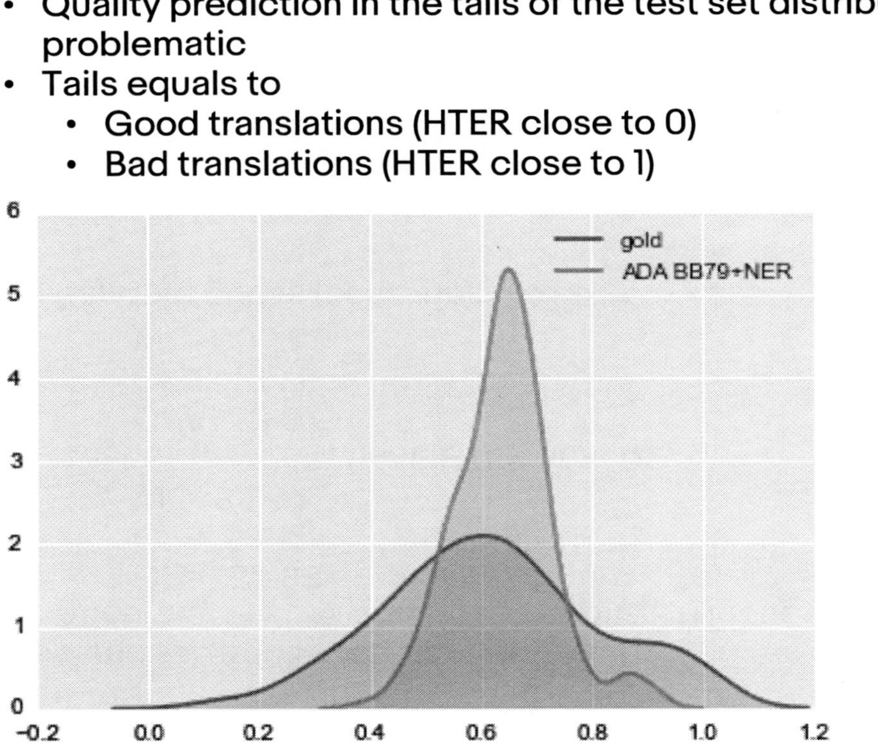

Analysis

Proceedings for AMTA 2018 Workshop: Translation Quality Estimation and Automatic Post-Editing

Quality Estimation

Analysis

Analysis

Best model, AdaBoost:
- Accuracy @ 25% worst translations (HTER near 1)
  - CPA: 52.83
  - CPS: 53.12
  - WC: 32.69
- Accuracy @ 25% best (HTER near 0)
  - CPA: 60.37
  - CPS: 43.75
  - WC: 30.76
- Random guess (baseline): ~25%

Proceedings for AMTA 2018 Workshop: Translation Quality Estimation and Automatic Post-Editing

Quality Estimation

Conclusion

- Best feature set on average: Quest79 + NER
- AdaBoost presents the best accuracy, but slow
- Extremely Randomized Trees offer best trade-off between accuracy and computing time
- Models can predict bad and good translations with more than 50% accuracy
- Models for single categories, no pooling

Proceedings for AMTA 2018 Workshop: Translation Quality Estimation and Automatic Post-Editing

Ongoing
research
ebay

Ongoing research

Ongoing research
- User feedback from star ratings => bandit learning
- Quality estimation for natural language generation (browse page titles)
  - Random forest with features, mix of common and task-specific
  - Neural approach
- (Potential) QE applications
  - Do not display low-quality MT/NLG on site
  - Decide about updating existing title / translation
  - Routing for post edition
  - Data selection for post edition

Proceedings for AMTA 2018 Workshop: Translation Quality Estimation and Automatic Post-Editing

References

Browse page title generation: APE approach and other MT-based methods described in:
International Conference on Natural Language Generation, Santiago de Compostela, Spain, September 2017
Generating titles for millions of browse pages on an e-Commerce site
Prashant Mathur, Nicola Ueffing, Gregor Leusch

Quality Estimation research described in:
MT Summit - User's Track, Miami, Florida, October 2015
MT Quality Estimation for E-Commerce Data
Jose G. C. de Souza, Marcello Federico, Hassan Sawaf

http://research.ebay.com/research-areas/research-machine-translation

Proceedings for AMTA 2018 Workshop: Translation Quality Estimation and Automatic Post-Editing

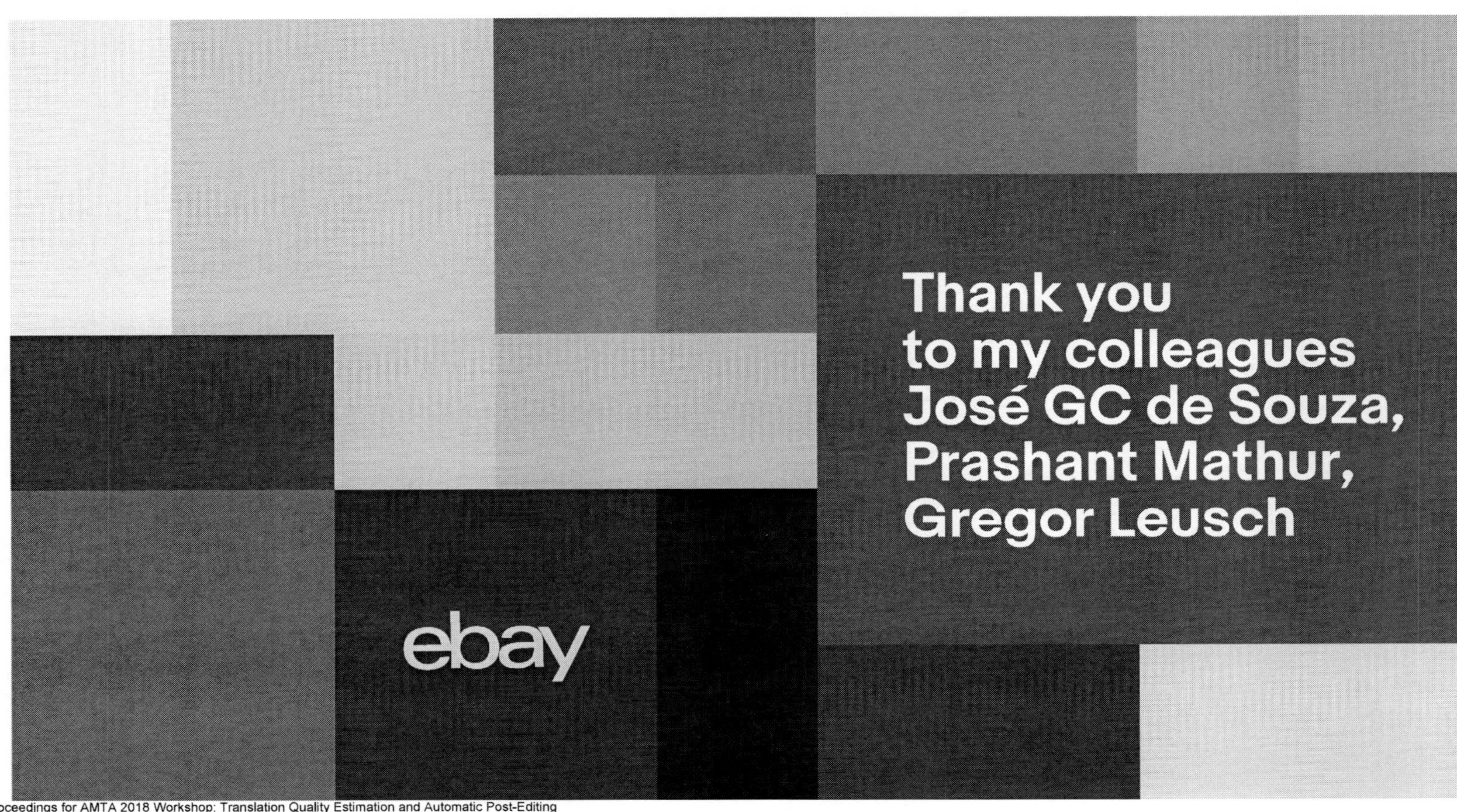

Thank you
to my colleagues
José GC de Souza,
Prashant Mathur,
Gregor Leusch
ebay

Thank You
ebay

Lightweight Word-Level Confidence Estimation
for Neural Interactive Translation Prediction

Rebecca Knowles and **Philipp Koehn**
Department of Computer Science
Center for Language and Speech Processing
Johns Hopkins University
`{rknowles,phi}@jhu.edu`

Abstract

In neural interactive translation prediction, a system provides translation suggestions ("auto-complete" functionality) for human translators. These translation suggestions may be rejected by the translator in predictable ways; being able to estimate confidence in the quality of translation suggestions could be useful in providing additional information for users of the system. We show that a very small set of features (which are already generated as byproducts of the process of translation prediction) can be used in a simple model to estimate confidence for interactive translation prediction.

1 Introduction

In neural interactive translation prediction (Wuebker et al., 2016; Knowles and Koehn, 2016), a human translator interacts with machine translation output by accepting or rejecting suggestions as they type a translation from beginning to end. By accepting a system suggestion, the translator implicitly provides an "OK" quality label for that token. Similarly, by rejecting a suggestion (and providing a correction), they implicitly provide a "BAD" quality label for the system's suggestion.

The system's suggestions may be wrong ("BAD") in predictable ways. For example, if one suggestion is incorrect, the subsequent suggestion may then be more likely to be incorrect. We seek to show that using these implicit labels and model scores we can predict whether subsequent tokens will be accepted as "OK" or rejected as "BAD" by the translator. This confidence estimation has a twofold purpose. First, if we can detect potentially "BAD" tokens before showing them to the translator, we may be able to increase translator trust in suggestions and reduce time spent reading incorrect suggestions, either by indicating confidence (by color, shading, or some other visual indication), providing multiple alternate translation options, or by simply not showing low-confidence predictions to the user. Second, if we can identify "BAD" tokens, we can save on computation. If we are confident that a prediction is wrong, we can wait to predict subsequent tokens until the human translator provides a correction rather than completing a translation that is likely to be rejected. Computer aided translation (CAT) tools such as Lilt[1] or CASMACAT[2] typically provide the translator with either full sentence predictions or predictions consisting of several tokens, which need to be recomputed each time the system is found to have made an erroneous prediction.

Speed is of the essence in interactive translation prediction; predictions (of several tokens or a full sentence) must be computed quickly enough that the translator does not experience lag in the user interface. For this reason, we focus on confidence estimation using a very small set of features that can be collected naturally in the process of the interactive translation prediction computation. We present results based on a simulation using reference text.

2 Related Work

In this work we use a neural machine translation (MT) model that consists of an encoder, a decoder, and an attention mechanism, based on the approach described in Bahdanau et al. (2015). Such systems have been highly successful in recent MT evaluations (Bojar et al., 2017).

Neural MT models have been applied to the task of interactive translation prediction. Interac-

---

[1] `https://lilt.com/`
[2] `http://www.casmacat.eu/`

Figure 1: Example of interactive translation prediction in CASMACAT. The system provides predictions for several tokens, conditioned on the source sentence and the prefix generated by the human translator. Figure from Knowles and Koehn (2016).

tive translation prediction provides a human translator using a CAT tool with functionality similar to "auto-complete" (as provided on smartphones, tablets, etc.). As the translator begins typing a translation, the interactive translation prediction system provides suggestions for the next target-language token(s). Figure 1 provides an example of an interactive translation prediction user interface in CASMACAT. The translator can accept these suggestions (for example by using the TAB key) or they can override them by typing different characters and tokens. Whenever the translator overrides the system suggestions, the system must adapt to the newly extended sentence prefix and provide new suggestions for how to continue the translation. In the case of neural interactive translation prediction,[3] this is quite simple: rather than feeding the originally predicted token (rejected as incorrect by the translator) back into the model to predict the next word, the system instead feeds the translator's token(s) into the model, then continues producing the translation token by token.

Knowles and Koehn (2016) note that the neural interactive translation prediction system recovers well from failure (predicting an incorrect token) when the correct token's model score is also (relatively) high. This suggests the feasibility of using features like the model score (which is already generated by the system) to predict when the system should be more or less confident in the quality of its predictions. Early work on word-level confidence estimation, such as Gandrabur and Foster (2003), focused on estimating the system's confidence in translations in a similar interactive translation prediction setting (using a maxent MT model). González-Rubio et al. (2010b) explored how confidence information might be able to be used in an interactive machine translation setting to lessen human effort, and González-Rubio et al. (2010a) suggested using confidence measures to determine which sentences need human intervention in the form of interactive translation prediction and which are likely to be of high enough quality for the MT output to be used without editing. Both of these focus on interactive machine translation using statistical machine translation.

Today, the task of word-level quality estimation typically focuses on assigning "OK"/"BAD" labels to individual tokens in a full sentence translation (Bojar et al., 2017). This task has been explored in-depth through the shared task on Quality Estimation at WMT, which was initially introduced in 2012 (Callison-Burch et al., 2012). The open-source tool QUEST++ (Specia et al., 2015) provides an implementation of word-, sentence-, and document-level quality estimation, using an extensive set of features that have been found to be useful for the task.

The vital difference between the word-level quality estimation task and confidence estimation for interactive translation prediction is that each human interaction in the interactive translation prediction setting provides a gold-standard "OK"/"BAD" label for a token, such that the full prefix of the sentence is labeled, and the task is now to predict the quality of the next token (potentially conditioning on the previous tokens). Additionally, in the standard word-level quality estimation task, it is possible to extract features from both the full source sentence and the full machine translation output. In the interactive translation prediction setting as we have described it, the target output is produced one word at a time, through interaction with the user, meaning that target side features can only be extracted from the prefix produced so far.

3 Experiments & Results

3.1 Data and MT Systems

We use University of Edinburgh's neural models from WMT 2016 (Sennrich et al., 2016) for the following language pairs and directions:

---

[3]As described in detail in Wuebker et al. (2016) and Knowles and Koehn (2016).

Label	Reference	Suggestion
BAD	here	at
OK	I	I
OK	should	should
BAD	confess	admit
OK	that	that
OK	I	I
OK	am	am
BAD	no	not
OK	expert	expert
OK	,	,
BAD	just	but
BAD	an	a
BAD	earth@@	Earth
BAD	bound	ed
OK	enthusiast	enthusiast
OK	.	.

Figure 2: An example sentence demonstrating how the labels are obtained. A "BAD" label is applied when the predicted token does not match the reference token. The @@ symbol is a product of byte-pair encoding (and would not be displayed to users in a CAT tool).

English-German (en-de), German-English (de-en), English-Czech (en-cs), and Czech-English (cs-en). The models were trained with Nematus (Sennrich et al., 2017) and are available publicly.[4]

We use WMT 2016 test data for training and development and report results on WMT 2017 test data. Both of these data sets consist of between 64,000 and 73,000 tokens.

For each sentence in the data set, we run neural interactive translation prediction (using a modified version of Nematus), simulating the actions of a real user with the reference translation. We use a beam size of 1 for speed. The interactive translation prediction system starts by producing a prediction for the first token; this is compared against the reference, generating an "OK" label if the prediction and reference are equal, and "BAD" otherwise. For each subsequent word, the system produces a prediction (adjusting to the reference as needed) and generates a label for each prediction by comparing it to the reference. Figure 2 provides an example, showing the source sentence, the reference sentence, the output of the interactive translation prediction system simulated against the reference, and the labels assigned. Each target language pair of gold token and prediction is associated with a label and constitutes a single training instance.

---

[4] http://data.statmt.org/rsennrich/
wmt16_systems/

Language Pair	WPA	BLEU
en-de	60.7%	24.2
de-en	62.7%	29.6
en-cs	56.1%	19.1
cs-en	57.0%	24.5

Table 1: Word prediction accuracy (WPA) of neural interactive translation prediction with beam size 1 and BLEU score for standard neural machine translation decoding with beam size 1 on WMT 2017 test set.

ing instance. Using the example in Figure 2, the first token (at) receives the label "BAD" because it does not match the reference, while the second token (I) receives the label "OK" because it does match.

Table 1 shows baseline word prediction accuracy scores on the WMT 2017 test data. Word prediction accuracy (WPA) is calculated as the percentage of the time that the system correctly predicts the next token of the sentence. The WPA is the percentage of the data that has the "OK" label. The slightly lower WPA scores for the Czech language tasks are consistent with the expectation that Czech-English translation is more difficult than German-English. We show the BLEU scores reported on standard decoding with beam size of 1 on WMT 2017 data in Table 1.[5]

3.2 Metrics

Following Logacheva et al. (2016), we report scores for F_1-BAD and F_1-mult (the product of F_1-BAD and F_1-OK scores). F_1-BAD is of interest because we seek in particular to be able to label incorrect predictions (of which there are fewer than correct predictions). F_1-mult has been shown to be more robust to pessimistic classifiers (those which label most tokens as "BAD").

3.3 Features

Here we describe the small set of simple features we explored, all of which are generated as byproducts of the neural interactive translation prediction system's computations. In Table 2 we show baseline results of using simple heuristics (based on the first five features) to predict labels on the training/development data. We also include a baseline

---

[5] Note that larger beam sizes and ensembling do improve performance, which is why these values are lower than the state-of-the-art.

Feature	en-de	de-en	en-cs	cs-en
Uniformly Random	40.9 (23.1)	39.9 (22.8)	44.6 (24.2)	44.1 (24.2)
Correctness of Previous Prediction	42.6 (29.7)	41.2 (29.1)	47.2 (30.4)	47.3 (31.2)
Threshold Gold Tok. Model Score (< 0.99)	51.0 (11.9)	50.0 (16.4)	56.2 (10.0)	55.9 (12.5)
Threshold Predicted Token Score (< 0.99)	50.8 (11.8)	49.9 (12.3)	56.1 (9.8)	55.8 (12.4)
Threshold Score Difference (> 0.99)	49.1 (21.9)	47.5 (21.4)	55.0 (23.1)	53.8 (22.6)
Current Token Model Score (< 0.99)	67.2 (51.9)	66.0 (51.6)	71.0 (52.7)	69.2 (51.6)

Table 2: Performance of simple heuristics for individual features on WMT 2016 data set (used for training and development). The first value is F_1-BAD, and the value in parentheses is F_1-mult.

that assigns the labels (uniformly) randomly.[6]

Correctness of Previous Prediction: Making one error can result in a sequence of errors, so the simplest feature we use is the gold-standard label assigned to the previous token. Since the first token has no previous token from which to draw a label, we set its value for this feature to "OK" (as the majority of tokens are "OK"). On the training data, using this feature as the label (that is, predicting the previous token's gold-standard label as the current token's label) provides an initial baseline.

Gold Token Model Score: We can examine the score that the model assigned to the previous gold-standard token. Knowles and Koehn (2016) note that even when the system did not correctly predict the previous token, it may be more likely to recover well (and predict subsequent tokens correctly) if the model assigned a relatively high score to the gold token. We can use this as a simple classifier by thresholding. While thresholding obtains a higher F_1-BAD score with the threshold of 0.99 (labeling the token as "OK" if the model score is greater than 0.99, and "BAD" otherwise), this produces a very pessimistic classifier, and the F_1-mult score suffers accordingly.

Predicted Token Model Score: In this case, we take the score that the model gave to its previous prediction (which may or may not have been correct), with the intuition that very high scores may indicate higher confidence. We again see that thresholding this value (labeling the token as "OK" if the model score is greater than 0.99, and "BAD" otherwise) produces a pessimistic model.

Score Difference: We compute the difference between the two previous features (gold token model score subtracted from the predicted token model score). This will be 0 when the predicted token was correct. A high difference may indicate a potential error being made by the system (when

the model assigns high probability to its prediction and very low probability to the gold token), which may have an impact on subsequent predictions. Thresholding (labeling the token as "OK" if the difference in scores is less than 0.99, and "BAD" otherwise) this feature results in a higher F_1-mult score and a less pessimistic labeling.

Current Token Model Score: We take the score that the model gave to the current prediction (for which we are currently trying to predict the "OK" or "BAD" label). Again, this is based on the intuition that very high scores may indicate higher confidence.

Index: We add the index of the word in the sentence as a feature.

First token: We add a feature that indicates if the token is the first token in a sentence.

3.4 Evaluation

In addition to using thresholding or simple heuristics with the features, we train logistic regression classifiers with scikit-learn (Pedregosa et al., 2011) on the WMT 2016 data set, using class weighting (with a weight of 2 on "BAD"). All other parameters are set to defaults, including the threshold. We report results on the WMT 2017 test sets in Table 3.

We find that the Current Token Model Score feature drastically outperforms all other features when thresholded, obtaining the best results in terms of F_1-BAD on train and test data. The logistic regression model that includes it and all other features shows slight improvements in terms of F_1-mult (at the cost of slight losses to F_1-BAD).

If we restrict ourselves to the features available before the new token is predicted, we find that the logistic regression model (without the Current Token Model Score) outperforms baselines in terms of F_1-BAD and the threshold score difference baseline in terms of F_1-mult on the en-cs and

---

[6]Averaged across 5 runs.

Model	en-de	de-en	en-cs	cs-en
Baseline (Random)	44.2 (24.3)	42.5 (23.6)	46.7 (24.7)	46.2 (24.6)
Baseline (Corr. of Prev. Pred.)	47.0 (31.0)	44.9 (30.3)	50.4 (31.1)	50.2 (31.5)
Baseline (Threshold Score Diff.)	53.7 (22.3)	51.5 (22.3)	58.0 (23.2)	57.2 (22.9)
Logistic Regression Model (w/o Curr. Tok.)	52.5 (30.1)	50.0 (30.8)	59.6 (25.2)	58.7 (27.2)
Baseline (Threshold Curr. Tok. Model Score)	69.6 (51.2)	68.2 (51.5)	73.0 (52.4)	70.5 (49.0)
Logistic Regression Model (with Curr. Tok.)	68.8 (53.5)	67.6 (52.8)	72.8 (54.3)	70.1 (51.1)

Table 3: Results on WMT 2017 test data. We show baselines and models built with and without the Current Token Model Score. The first value is F_1-BAD, and the value in parentheses is F_1-mult.

cs-en data. For the en-de and de-en data, we find that it outperforms the threshold score difference baseline in terms of F_1-mult and the correctness of previous prediction baseline in terms of F_1-BAD.

4   Conclusions and Future Work

A very small set of features can be used in a simple trained model or even with simple heuristics to estimate confidence for interactive translation prediction. This work provides a proof-of-concept of how this can be done for neural interactive translation in particular, using the sorts of features that are already produced in the process of generating predictions, which is desirable in a setting that requires very fast computation in order to serve translations to the user without lag.

We worked with a very limited feature set here, drawing on intuitions from previous work on interactive translation prediction. One could certainly explore a wide range of more complex features, such as the number of previous errors, the number of tokens since the last error, sparse word-specific features, or even features derived from the attention mechanism (as proposed by Rikters and Fishel (2017) for general MT confidence estimation). It would also be interesting to explore the types of features used in QUEST++ (Specia et al., 2015) and other word-level quality estimation systems which are applicable to this setting.[7] In this model, we only use features that reference the current or previous token or the position of the token in the sentence; a longer history (such as sequences of errors) may also be a fruitful avenue to explore. We have used a simple, out-of-the-box

model; in particular we did not optimize specifically for either of the metrics, nor did we make significant efforts to elegantly handle the label imbalance in labels. Attention to both of these areas could easily result in improvement.

While we evaluated with F_1-BAD and F_1-mult, it may also be useful to evaluate the system in terms of the computational costs saved by holding off on making full sentence predictions following low-confidence tokens. This, or a user-centric metric (like those described in Gandrabur and Foster (2003)) could also be valuable. Ueffing and Ney (2005) propose an evaluation metric called prediction F-measure, which incorporates the keystroke ratio that models human effort by the number of keystroke actions needed to complete translations.

Additionally, there is work to be done on the user interface side to determine how best to use confidence estimation for interactive translation prediction. What is the best way to communicate the confidence estimate to the user? Is it sufficient to use a visual representation (color, shading), or would it be preferable to show multiple suggestions or (no suggestions) when the system is not confident? Answering these questions would certainly require user studies rather than simulations. It would also be interesting to explore possible differences between real data from user interactions and our simulations using references.

Acknowledgments

We thank the reviewers for their thoughtful comments, suggestions, and advice. This work was partially supported by a National Science Foundation Graduate Research Fellowship under Grant No. DGE-1232825 (to the first author). The first author thanks her 2018 Raymond Kayser Bonspiel teammates for their patience during the submission process.

---

[7]Since QUEST++ is used for quality estimation after a full translation is produced, we would need to use a modified subset of these features for interactive translation prediction confidence estimation. For example, we could not use n-gram features that include target context beyond the sequence of tokens generated so far.

References

Dzmitry Bahdanau, Kyunghyun Cho, and Yoshua Bengio. 2015. Neural machine translation by jointly learning to align and translate. In *ICLR*.

Ondřej Bojar, Rajen Chatterjee, Christian Federmann, Yvette Graham, Barry Haddow, Shujian Huang, Matthias Huck, Philipp Koehn, Qun Liu, Varvara Logacheva, Christof Monz, Matteo Negri, Matt Post, Raphael Rubino, Lucia Specia, and Marco Turchi. 2017. Findings of the 2017 conference on machine translation (wmt17). In *Proceedings of the Second Conference on Machine Translation, Volume 2: Shared Task Papers*, pages 169–214, Copenhagen, Denmark. Association for Computational Linguistics.

Chris Callison-Burch, Philipp Koehn, Christof Monz, Matt Post, Radu Soricut, and Lucia Specia. 2012. Findings of the 2012 workshop on statistical machine translation. In *Proceedings of the Seventh Workshop on Statistical Machine Translation*, pages 10–48, Montreal, Canada. Association for Computational Linguistics.

Simona Gandrabur and George Foster. 2003. Confidence estimation for translation prediction. In *Proceedings of the Seventh Conference on Natural Language Learning at HLT-NAACL 2003 - Volume 4*, CONLL '03, pages 95–102, Stroudsburg, PA, USA. Association for Computational Linguistics.

Jesús González-Rubio, Daniel Ortiz-Martínez, and Francisco Casacuberta. 2010a. Balancing user effort and translation error in interactive machine translation via confidence measures. In *Proceedings of the ACL 2010 Conference Short Papers*, ACLShort '10, pages 173–177, Stroudsburg, PA, USA. Association for Computational Linguistics.

Jesús González-Rubio, Daniel Ortiz-Martínez, and Francisco Casacuberta. 2010b. On the use of confidence measures within an interactive-predictive machine translation system. In *Proceedings of 14th Annual Conference of the European Association for Machine Translation*.

Rebecca Knowles and Philipp Koehn. 2016. Neural interactive translation prediction. In *Proceedings of the Conference of the Association for Machine Translation in the Americas (AMTA)*.

Varvara Logacheva, Michal Lukasik, and Lucia Specia. 2016. Metrics for evaluation of word-level machine translation quality estimation. In *Proceedings of the 54th Annual Meeting of the Association for Computational Linguistics (Volume 2: Short Papers)*, pages 585–590, Berlin, Germany. Association for Computational Linguistics.

F. Pedregosa, G. Varoquaux, A. Gramfort, V. Michel, B. Thirion, O. Grisel, M. Blondel, P. Prettenhofer, R. Weiss, V. Dubourg, J. Vanderplas, A. Passos, D. Cournapeau, M. Brucher, M. Perrot, and E. Duchesnay. 2011. Scikit-learn: Machine learning in Python. *Journal of Machine Learning Research*, 12:2825–2830.

Matss Rikters and Mark Fishel. 2017. Confidence Through Attention. In *Proceedings of the 16th Machine Translation Summit (MT Summit 2017)*, Nagoya, Japan.

Rico Sennrich, Orhan Firat, Kyunghyun Cho, Alexandra Birch, Barry Haddow, Julian Hitschler, Marcin Junczys-Dowmunt, Samuel Läubli, Antonio Valerio Miceli Barone, Jozef Mokry, and Maria Nadejde. 2017. Nematus: a toolkit for neural machine translation. In *Proceedings of the Software Demonstrations of the 15th Conference of the European Chapter of the Association for Computational Linguistics*, pages 65–68, Valencia, Spain. Association for Computational Linguistics.

Rico Sennrich, Barry Haddow, and Alexandra Birch. 2016. Edinburgh neural machine translation systems for WMT 16. In *Proceedings of the First Conference on Machine Translation (WMT)*.

Lucia Specia, Gustavo Paetzold, and Carolina Scarton. 2015. Multi-level translation quality prediction with quest++. In *ACL-IJCNLP 2015 System Demonstrations*, pages 115–120, Beijing, China.

Nicola Ueffing and Hermann Ney. 2005. Application of word-level confidence measures in interactive statistical machine translation. In *In Proceedings of EAMT 2005 (10th Annual Conference of the European Association for Machine Translation*, pages 262–270.

Joern Wuebker, Spence Green, John DeNero, Sasa Hasan, and Minh-Thang Luong. 2016. Models and inference for prefix-constrained machine translation. In *Proceedings of the 54th Annual Meeting of the Association for Computational Linguistics (Volume 1: Long Papers)*, pages 66–75, Berlin, Germany. Association for Computational Linguistics.

Building universal understanding

Combining Crowd and AI
to scale professional-quality translation

João Graça
CTO

Proceedings for AMTA 2018 Workshop: Translation Quality Estimation and Automatic Post-Editing

The internet, 1997

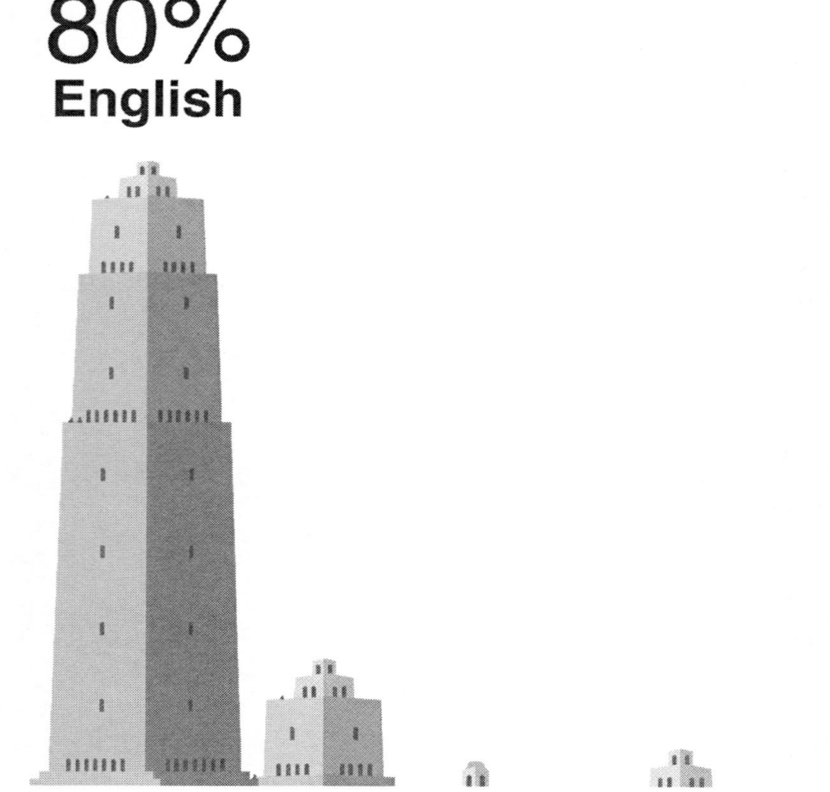

Proceedings for AMTA 2018 Workshop: Translation Quality Estimation and Automatic Post-Editing

The internet, 2017

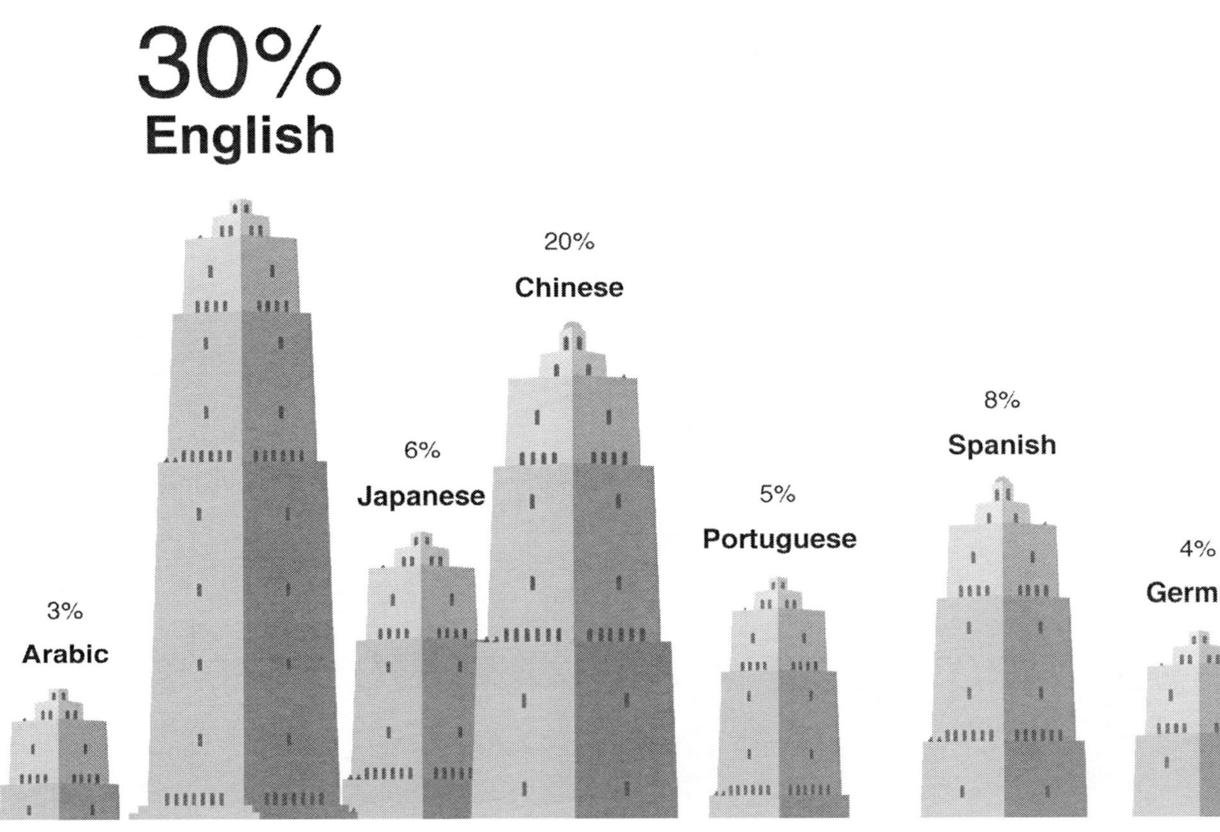

Proceedings for AMTA 2018 Workshop: Translation Quality Estimation and Automatic Post-Editing

Language barriers = trade barriers

Proceedings for AMTA 2018 Workshop: Translation Quality Estimation and Automatic Post-Editing

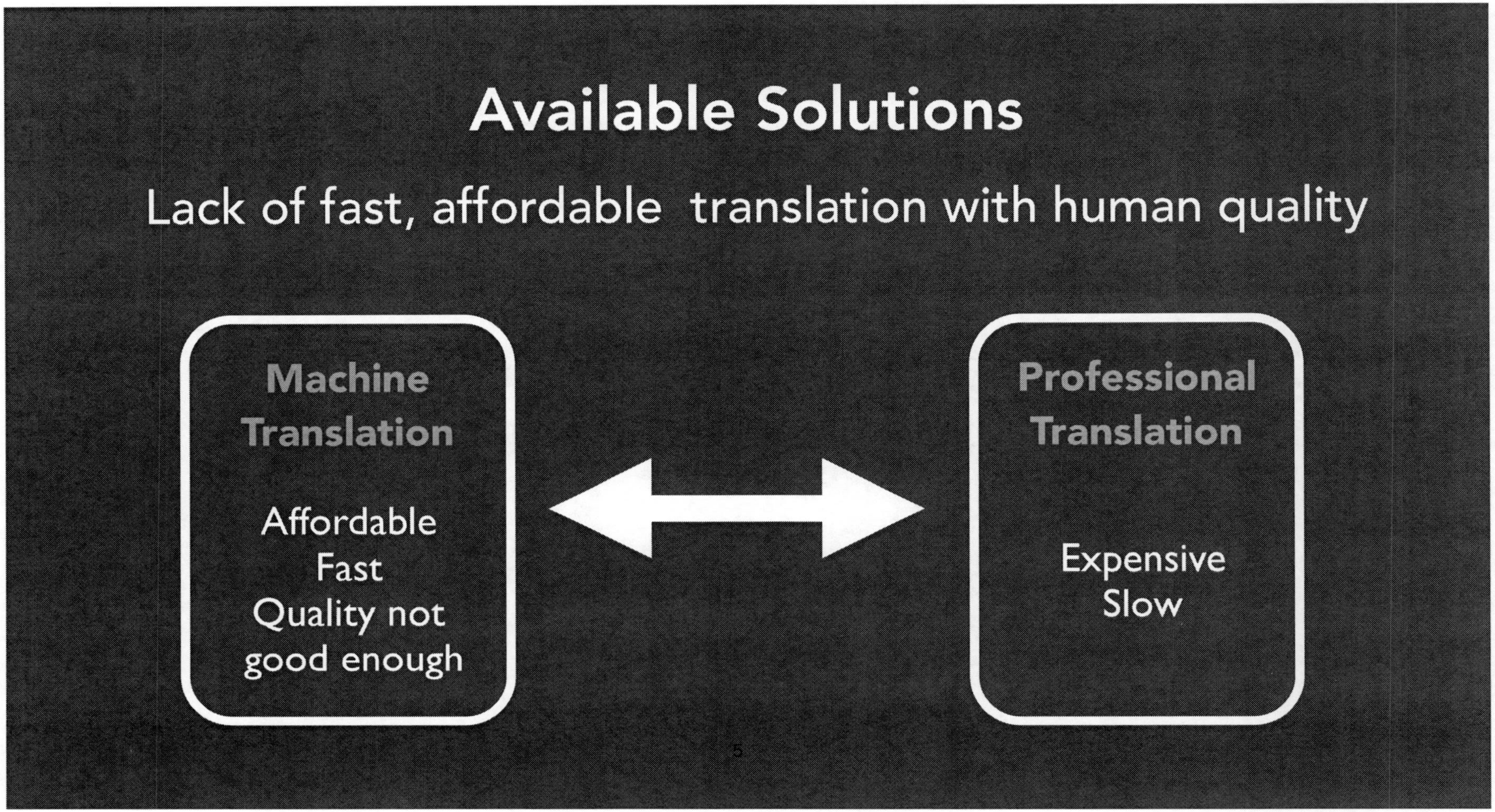

Proceedings for AMTA 2018 Workshop: Translation Quality Estimation and Automatic Post-Editing

"All translation firms together are able to translate **far less than 1%** of relevant content produced everyday"

CSA – MT Is Unavoidable to Keep Up with Content Volumes

Will AI solve translation?

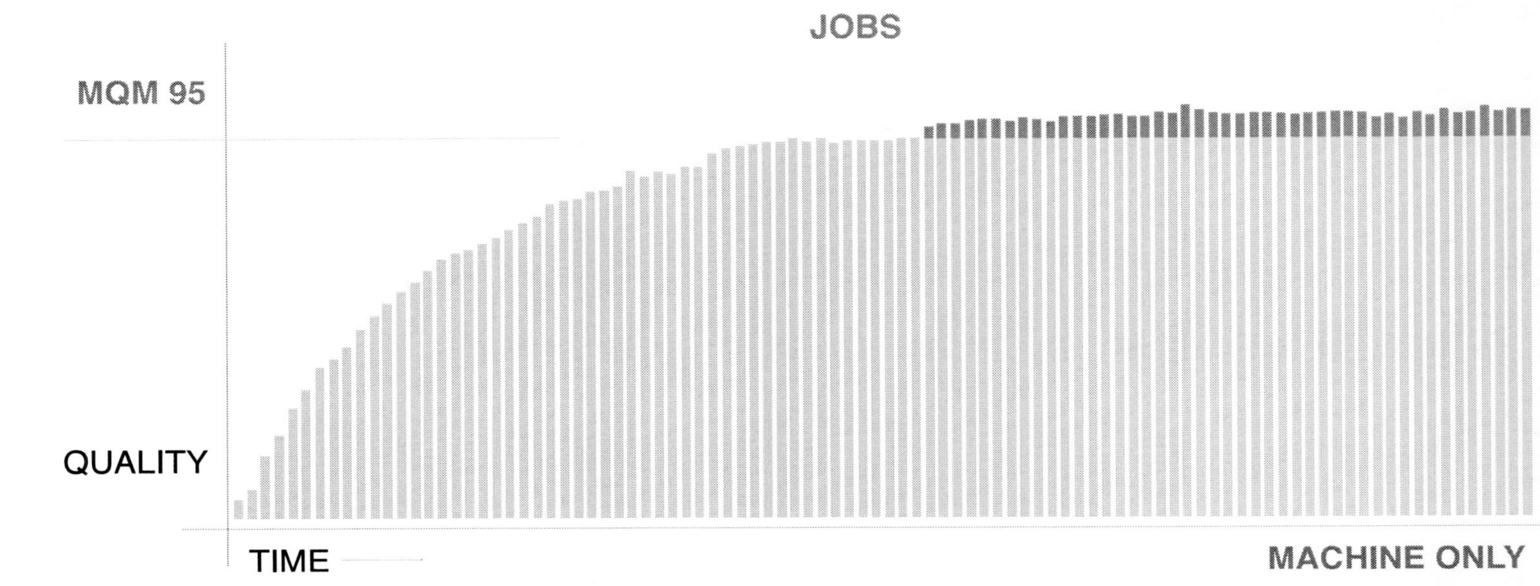

Proceedings for AMTA 2018 Workshop: Translation Quality Estimation and Automatic Post-Editing

Will AI solve translation?

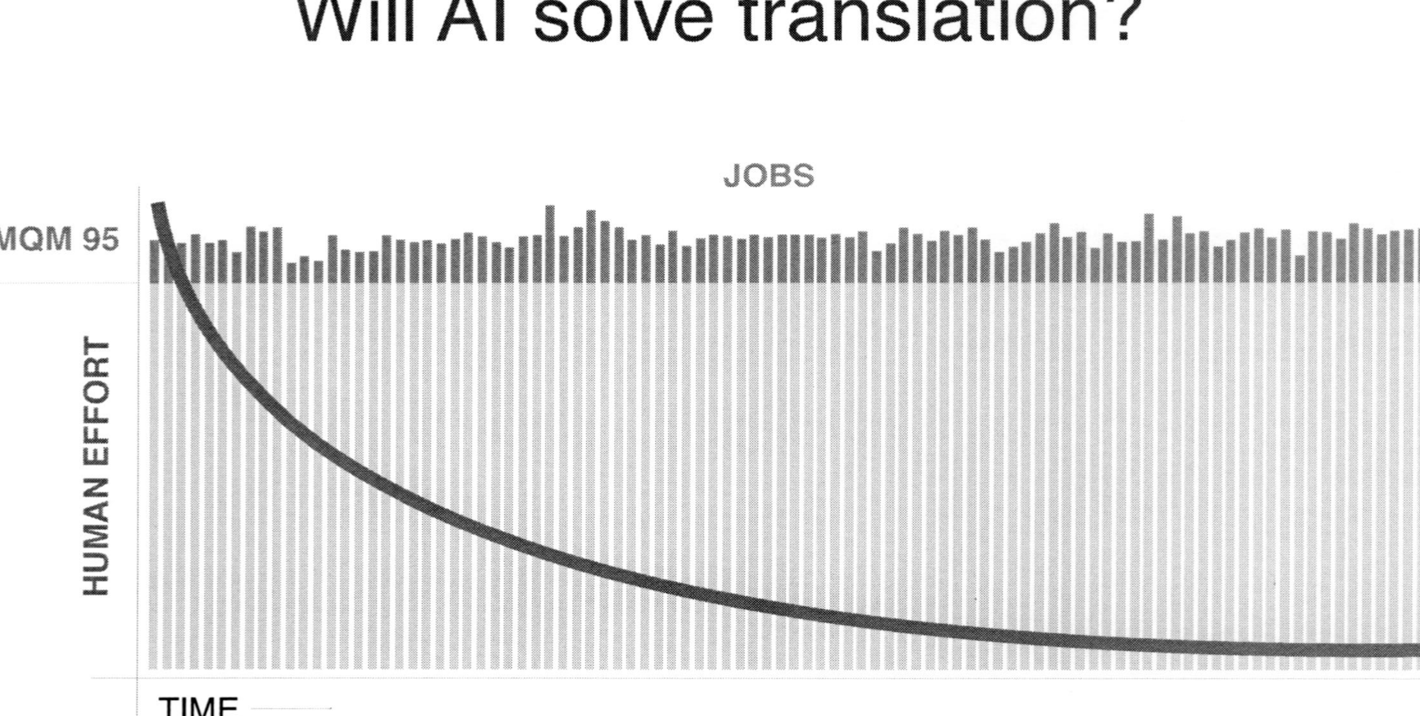

Proceedings for AMTA 2018 Workshop: Translation Quality Estimation and Automatic Post-Editing

Quality per Job

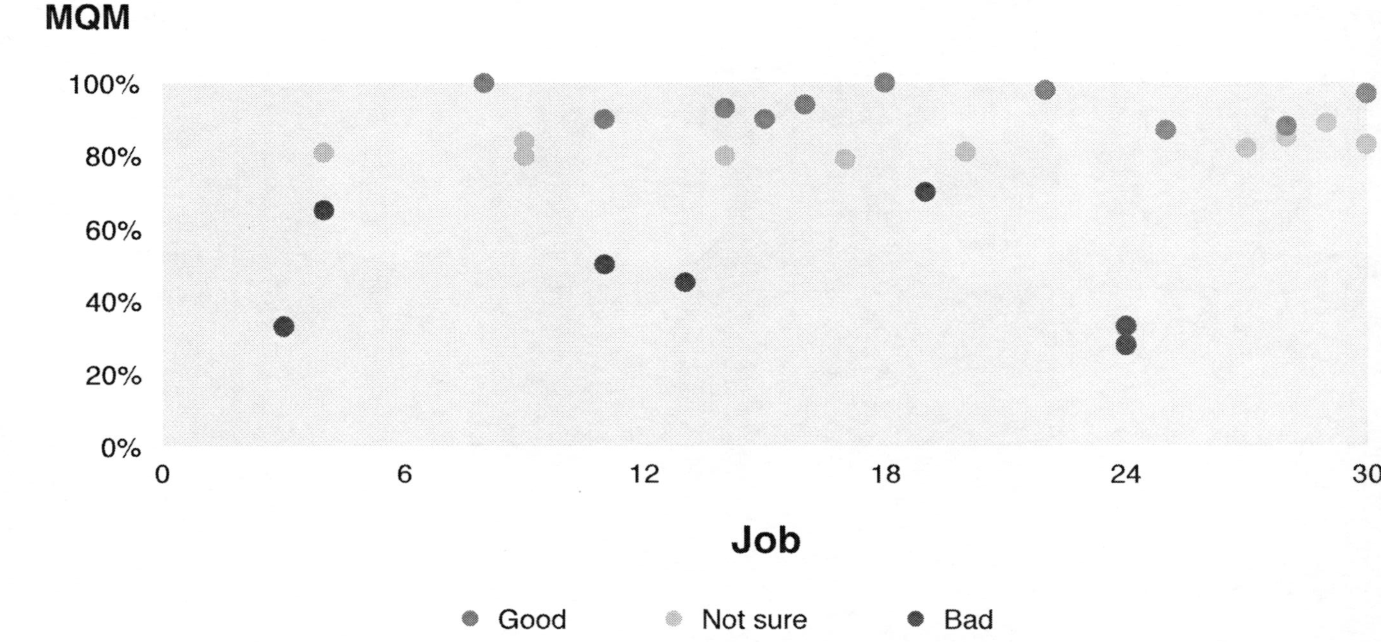

Proceedings for AMTA 2018 Workshop: Translation Quality Estimation and Automatic Post-Editing

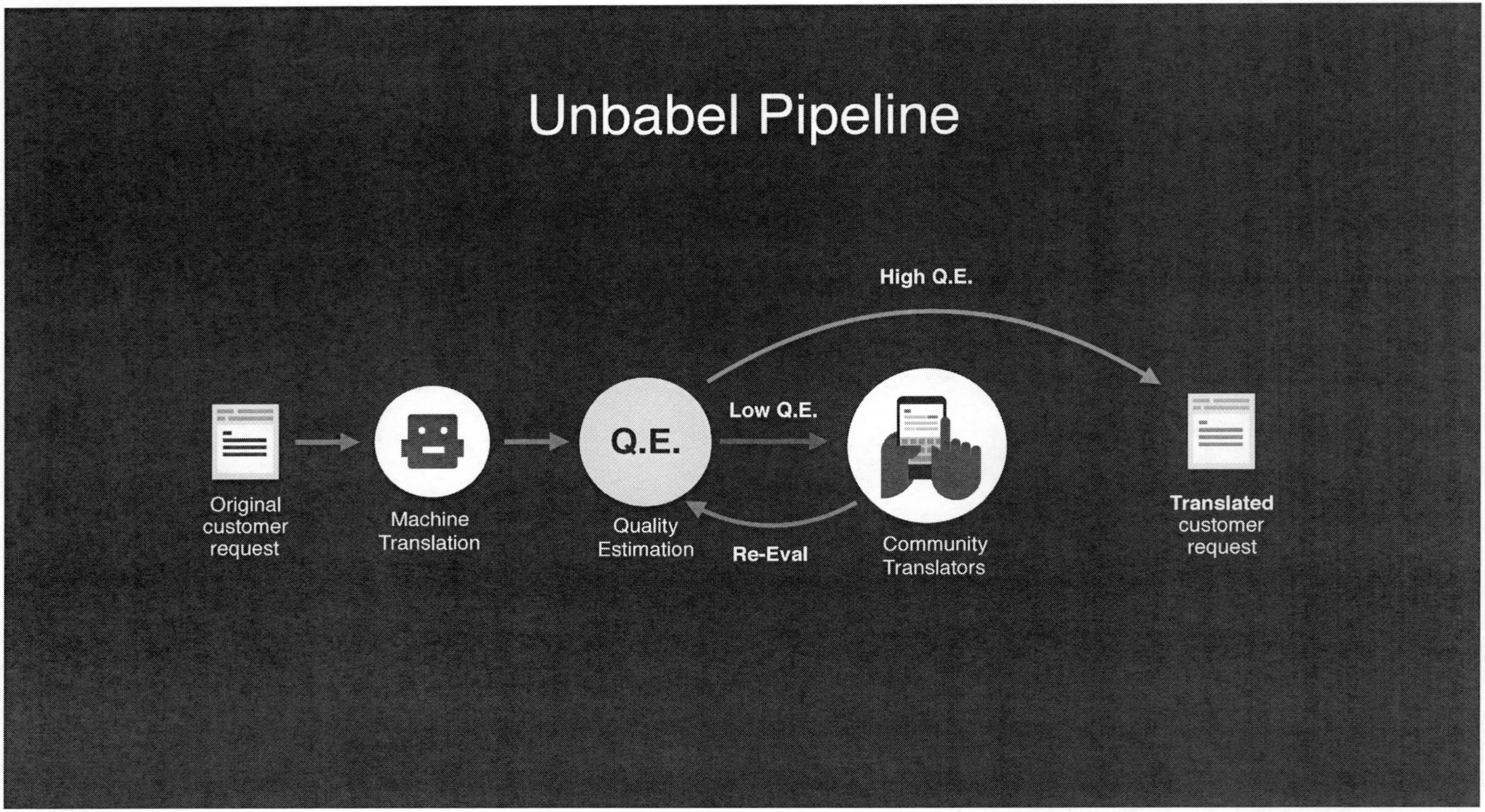

Unbabel Pipeline

Proceedings for AMTA 2018 Workshop: Translation Quality Estimation and Automatic Post-Editing

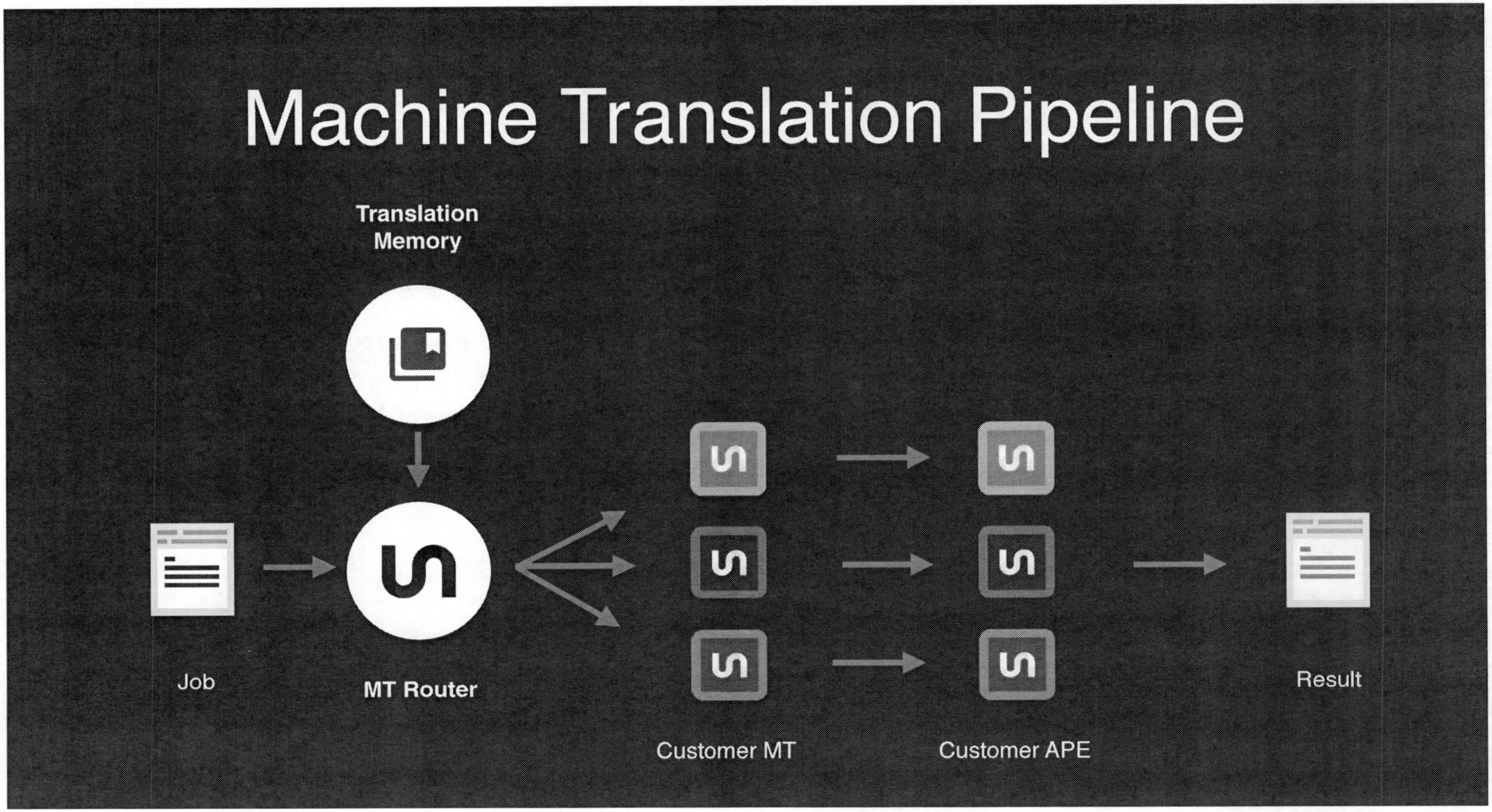

Machine Translation Pipeline

Proceedings for AMTA 2018 Workshop: Translation Quality Estimation and Automatic Post-Editing

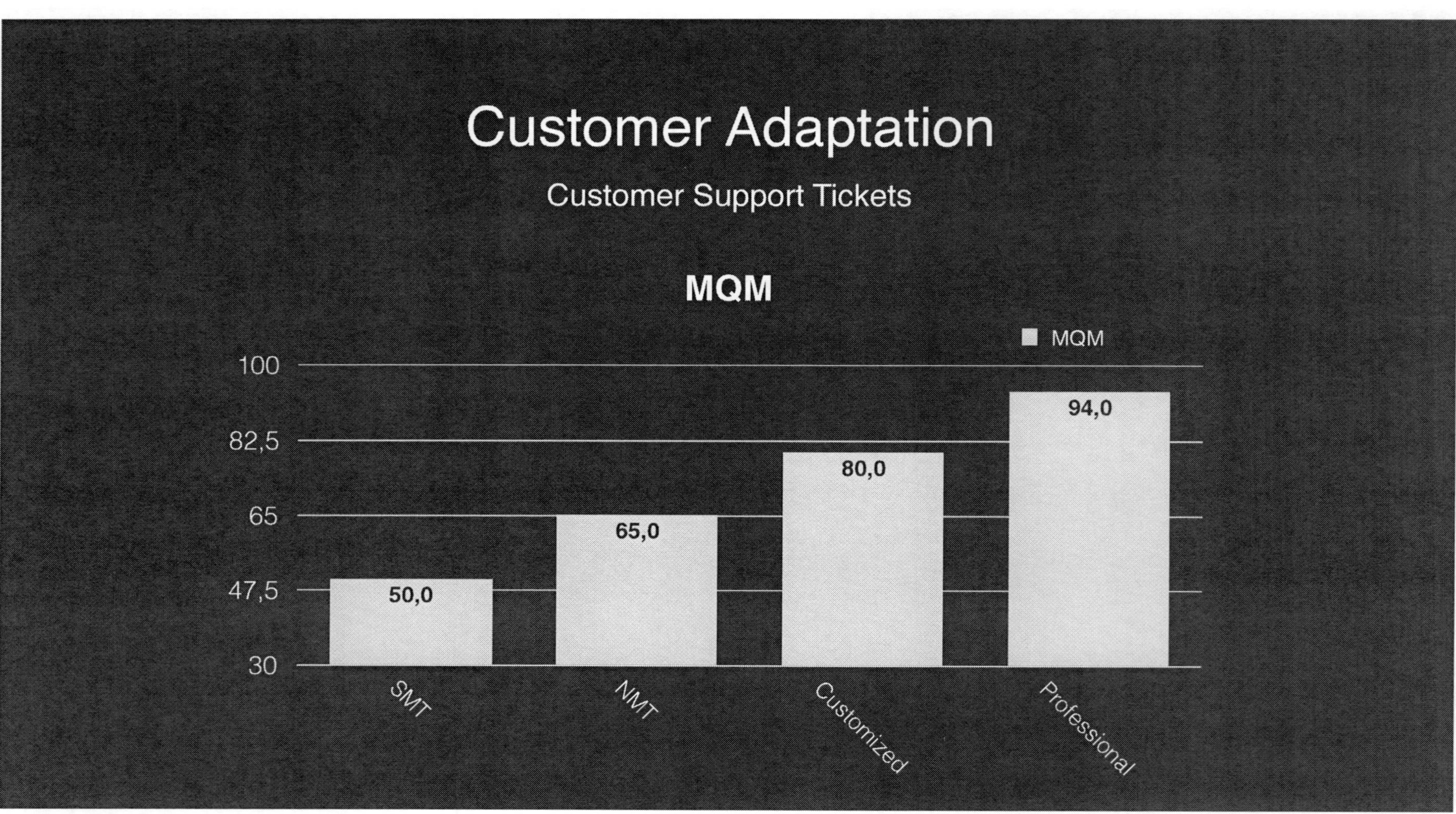

Proceedings for AMTA 2018 Workshop: Translation Quality Estimation and Automatic Post-Editing

Proceedings for AMTA 2018 Workshop: Translation Quality Estimation and Automatic Post-Editing

Quality Estimation

Word-level QE example

Hey lá , eu sou pesaroso sobre aquele !

BA BA OK BA BA BA OK OK OK
D D D D D

Proceedings for AMTA 2018 Workshop: Translation Quality Estimation and Automatic Post-Editing

QE Training

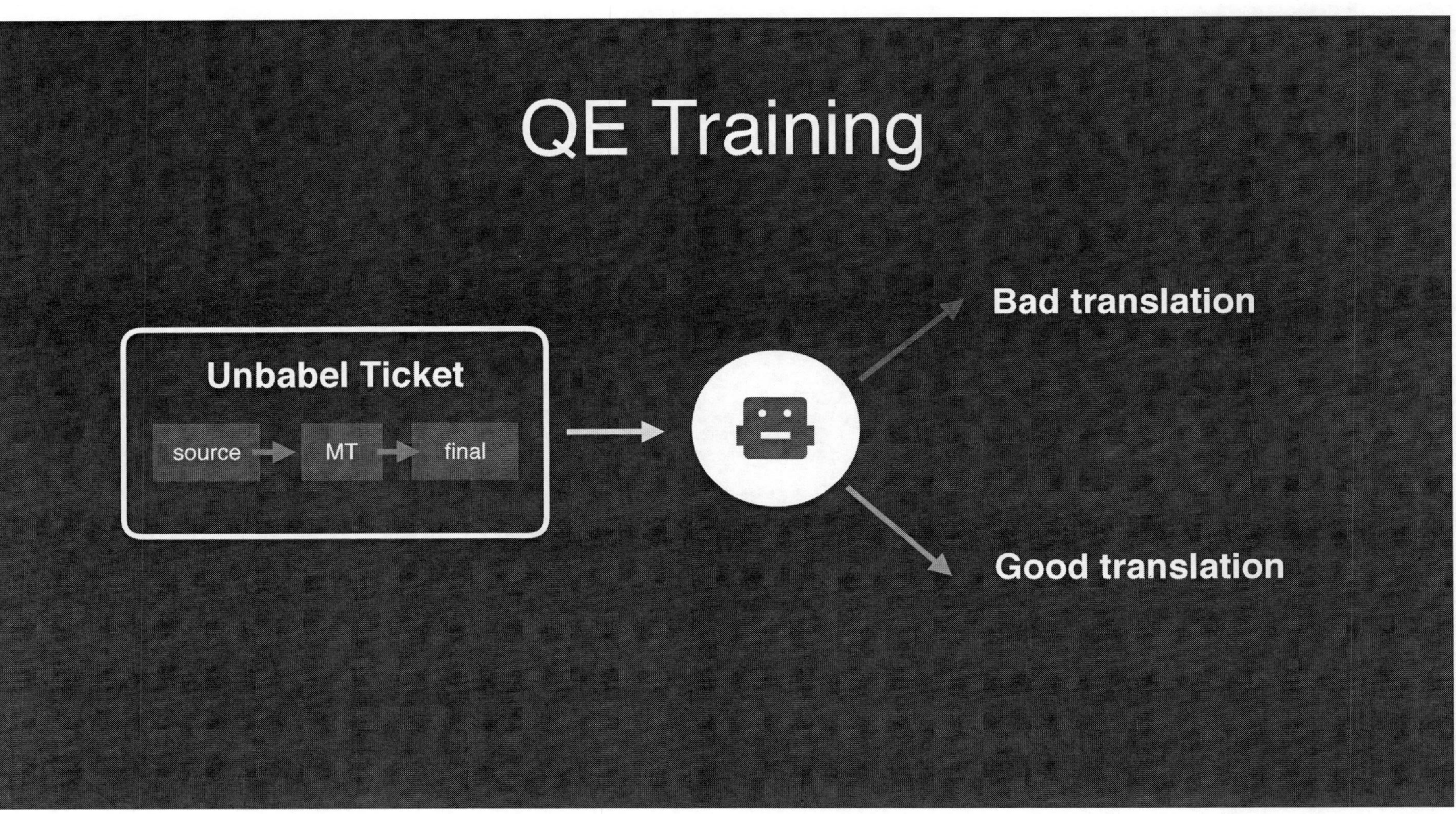

Proceedings for AMTA 2018 Workshop: Translation Quality Estimation and Automatic Post-Editing

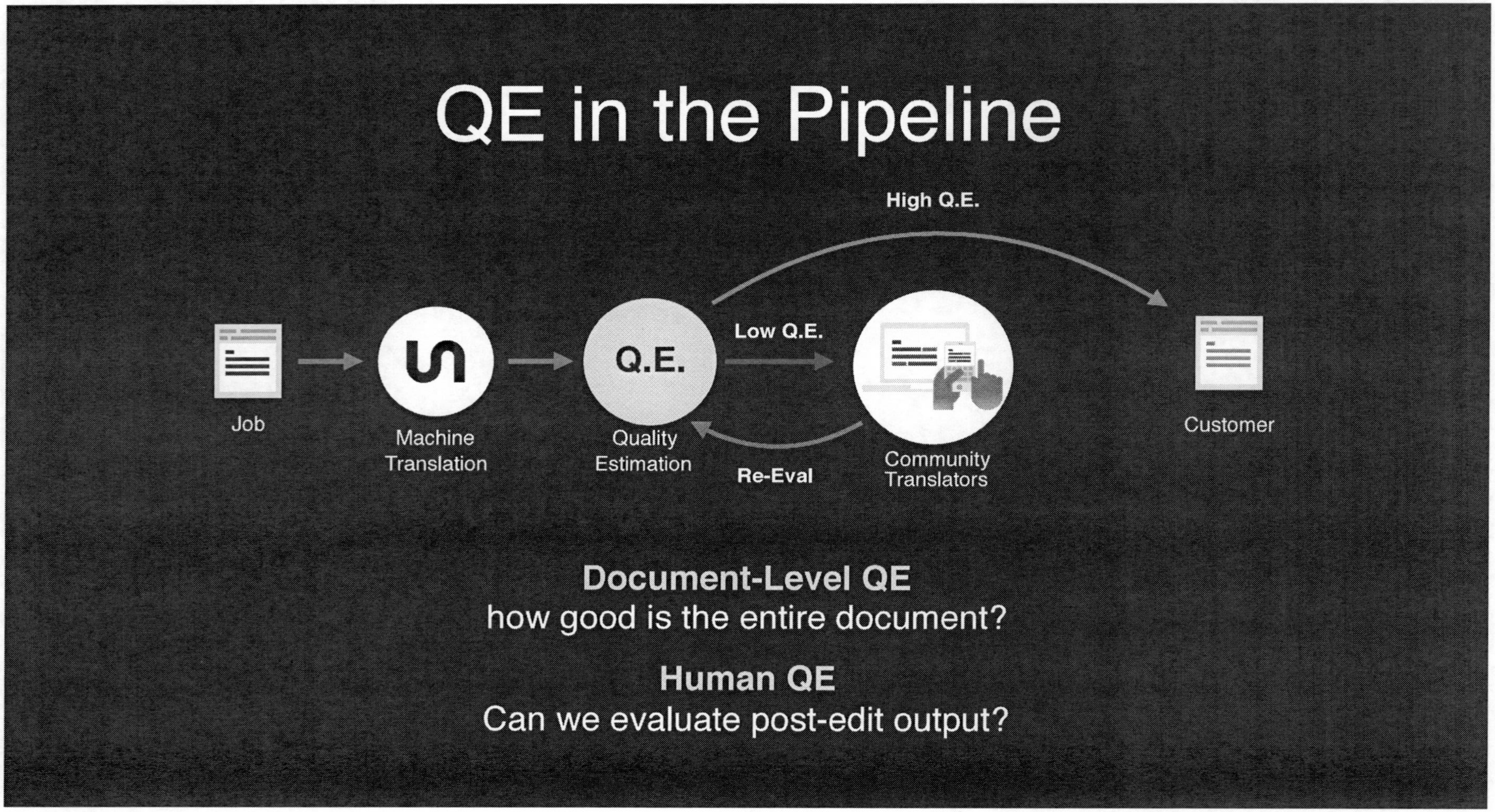

QE in the Pipeline

Document-Level QE
how good is the entire document?

Human QE
Can we evaluate post-edit output?

Proceedings for AMTA 2018 Workshop: Translation Quality Estimation and Automatic Post-Editing

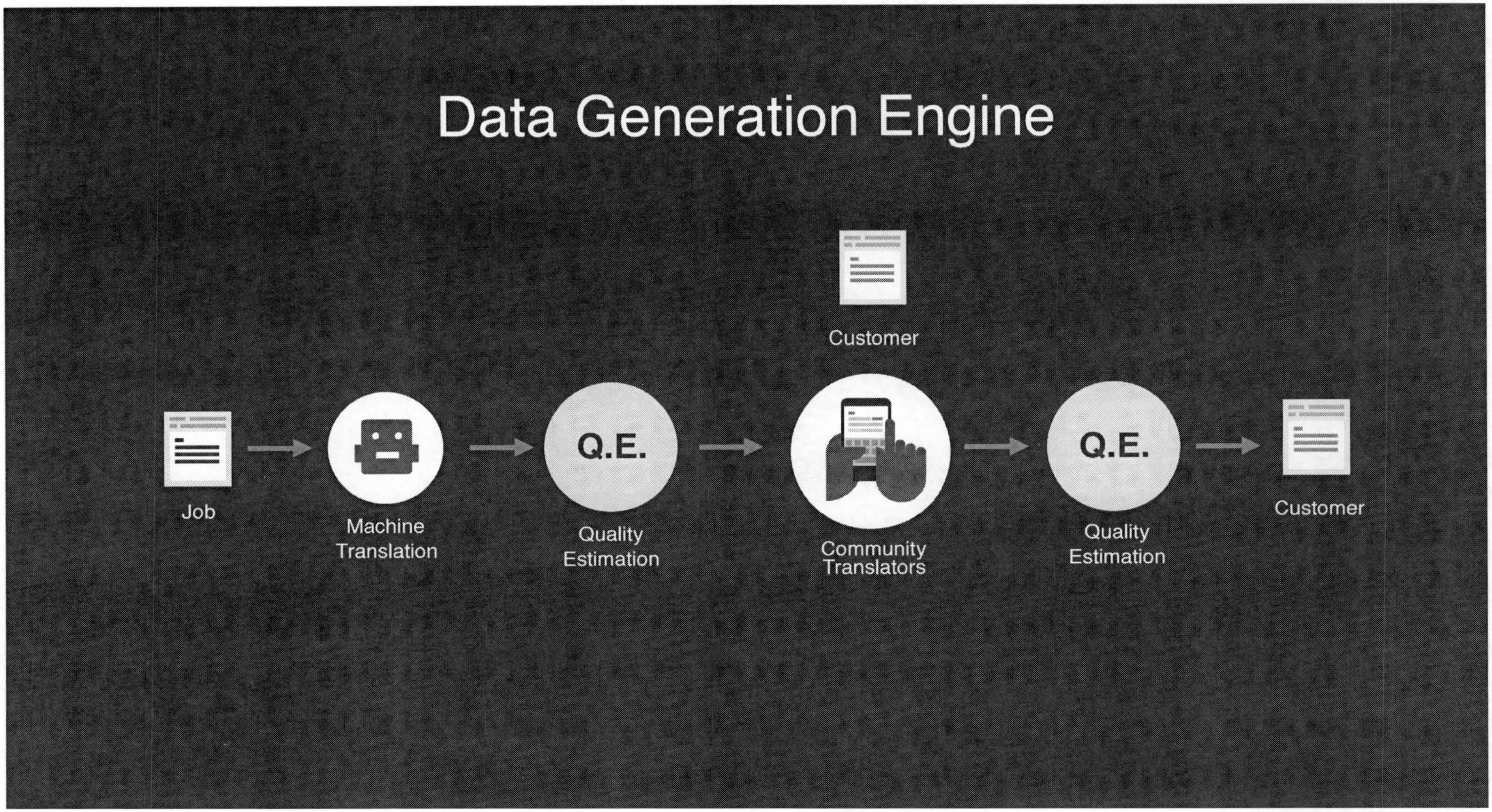

Proceedings for AMTA 2018 Workshop: Translation Quality Estimation and Automatic Post-Editing

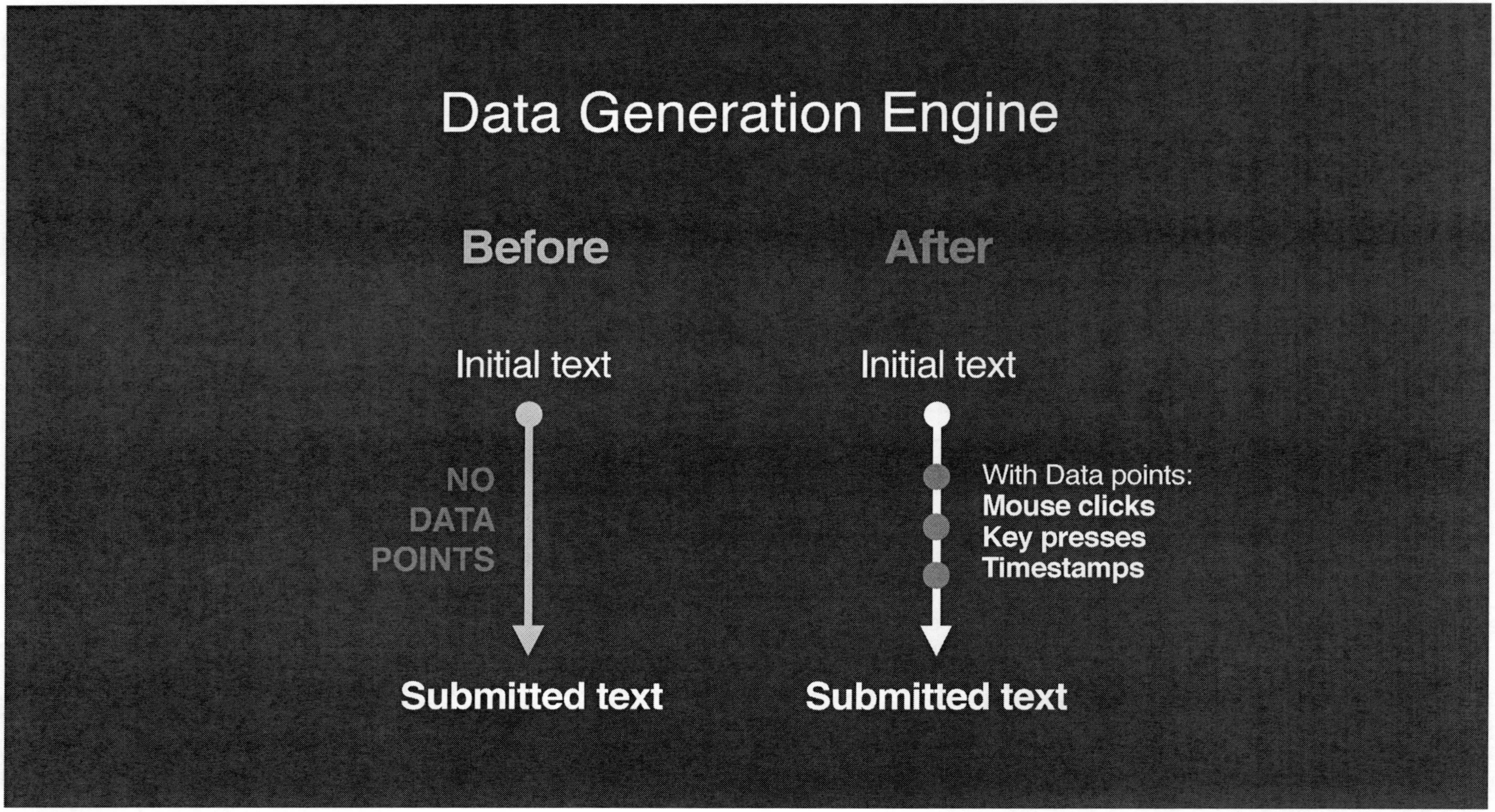

Proceedings for AMTA 2018 Workshop: Translation Quality Estimation and Automatic Post-Editing

Keystroke Analysis

Raw data

At 18:03:30:	At 18:03:35:	At 18:03:30:
In nugget 3	In nugget 3	In nugget 3
mouseClick	Pressed Shift	mouseClick
Cursor at 16	Cursor at 25	Cursor at 16
Selected: 0	Selected: 0	Selected: 0
At 18:03:31:	At 18:03:35:	At 18:03:31:
In nugget 3	In nugget 3	In nugget 3
Pressed Backspace	Pressed s	Pressed Backspace
Cursor at 16	Cursor at 25	Cursor at 16
Selected: 0	Selected: 0	Selected: 0
At 18:03:31:	At 18:03:35:	At 18:03:31:
In nugget 3	In nugget 3	In nugget 3
Pressed Backspace	Pressed i	Pressed Backspace
Cursor at 15	Cursor at 26	Cursor at 15
Selected: 0	Selected: 0	Selected: 0
At 18:03:31:	At 18:03:35:	At 18:03:31:
In nugget 3	In nugget 3	In nugget 3
Pressed Backspace	Pressed e	Pressed Backspace
Cursor at 14	Cursor at 27	Cursor at 14
Selected: 0	Selected: 0	Selected: 0

Processed information

Initial text
"Espero que esto es útil"

- Deleted word "es"
- Inserted word "sea"

Submitted text
"Espero que esto sea útil"

Proceedings for AMTA 2018 Workshop: Translation Quality Estimation and Automatic Post-Editing

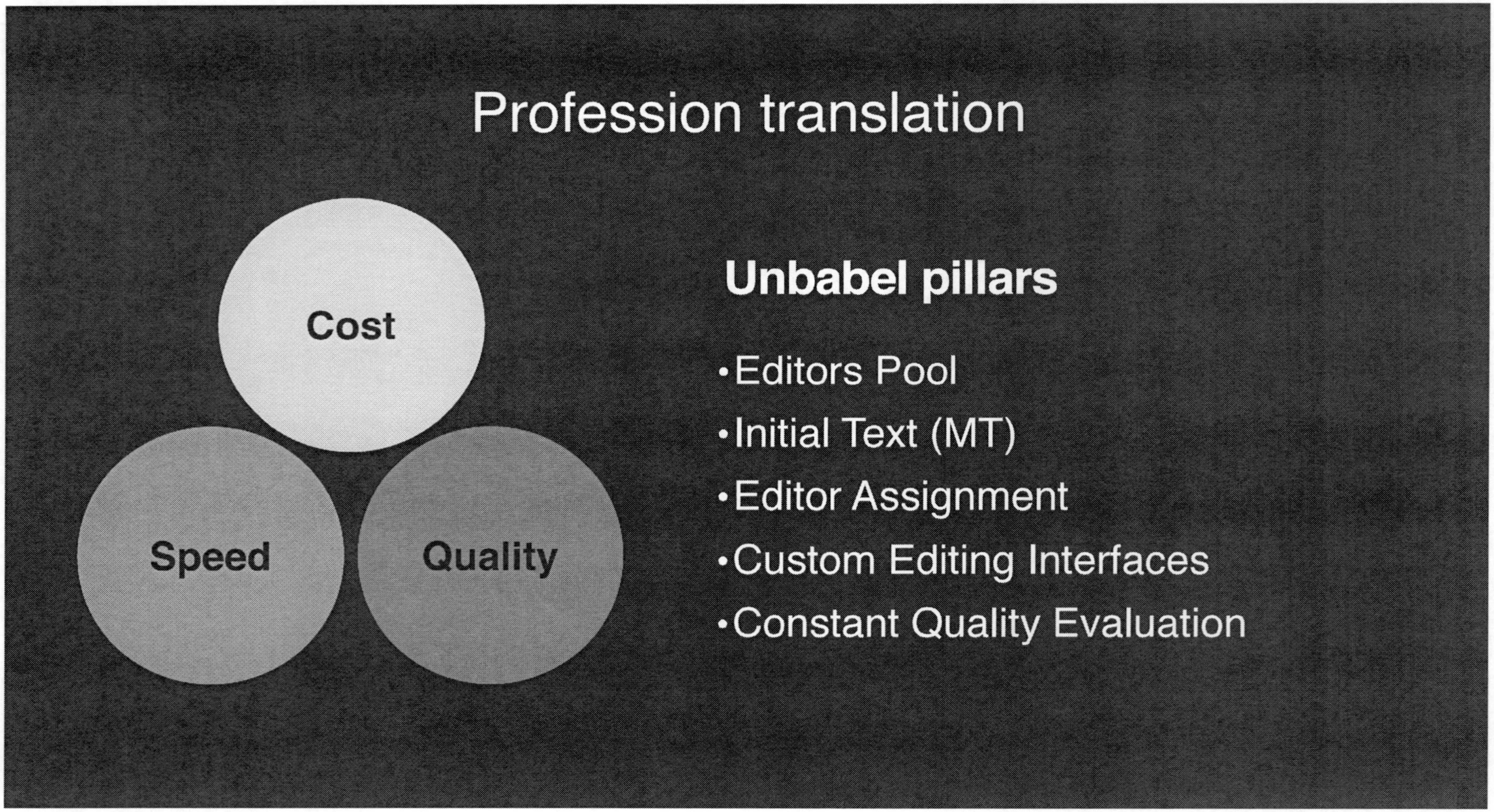

Proceedings for AMTA 2018 Workshop: Translation Quality Estimation and Automatic Post-Editing

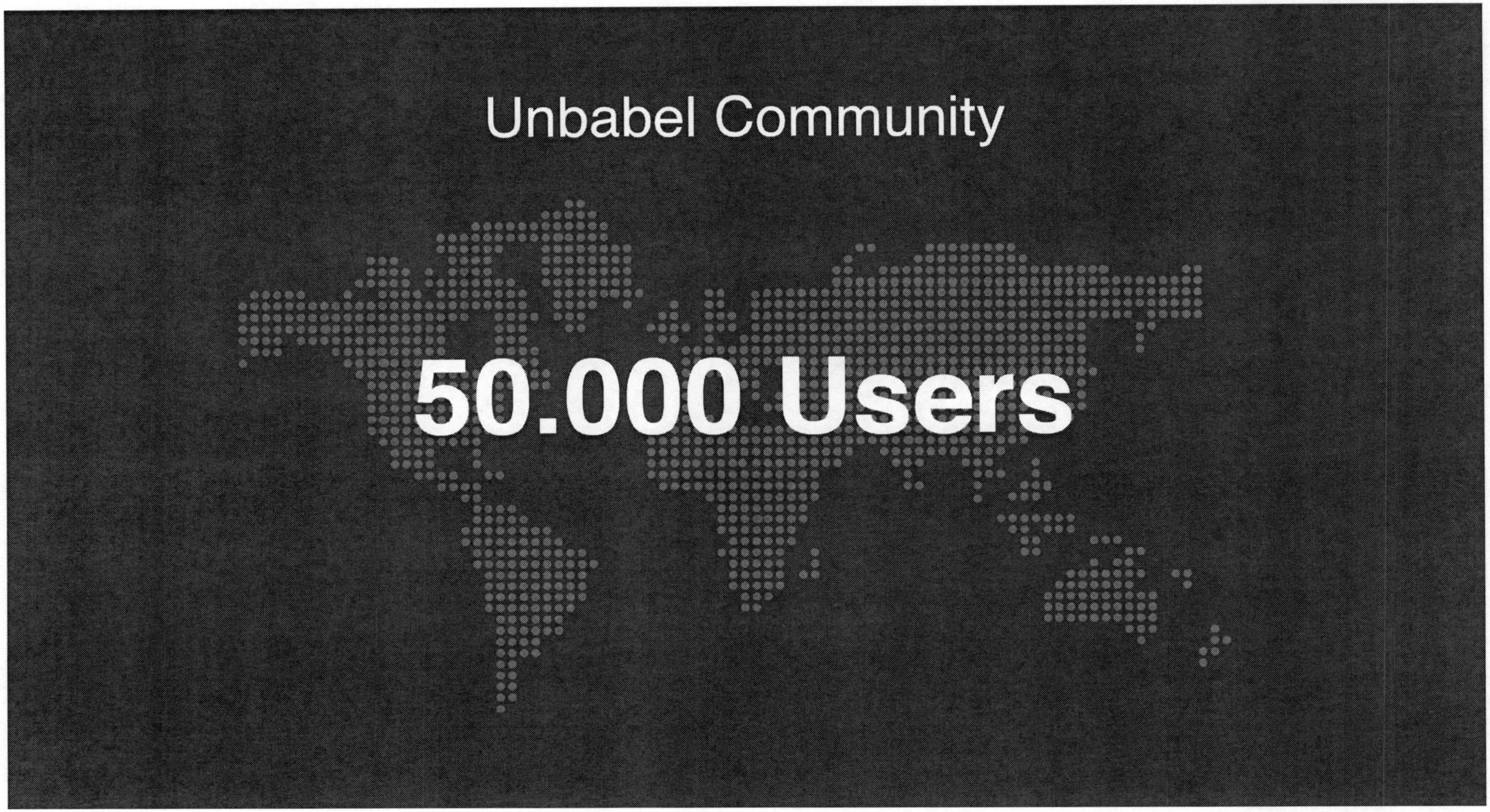

Unbabel Community
50.000 Users

Editors Pool

4 More specialization layers
will be created

**3 Only the best rated editors
have access to customer tasks**

2 Editors get rated
with training tasks

1 First tests right after signup

Proceedings for AMTA 2018 Workshop: Translation Quality Estimation and Automatic Post-Editing

Evaluation Tool

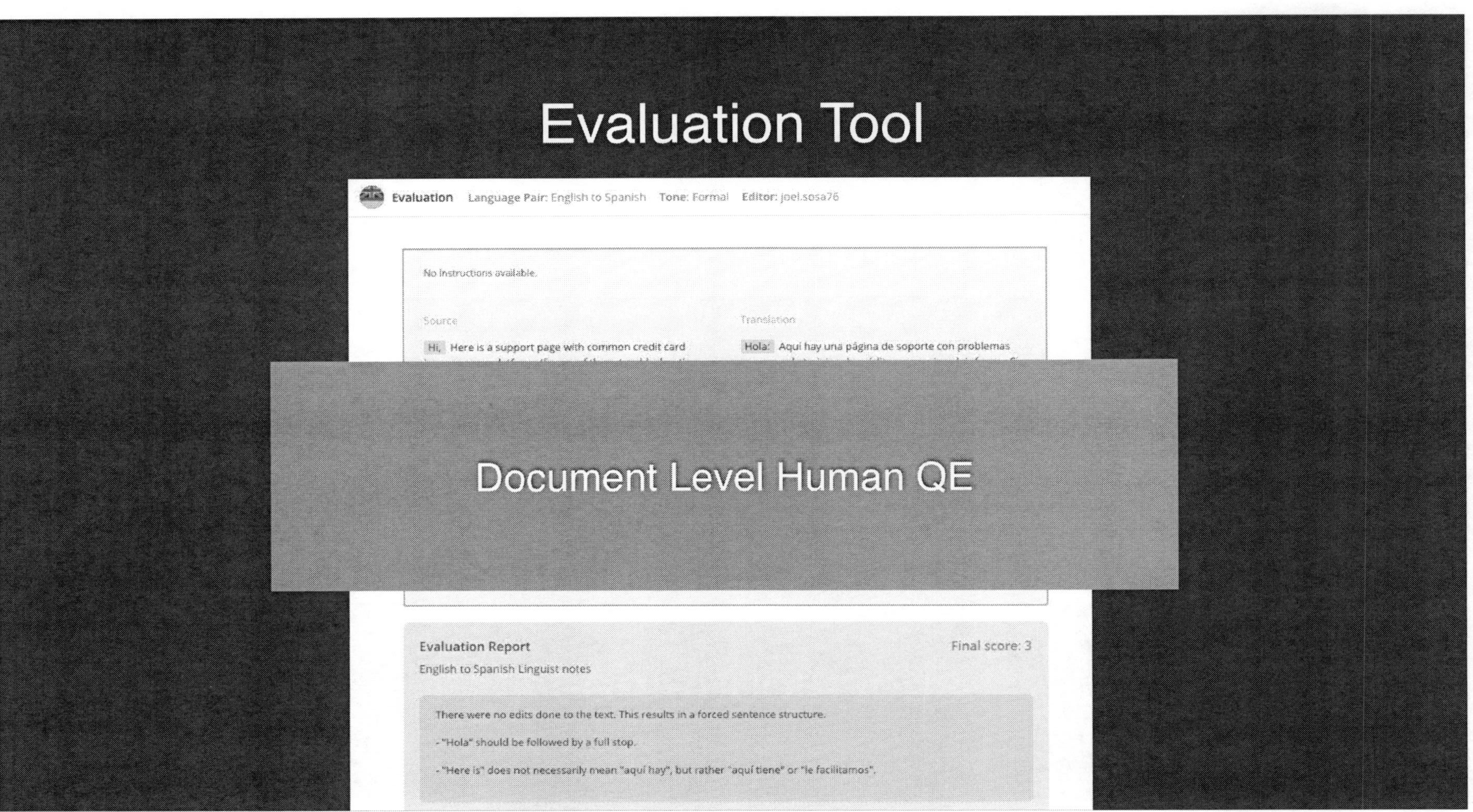

Proceedings for AMTA 2018 Workshop: Translation Quality Estimation and Automatic Post-Editing

Deep Annotations

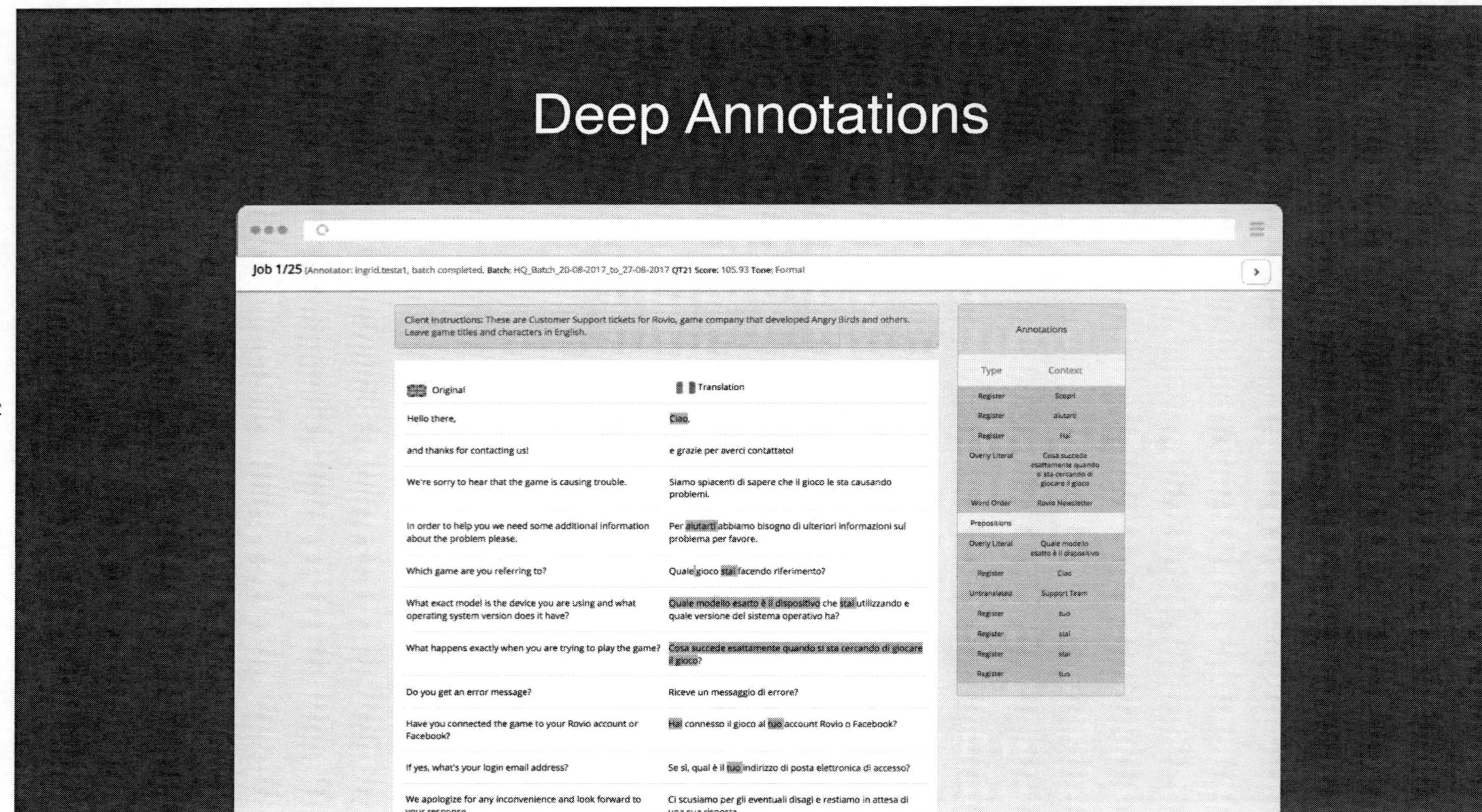

Proceedings for AMTA 2018 Workshop: Translation Quality Estimation and Automatic Post-Editing

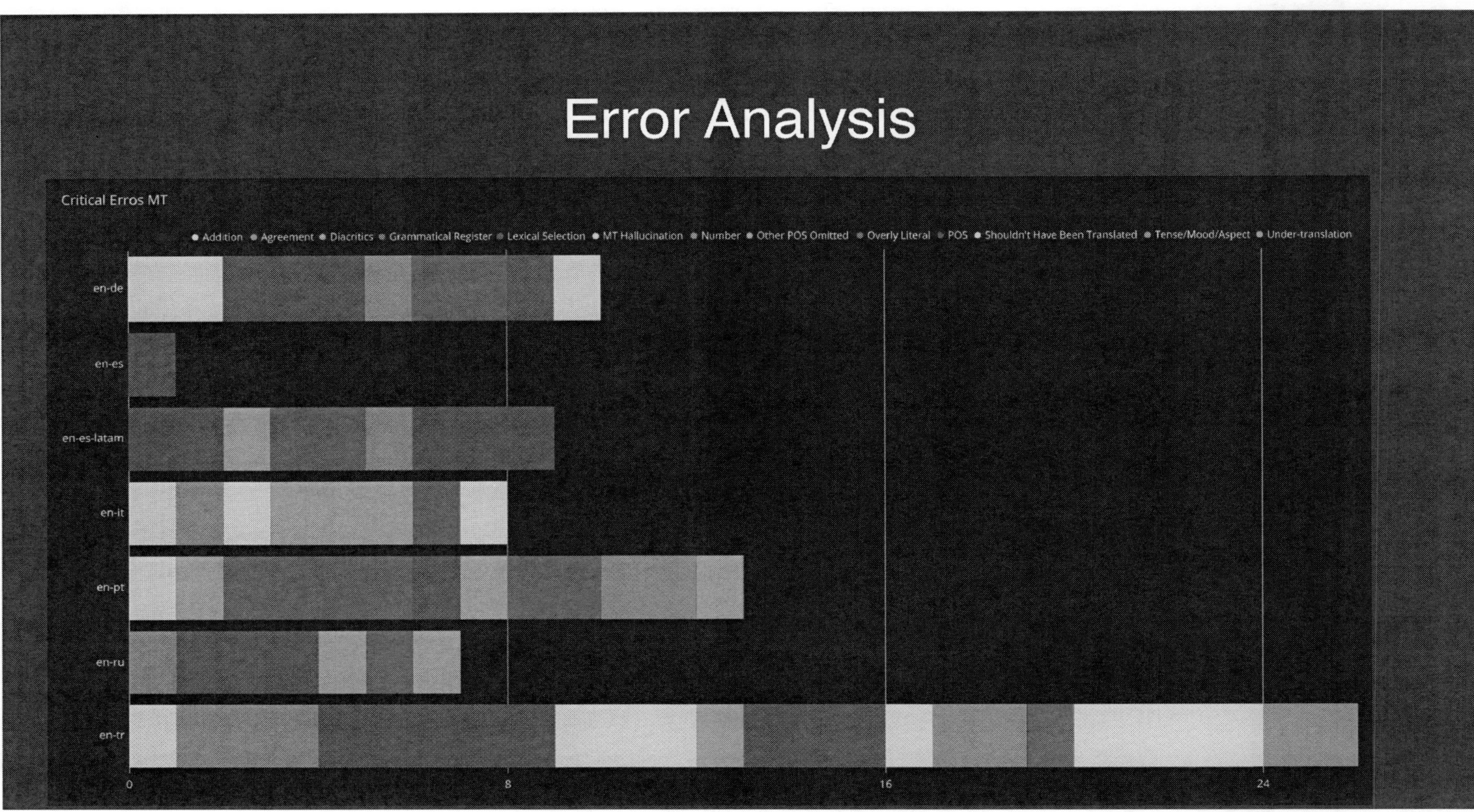

Proceedings for AMTA 2018 Workshop: Translation Quality Estimation and Automatic Post-Editing

QE for Annotation

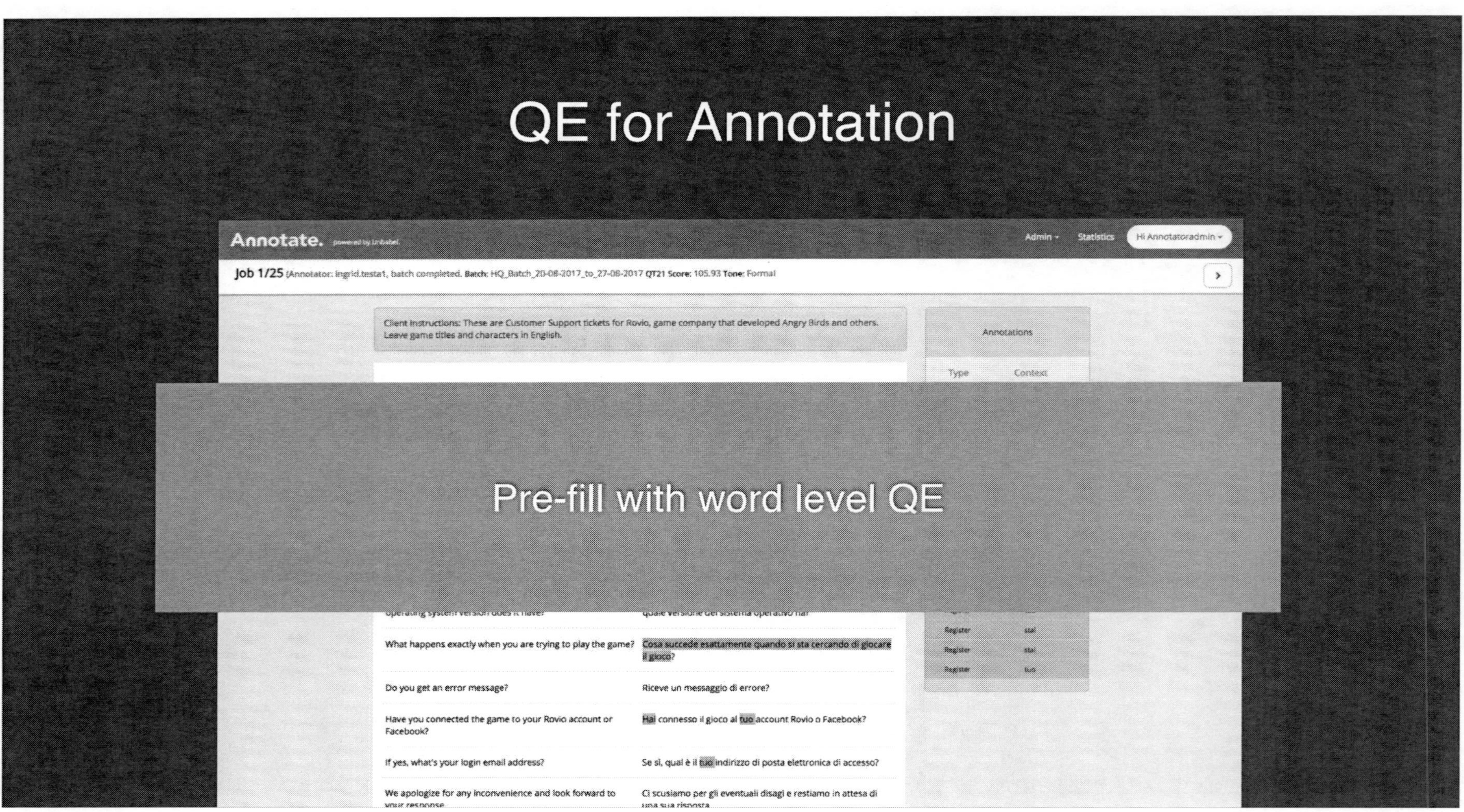

Proceedings for AMTA 2018 Workshop: Translation Quality Estimation and Automatic Post-Editing

Editors Profiling

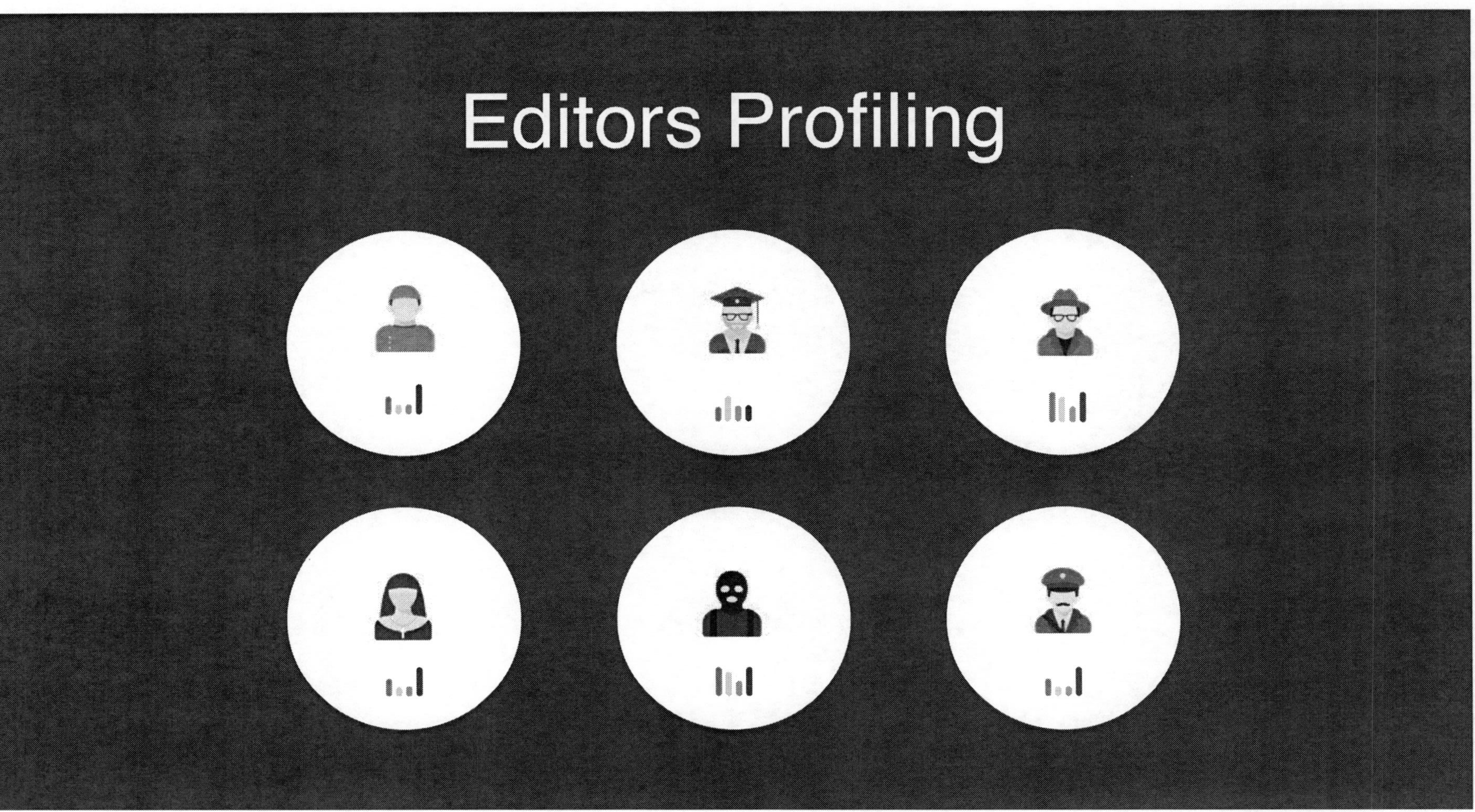

Proceedings for AMTA 2018 Workshop: Translation Quality Estimation and Automatic Post-Editing

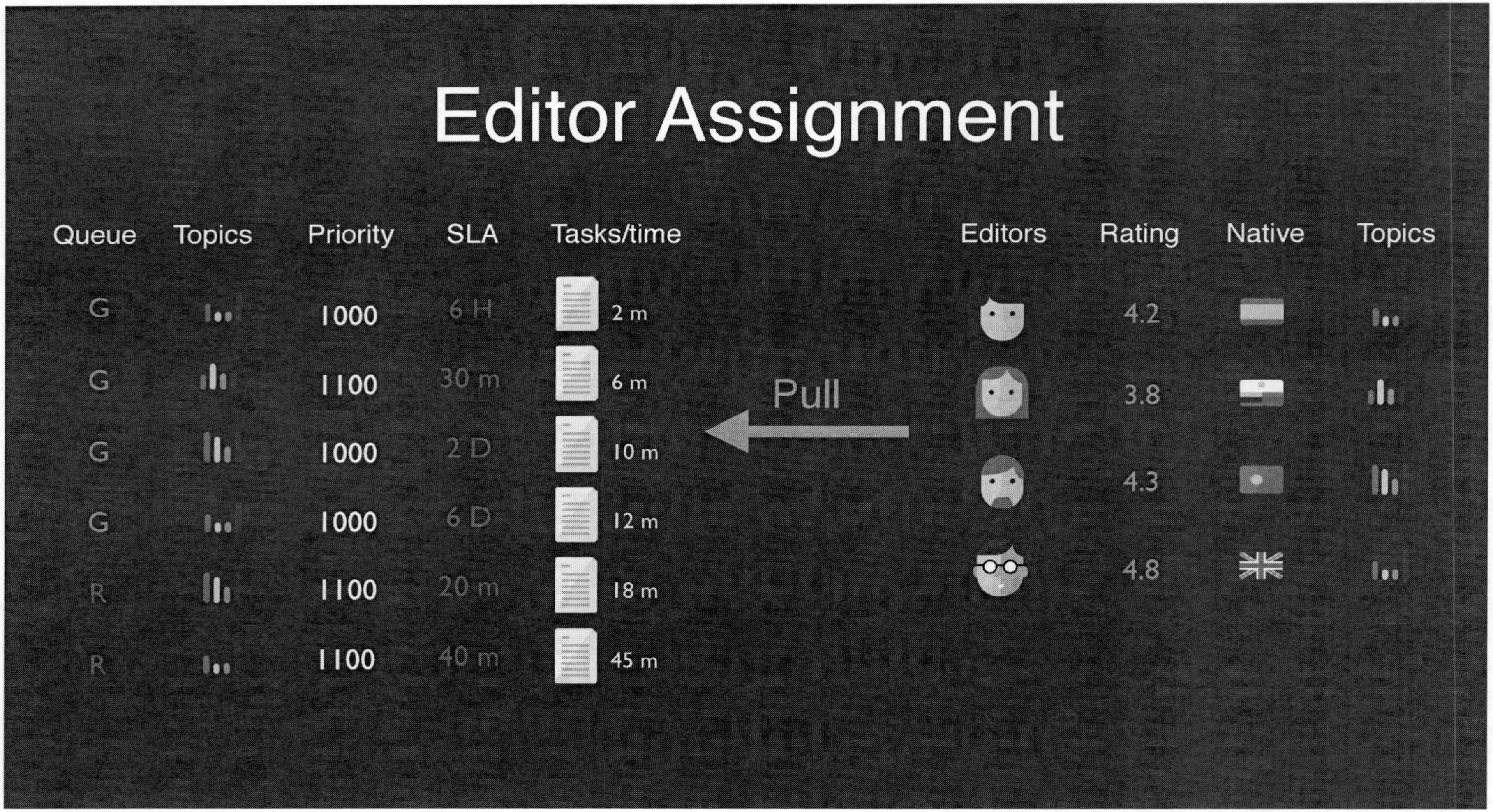
Editor Assignment
Queue
Topics
Priority
SLA
Tasks/time
Editors
Rating
Native
Topics
G
1000
6 H
2 m
4.2
G
1100
30 m
6 m
3.8
G
1000
2 D
10 m
4.3
G
1000
6 D
12 m
4.8
R
1100
20 m
18 m
R
1100
40 m
45 m
Pull

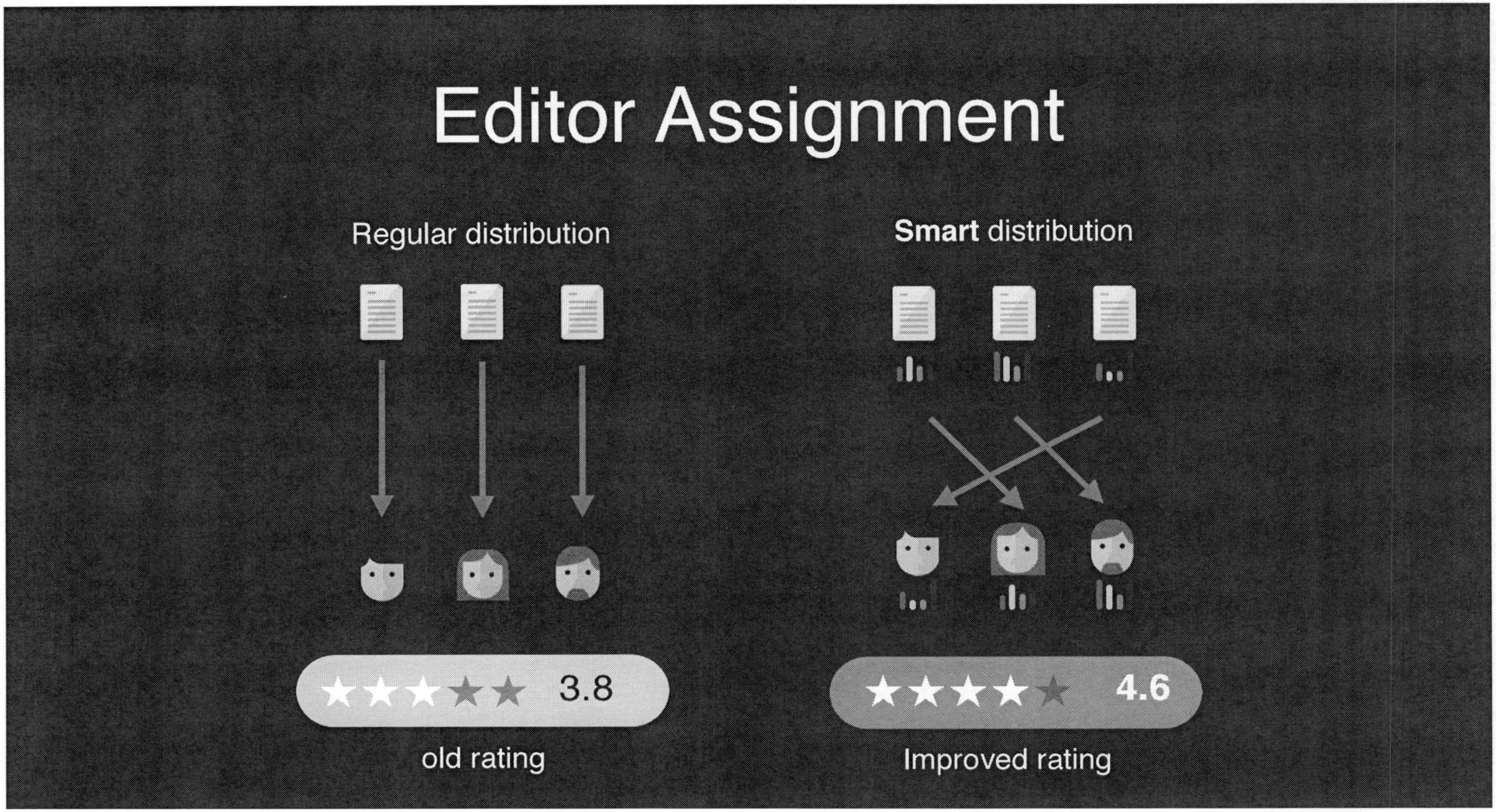

Editor Assignment

Proceedings for AMTA 2018 Workshop: Translation Quality Estimation and Automatic Post-Editing

Post-Editing Interfaces

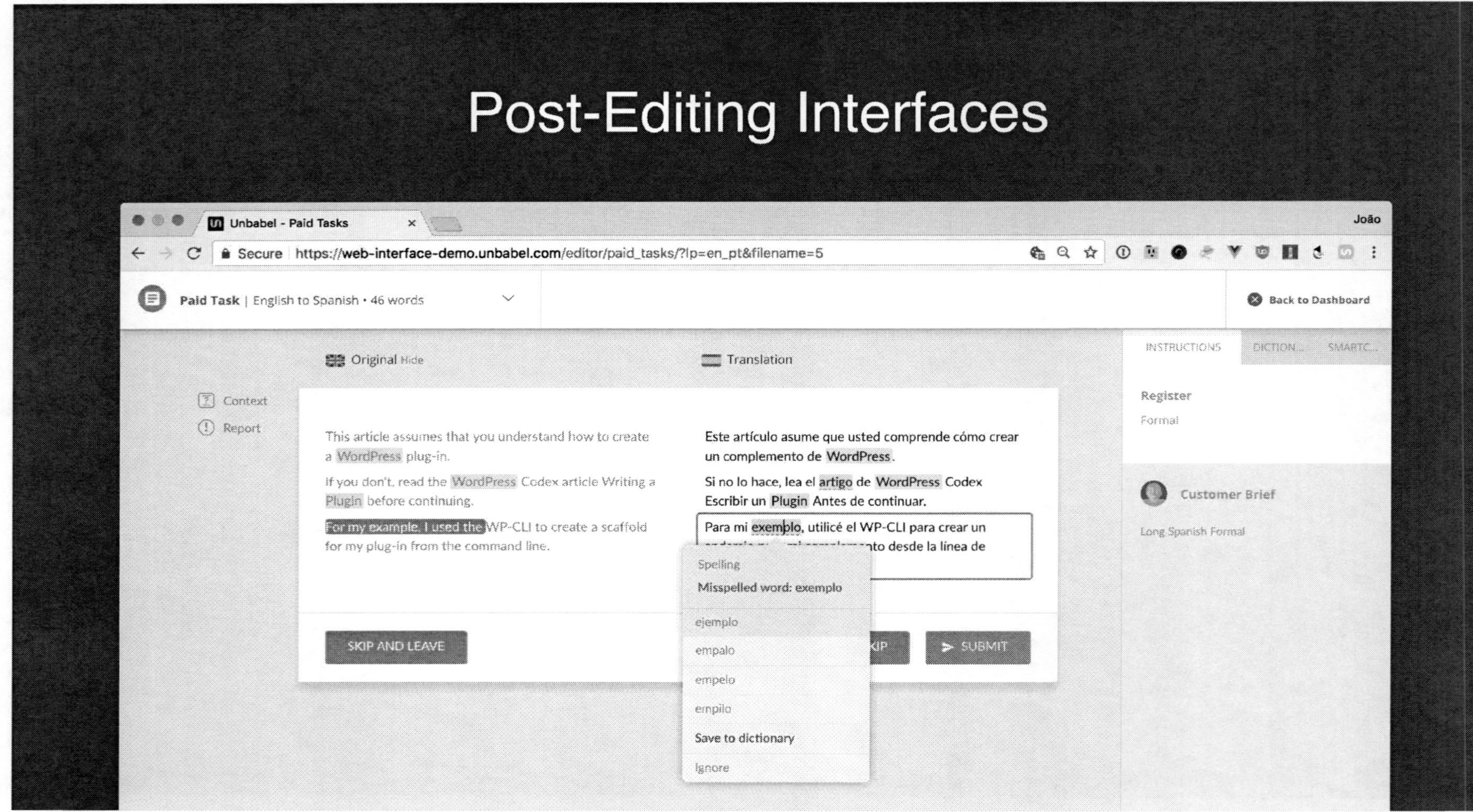

Proceedings for AMTA 2018 Workshop: Translation Quality Estimation and Automatic Post-Editing

QE on Interfaces

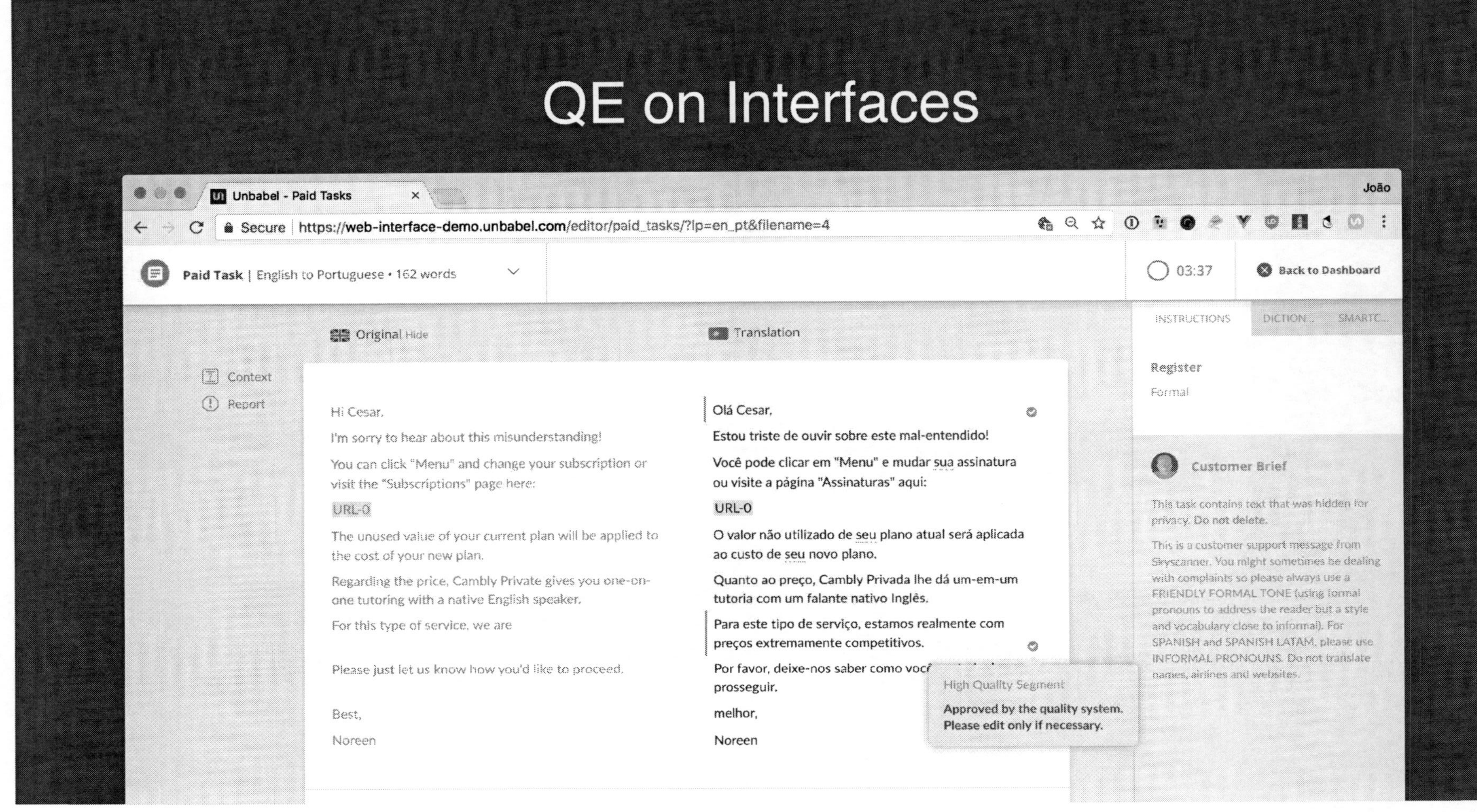

Post-Editing Interfaces

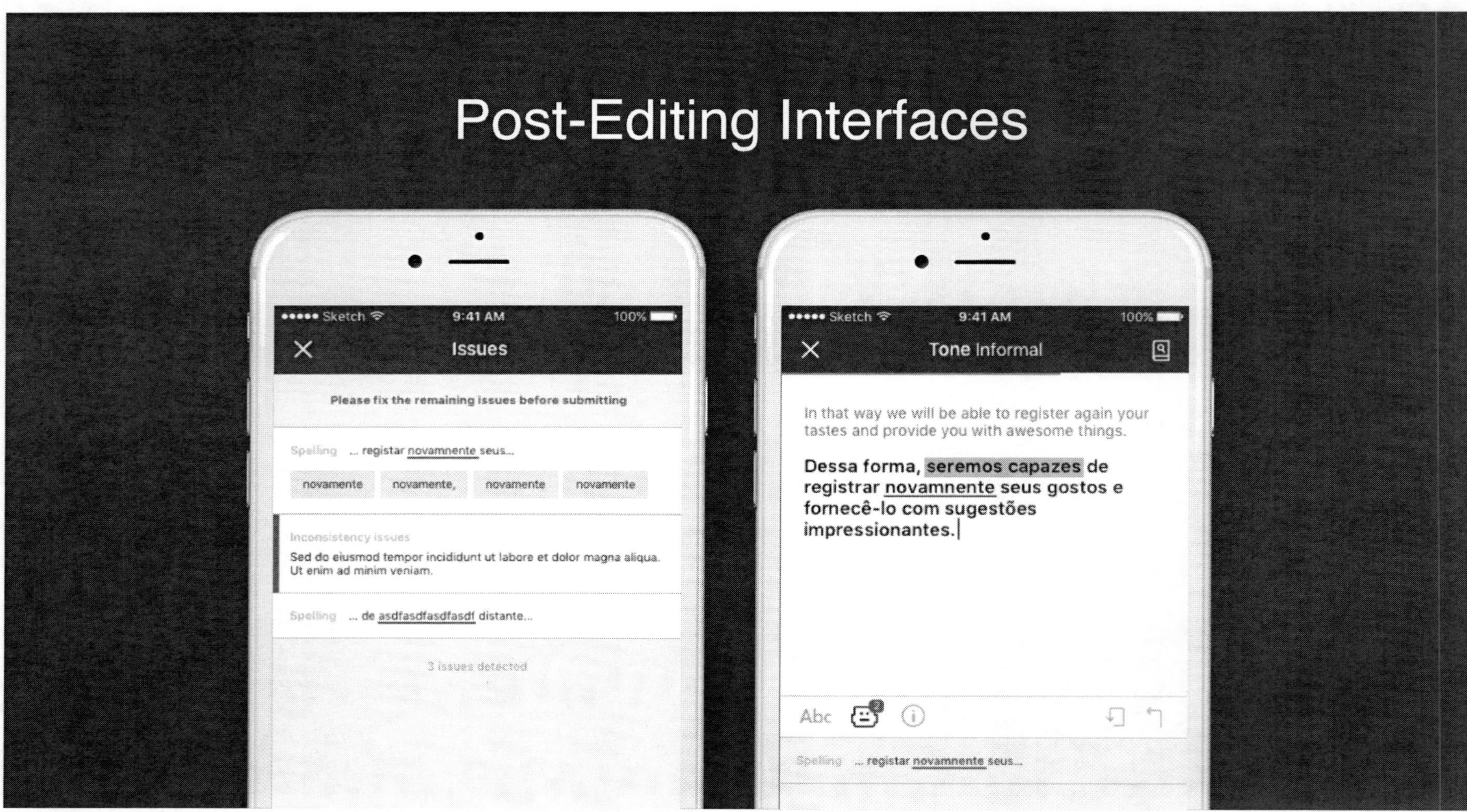

Proceedings for AMTA 2018 Workshop: Translation Quality Estimation and Automatic Post-Editing

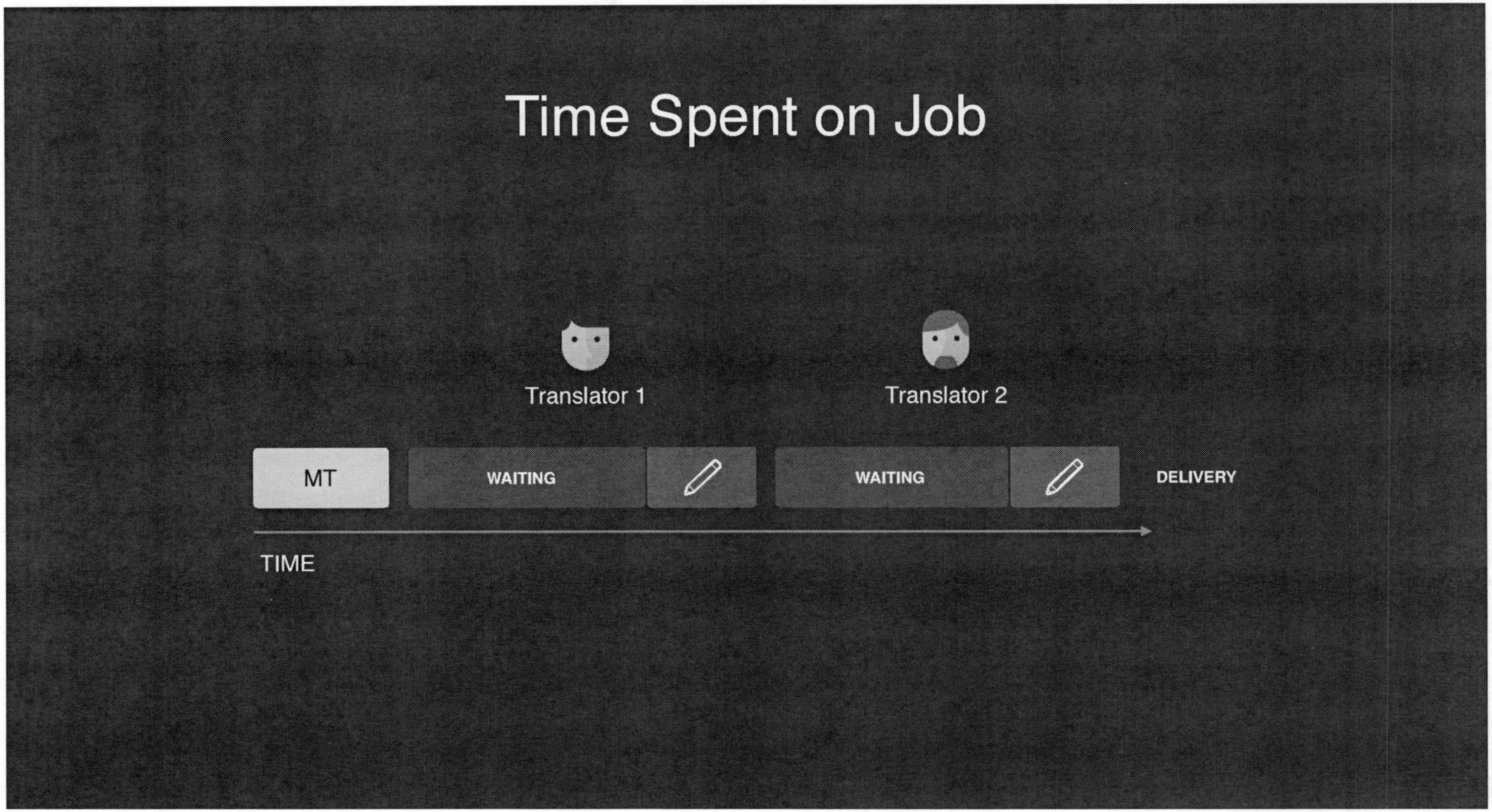

Proceedings for AMTA 2018 Workshop: Translation Quality Estimation and Automatic Post-Editing

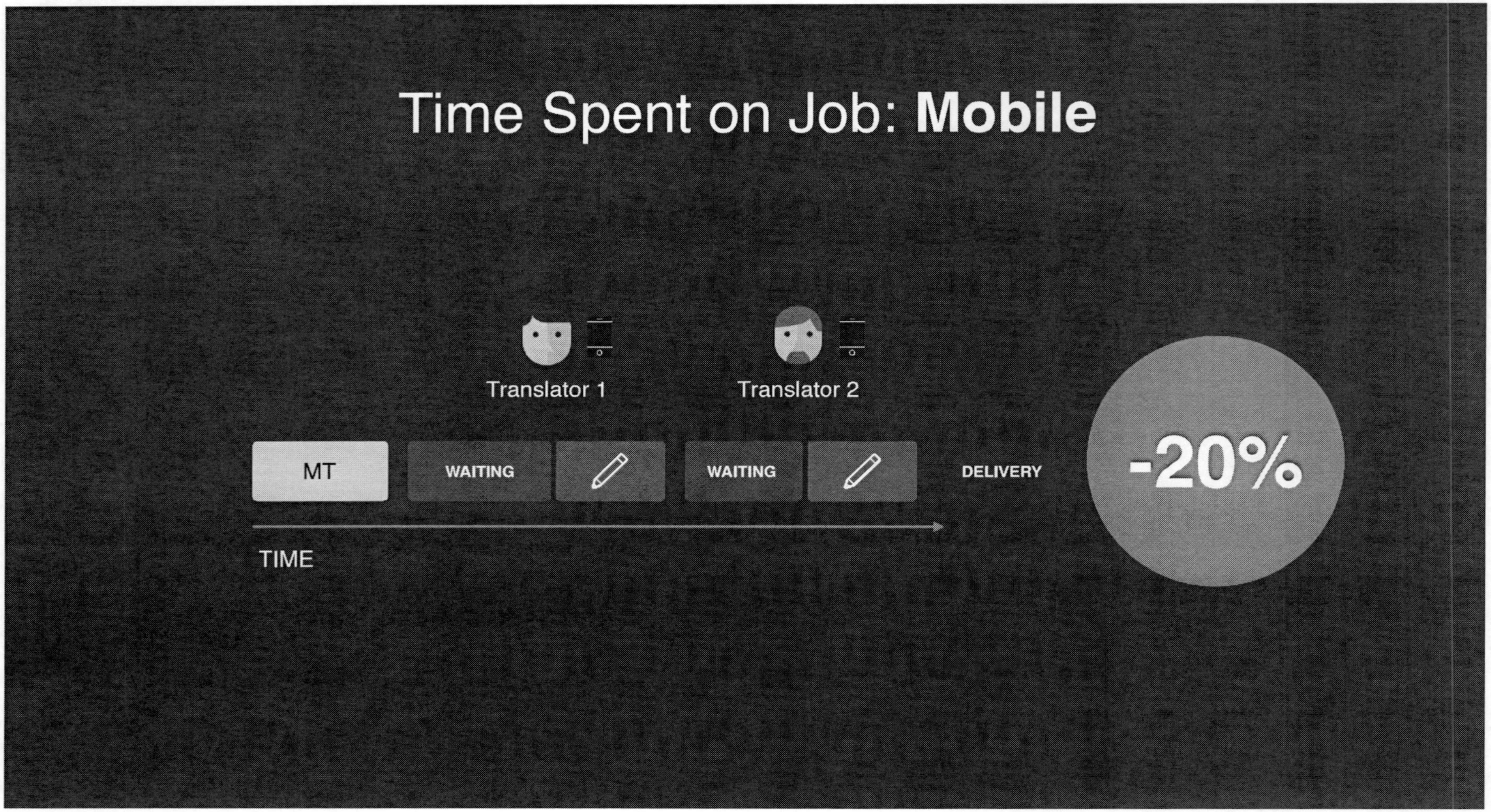

Time Spent on Job: **Mobile**

Proceedings for AMTA 2018 Workshop: Translation Quality Estimation and Automatic Post-Editing

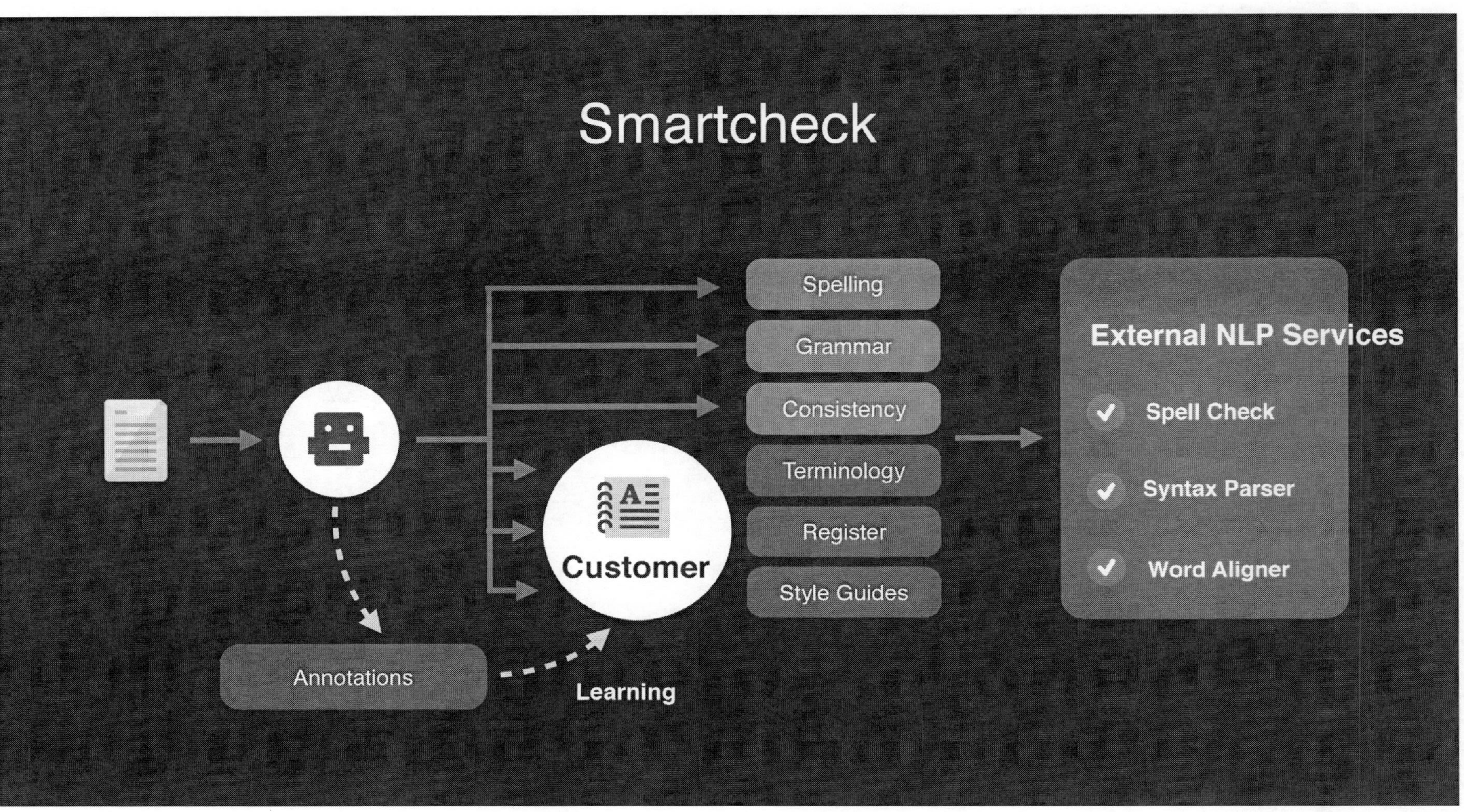

Smartcheck
Spelling
Grammar
Consistency
Terminology
Register
Style Guides
Customer
Annotations
Learning
External NLP Services
Spell Check
Syntax Parser
Word Aligner

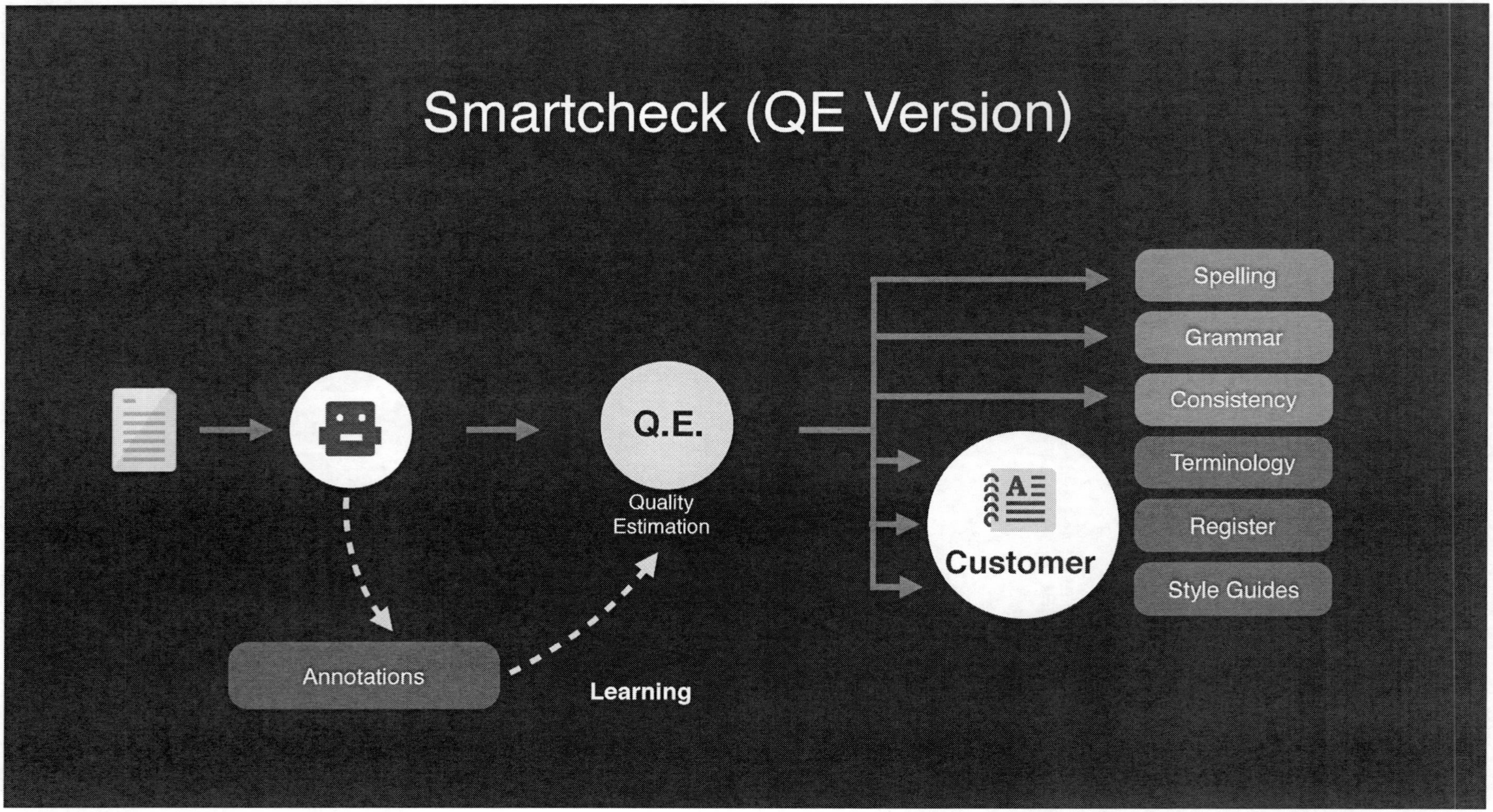

Proceedings for AMTA 2018 Workshop: Translation Quality Estimation and Automatic Post-Editing

Conversational
Customer Service
Bots
Messenger
slack
zendesk
salesforce
CYRANO API
CHAT API
MESSAGING API
CORE API
Language OS
Language Engine
MACHINE + HUMAN

Unbabel for Customer Service

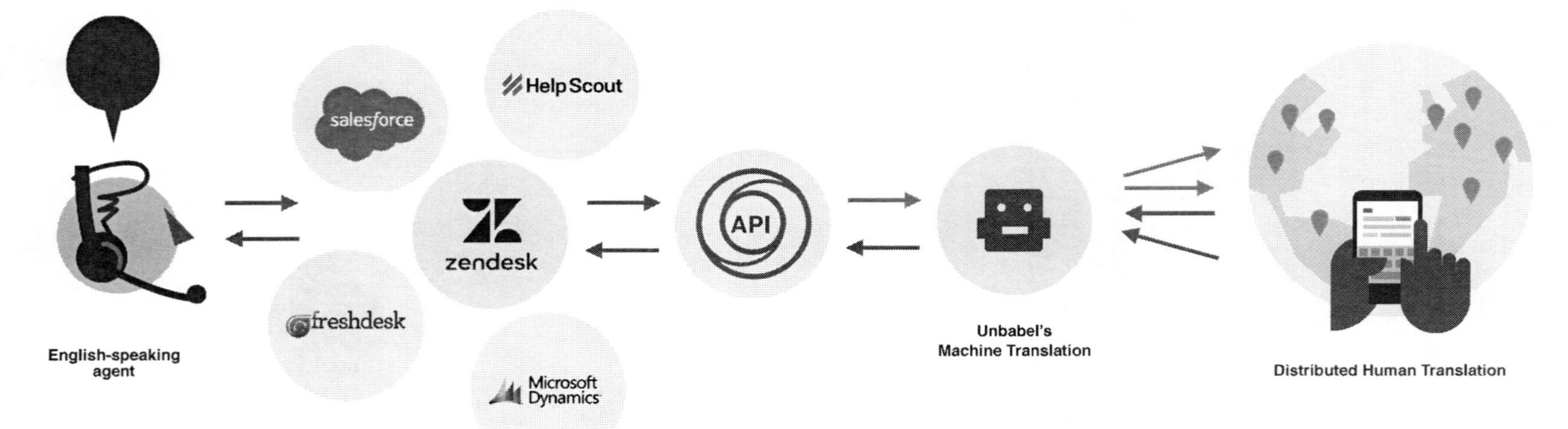

Unbabel adapts to any workflow

Proceedings for AMTA 2018 Workshop: Translation Quality Estimation and Automatic Post-Editing

Customer Replies: **Speed & Quality**

20 minutes

94

Proceedings for AMTA 2018 Workshop: Translation Quality Estimation and Automatic Post-Editing

Unbabel Chat

Native speaking
in multiple languages

chatter

API

Chat

Unbabel Chat

Understand and be understood in multiple languages.

with Juan Torres

Start typing here, or paste the text you'd like to be translated.

Translate to   Portuguese   Translate

Good morning, that's great! What color do you like?

Translating...

Good morning, I would like to buy a hat

Bom dia, gostava de comprar um chapéu

Proceedings for AMTA 2018 Workshop: Translation Quality Estimation and Automatic Post-Editing

Chat Translation Flow

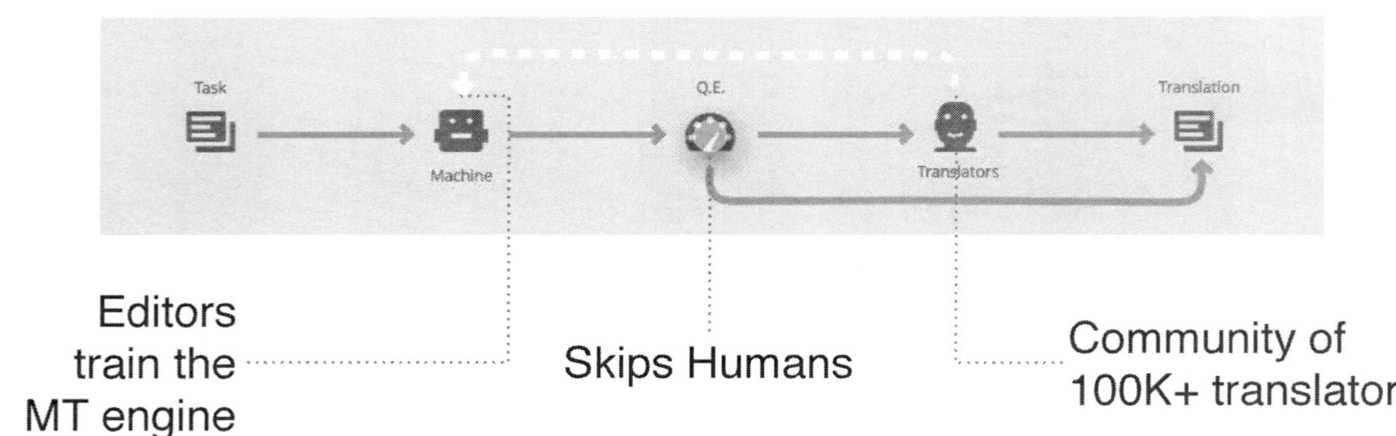

Editors train the MT engine

Skips Humans

Community of 100K+ translators

Proceedings for AMTA 2018 Workshop: Translation Quality Estimation and Automatic Post-Editing

Chat Messages: **Speed & Quality**

Proceedings for AMTA 2018 Workshop: Translation Quality Estimation and Automatic Post-Editing

Other Use Cases

Proceedings for AMTA 2018 Workshop: Translation Quality Estimation and Automatic Post-Editing

We're Hiring
https://unbabel.com/careers/
Unbabel

Proceedings for AMTA 2018 Workshop: Translation Quality Estimation and Automatic Post-Editing

Booking.com.

The world's #1 website for booking hotels and other accommodations.

- Founded in 1996 in Amsterdam
- Part of the Priceline Group (NASDAQ: PCLN) since 2005
- 1,500,000+ properties in more than 220 countries and territories representing over 27M rooms
- Over 1,550,000 room nights every 24 hours
- Number of unique destinations worldwide: 120,000+
- Total number of guest reviews: 173,000,000+
- 43 languages
- 198 offices worldwide
- More than 15,500 employees

Use case of MT at Booking.com

Mission: Empower people to experience the world without any language barrier.

2/3 of daily bookings on Booking.com is made in a language other than English

… thus it is important to have **locally relevant content at scale**

How Locally Relevant?

Allow partners and guests to **consume and produce content in their own language**
- Hotel Descriptions
- Customer Reviews
- Customer Service Support

Why At Scale?

- **One Million+ properties** and growing very fast
- **Frequent change requests** to update the content
- **43 languages** and more
- New user-generated **customer reviews / tickets** every second

Why MT?

Limited domain	One product
Lots of in-domain data	Av. 10M parallel sent. for big languages
Language expertise	In-house evaluators for 43 languages

Use Case #1: Hotel descriptions – currently translated by human in 43 languages based on visitor demand.

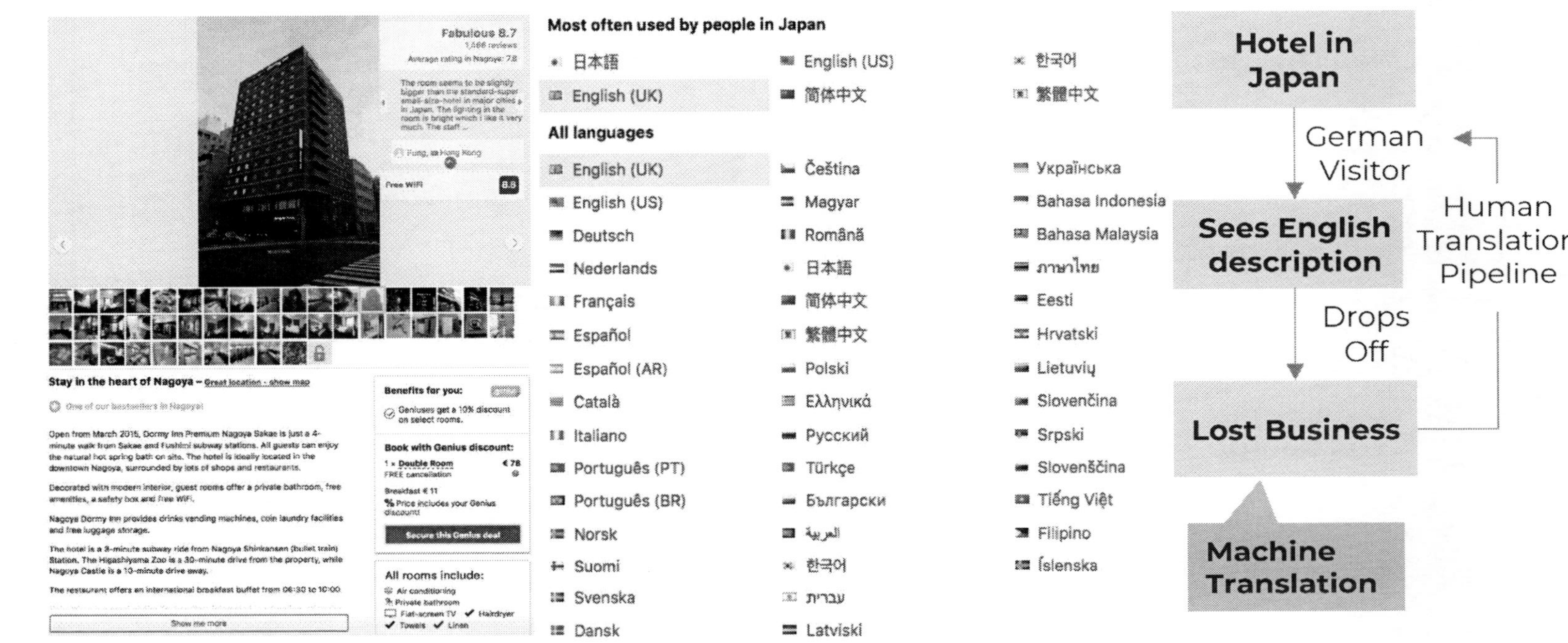

Use Case #2: Customer Reviews – currently not translated; available only if user leaves a review in that language.

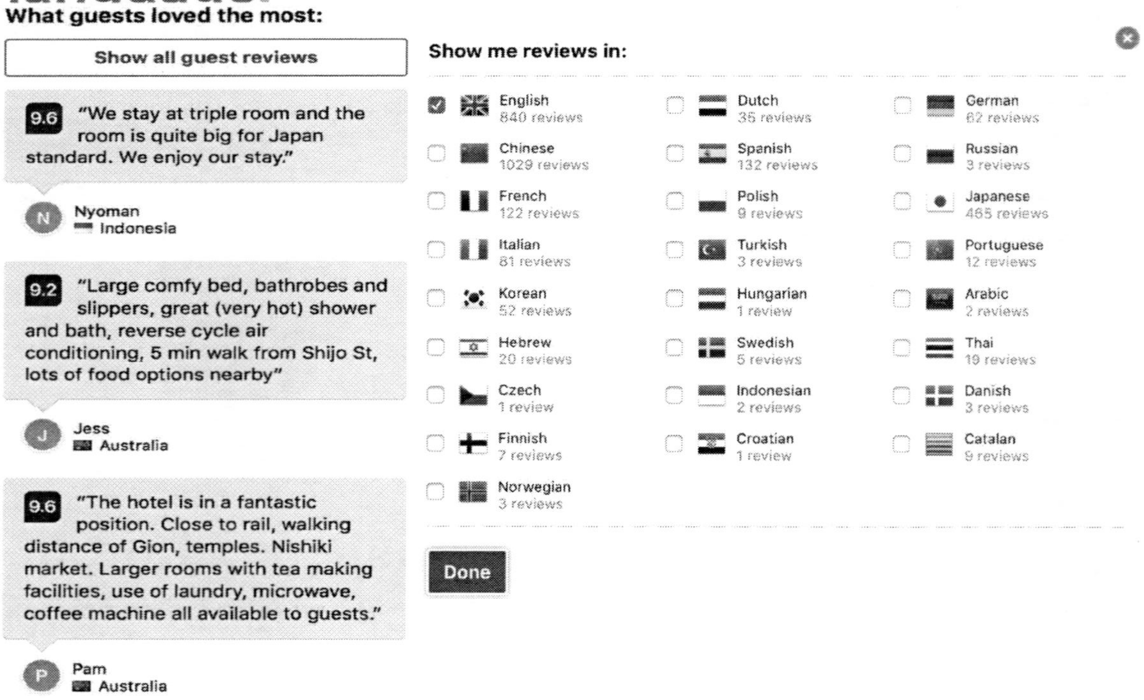

What guests loved the most:

Show all guest reviews

9.6 "We stay at triple room and the room is quite big for Japan standard. We enjoy our stay."

N Nyoman — Indonesia

9.2 "Large comfy bed, bathrobes and slippers, great (very hot) shower and bath, reverse cycle air conditioning, 5 min walk from Shijo St, lots of food options nearby"

J Jess — Australia

9.6 "The hotel is in a fantastic position. Close to rail, walking distance of Gion, temples. Nishiki market. Larger rooms with tea making facilities, use of laundry, microwave, coffee machine all available to guests."

P Pam — Australia

Show me reviews in:

English — 840 reviews
Chinese — 1029 reviews
French — 122 reviews
Italian — 81 reviews
Korean — 52 reviews
Hebrew — 20 reviews
Czech — 1 review
Finnish — 7 reviews
Norwegian — 3 reviews

Dutch — 35 reviews
Spanish — 132 reviews
Polish — 9 reviews
Turkish — 3 reviews
Hungarian — 1 review
Swedish — 5 reviews
Indonesian — 2 reviews
Croatian — 1 review

German — 62 reviews
Russian — 3 reviews
Japanese — 465 reviews
Portuguese — 12 reviews
Arabic — 2 reviews
Thai — 19 reviews
Danish — 3 reviews
Catalan — 9 reviews

Done

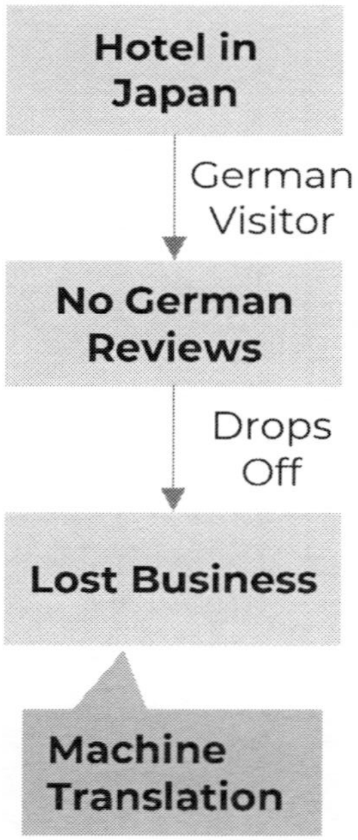

Use Case #3: Partner support – Partner-facing localization and customer/partner support.

Use Case #4: Translation support – make translation cheaper by providing high-quality productivity tools.

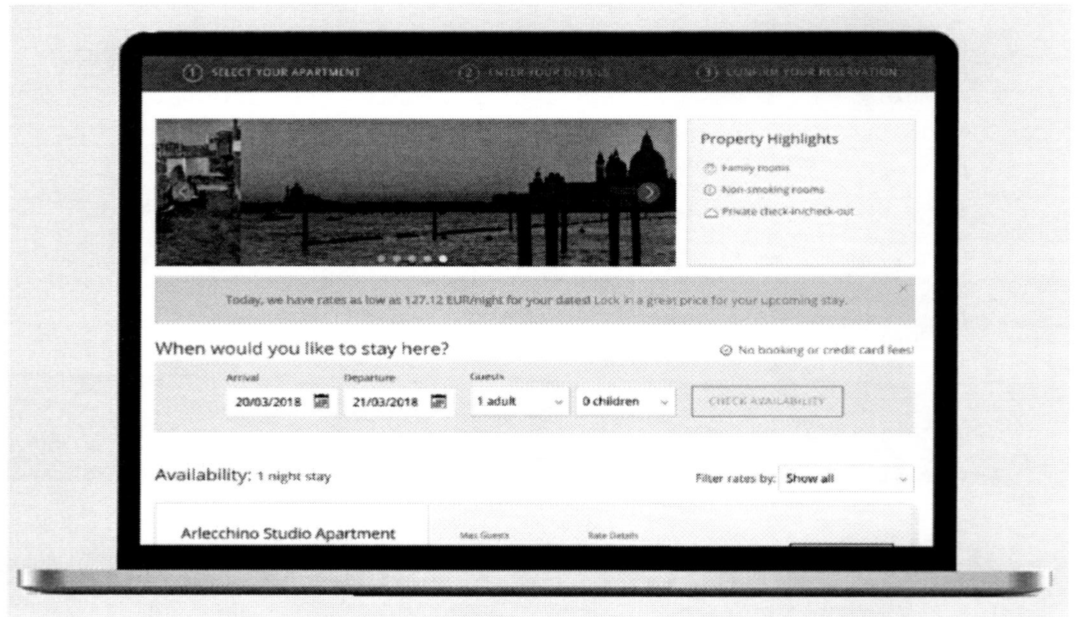

And there is even more..

Messages.

Ask a question

Say hello to your host or send a request!
Please write your requests in English or German.
Special requests cannot be guaranteed—but the accommodation will do its best to meet your needs.
You can always make a special request after your booking is complete!

我想要一个安静的房间

- ✔ Introduce yourself to your host
- ✔ What brings you to the area?
- ✔ Who are you travelling with?

Attractions .

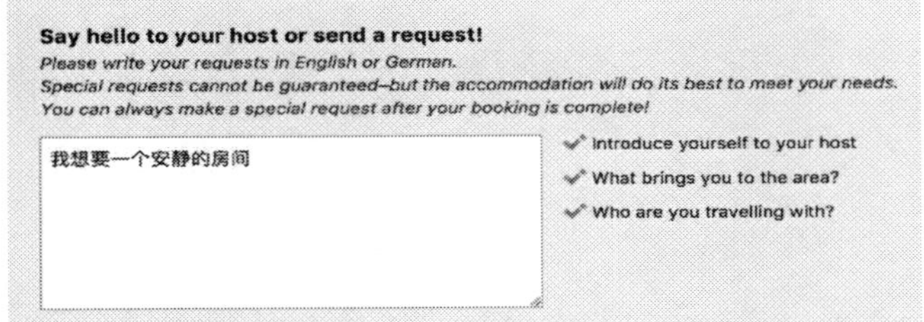

Attractions Recommended by Locals:

Hackescher Höfe
(0.7 km)
This collection of 8 courtyards has developed into a real entertainment hub. Both locals and tourists flock to the art galleries, independent shops and lively bars.

Mauerpark
(1.9 km)
With outdoor karaoke and dozens of market stalls, weekends at Mauerpark are certainly not a quiet affair. The basketball courts are where sports fans can show off their skills.

Tiergarten
(2.9 km)
This park is popular with locals who want to picnic on the grass or kick a ball around. In the winter, skaters spin circles on the frozen lakes.

Room descriptions.

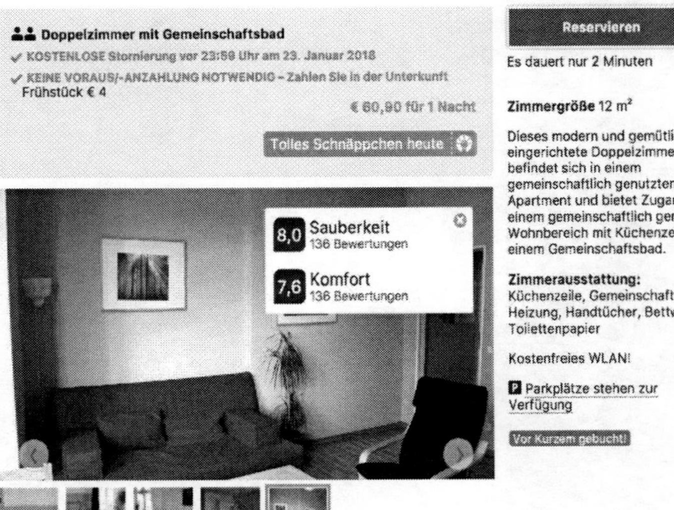

👥 Doppelzimmer mit Gemeinschaftsbad
✔ KOSTENLOSE Stornierung vor 23:59 Uhr am 23. Januar 2018
✔ KEINE VORAUS/-ANZAHLUNG NOTWENDIG – Zahlen Sie in der Unterkunft
Frühstück € 4

€ 60,90 für 1 Nacht

Tolles Schnäppchen heute

8,0 Sauberkeit 136 Bewertungen
7,6 Komfort 136 Bewertungen

Reservieren

Es dauert nur 2 Minuten

Zimmergröße 12 m²

Dieses modern und gemütlich eingerichtete Doppelzimmer befindet sich in einem gemeinschaftlich genutzten Apartment und bietet Zugang zu einem gemeinschaftlich genutzten Wohnbereich mit Küchenzeile und einem Gemeinschaftsbad.

Zimmerausstattung:
Küchenzeile, Gemeinschaftsbad, Heizung, Handtücher, Bettwäsche, Toilettenpapier

Kostenfreies WLAN!

P Parkplätze stehen zur Verfügung

Vor Kurzem gebucht!

Why not general purpose MT engines?

3

Reasons

1. Quality

Customized MT can do much better for our own content.

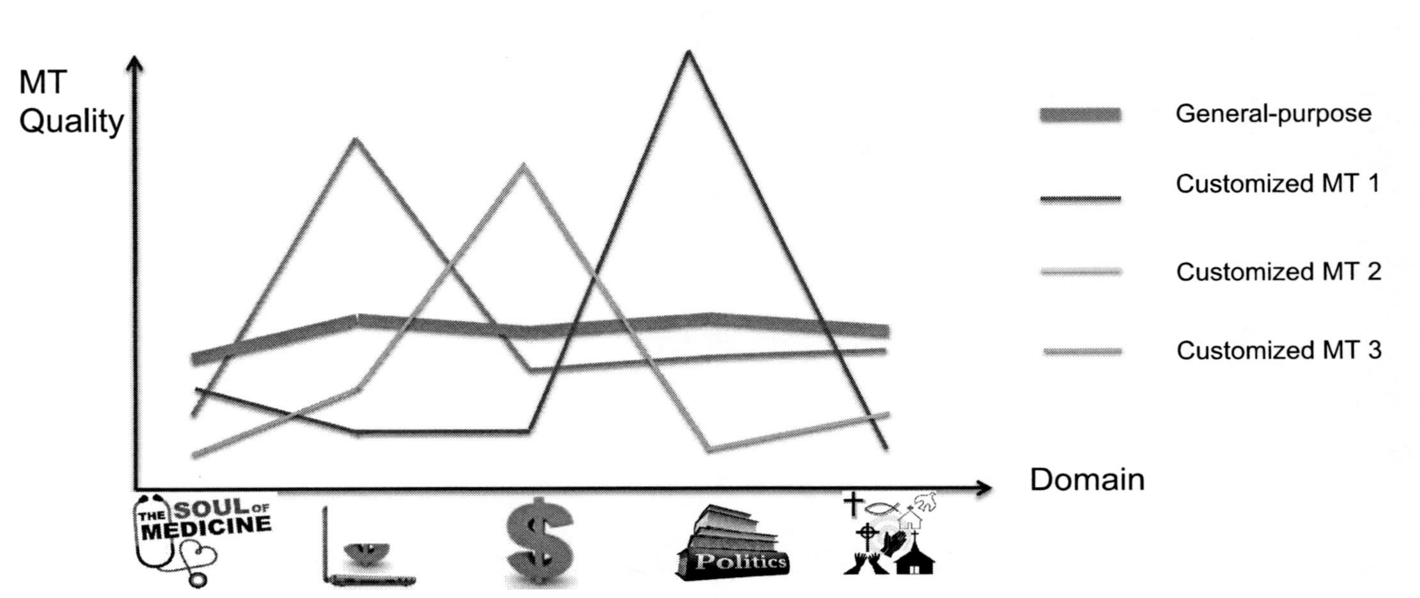

Hotel Description: Evaluation Results

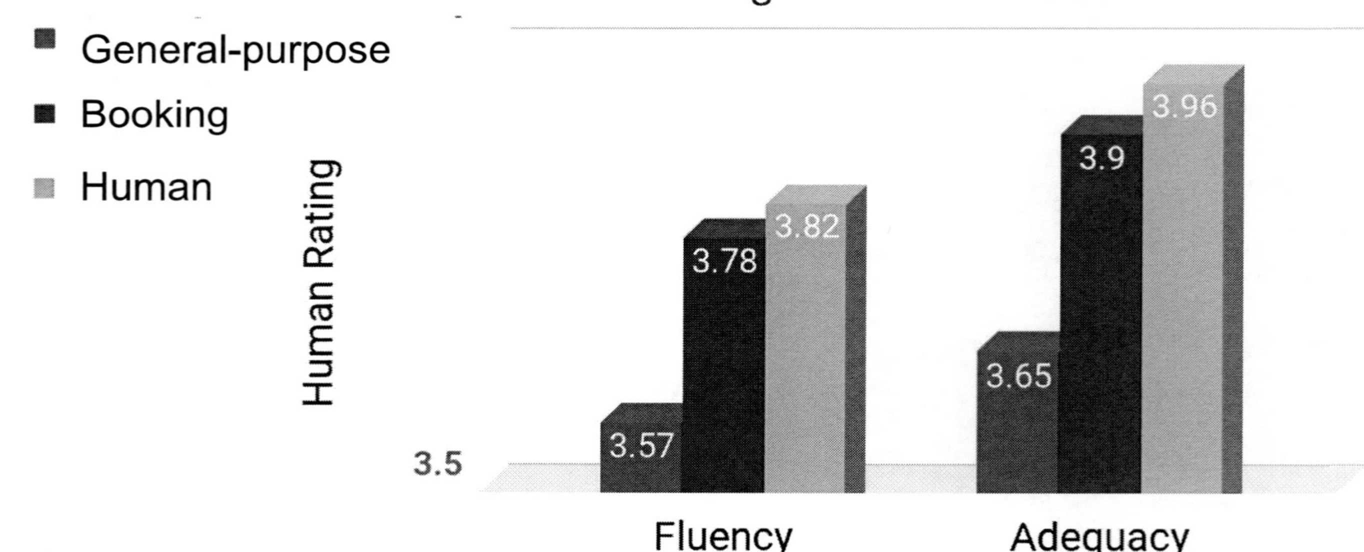

Customer Review: Evaluation Results

- General purpose
- Booking:
  - Hotel Description
- Booking:
  - Customer Review

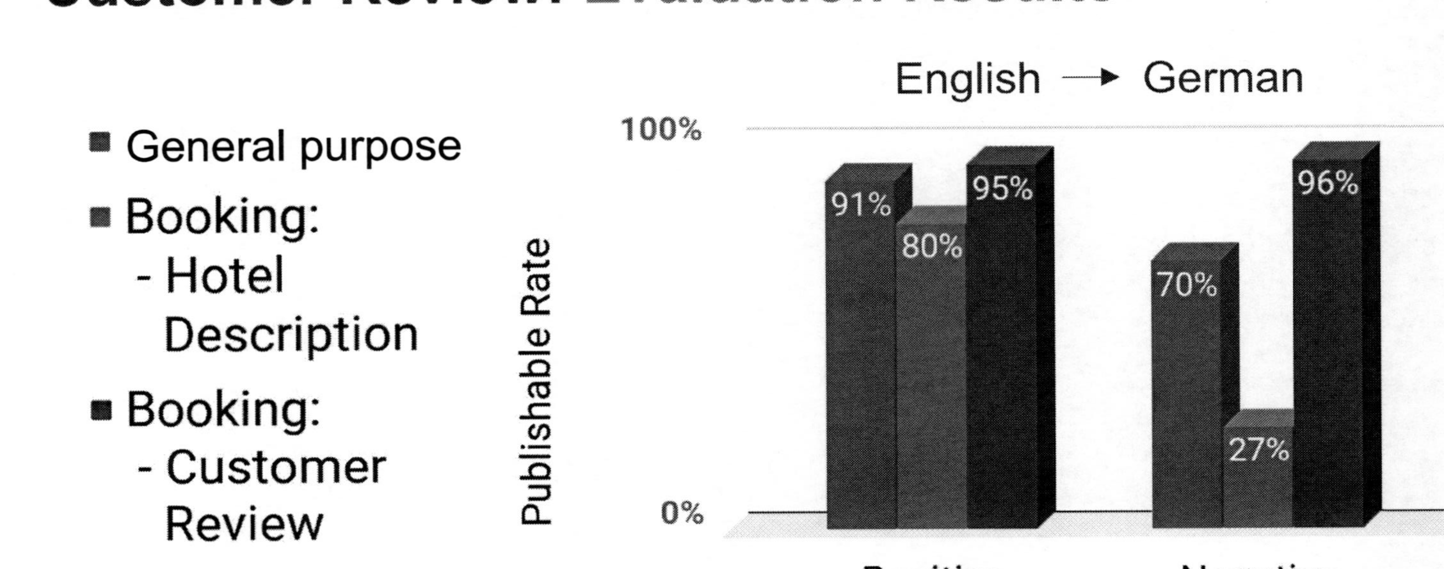

1. Quality
2. Risk

Can machine translation be **dangerous?**

The imperfection of MT might mislead users, have legal consequences for the company or damage brand's reputation and customer's confidence of translated content.

Examples of **business sensitive errors**

Offering a restaurant with WiFi, Hodor Ecolodge is located in Winterfell. On-site **parking is free**.

Die Hodor Ecolodge in Winterfell bietet ein Restaurant mit WLAN. **Parkplatz vor Ort ist verfügbar**.

The hotel offers 24-hour concierge service and free-use bicycles. **Pets can be accommodated** with advance reservation.

Der Conciergeservice steht rund um die Uhr zu Ihrer Verfügung und die Leihfahrräder nutzen Sie kostenfrei.

1. Quality
2. Risk
3. Cost

Cost

Cost
3XX M Euros
Today: XX M Euros
Untranslated Properties
Year
2018
2019
2020

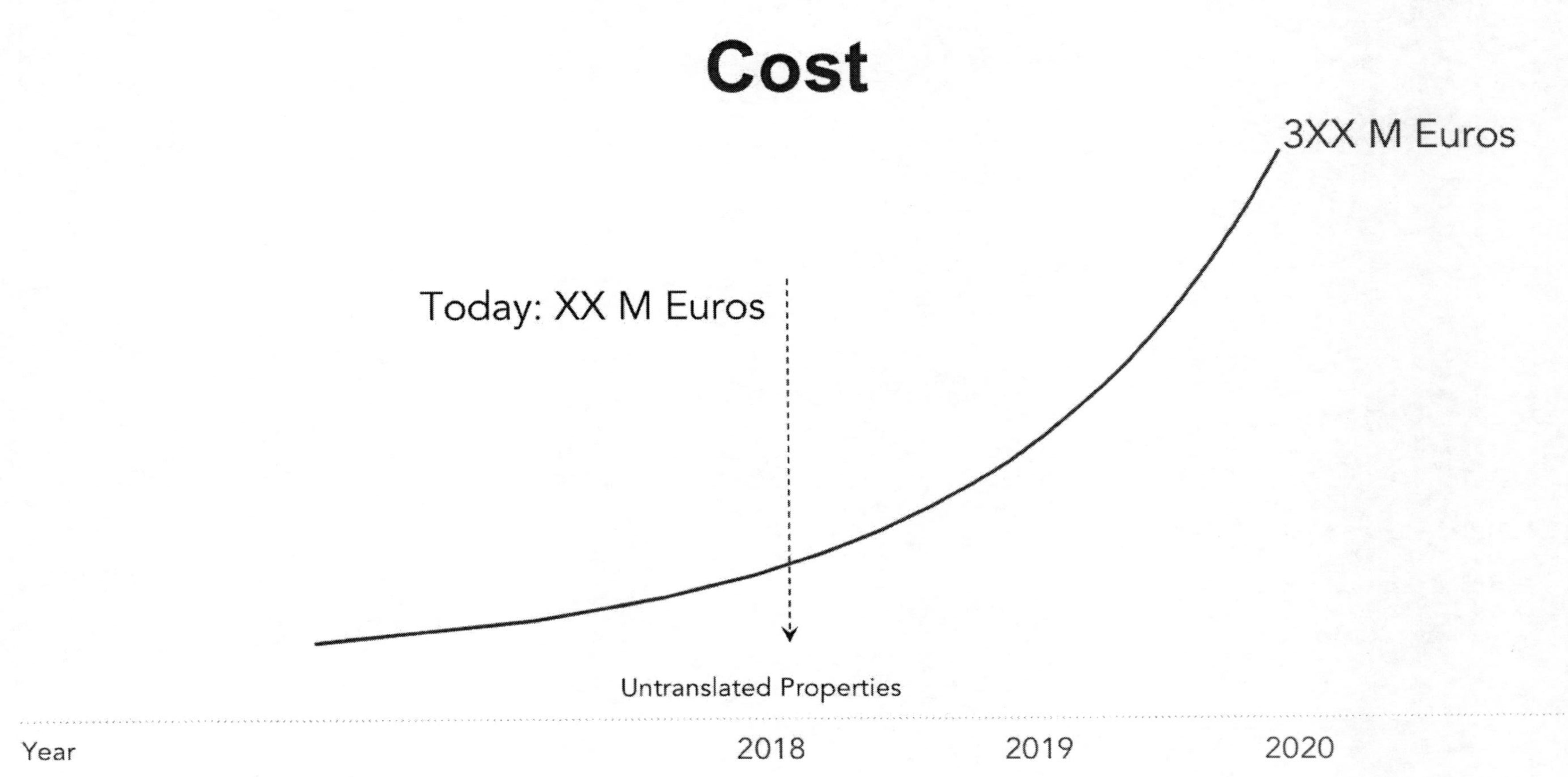

But why neural?

Adequacy / Fluency Scores for EN->DE hotel description translations

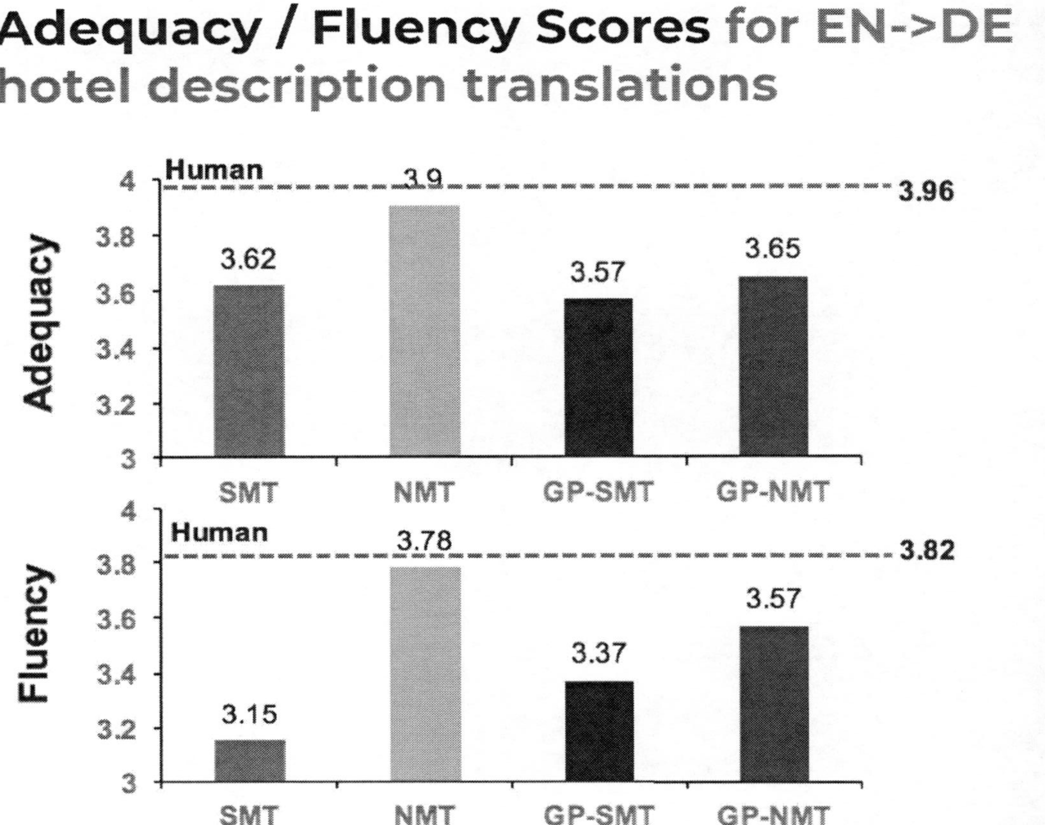

The Data

Hotel descriptions translated by human in 43 languages resulting in lots of in-domain data for MT

Monolingual reviews never translated in 43 languages resulting in lots of out-of-domain data potentially useful for MT

„Es war alles ziemlich nach vorne, das Zimmer hatte eine schöne Größe, die Betten waren bequem, wir brauchten keine Aussicht."

Übersetzt aus: English – Original anzeigen

Morgan
Großbritannien

„Sauber, tolle Lage, wunderbare und große Bar für die Gäste mit ausgezeichneten großen Bildschirmen (Football an diesem Abend)"

Übersetzt aus: English – Original anzeigen

Markus
Deutschland

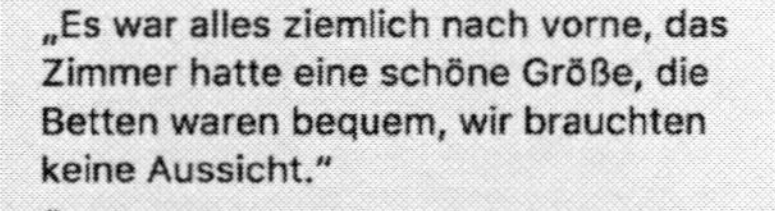

173M	Total reviews
17	Languages >1M reviews
37%	Properties w/o reviews

Few specific challenges and proposed solutions

Our NMT Model Configuration Details

Data Preparation	
Split Data	Train, Val, Test
Input Text Unit	Word Level
Tokenization	Aggressive
Max Sentence Length	50
Vocabulary Size	50,000

Model	
Model Type	seq2seq
Input Embedding Dimension	1,000
RNN Type	LSTM
# of hidden layers	4
Hidden Layer Dimension	1,000
Attention Mechanism	Global Attention

** Approx. 220 Million Parameters

Training	
Optimization Method	Stochastic Gradient Descent
Initial Learning Rate	1
Decay Rate	0.5
Decay Strategy	Decrease in Validation Perplexity <=0
Number of Epochs	5 - 13
Stopping Criteria	BLEU + sensitive sentences +constraints
Dropout	0.3
Batch Size	250

** 1 Epoch takes approx. 2 days on a single NVIDIA Tesla K80 GPU

Translate	
Beam Size	10
Unknown Words Handling	Source with Highest Attention

Evaluate	
Auto	BLEU
Human	A/F
Other	A/B Test

** MT pipeline based on Harvard implementation of OpenNMT

Our challenges

Real-world content

- Named entities
- Rare words

Customer facing output

- Human loop
- BLEU & human evaluation correlation
- Business sensitive issues

Lack of parallel training data

- Use and sources of data
- Domain adaptation

Our challenges

Real-world content

- Named entities
- Rare words

Customer facing output

- Human loop
- BLEU & human evaluation correlation
- Business sensitive issues

Lack of parallel training data

- Use and sources of data
- Domain adaptation

End-to-end approach insufficient to handle Named Entities, pre-processing improves performance

Problem

Hotel Shirakawa is just a **5-minute** walk from **Fushimi Subway Station**. **Nagoya Castle** is a **10-minute** drive, and the **Sakae shopping area** is **500 m** away.

Approach

Search for named entities in source → Replace with placeholders → Translate → Substitute as per target format

- Regular expression for distance, date, time
- Hybrid dictionary, conditional random field NER for names

Results

Raw source	Winterfell Railway Station can be reached in a **55-minute** car ride.
Pure NMT Translation	Den Bahnhof Winterfell erreichen Sie nach einer **5-mintigen** Autofahrt.
NMT with distance placeholders	Den Bahnhof Winterfell erreichen Sie nach einer **55-mintigen** Autofahrt.

Better handling of rare words and 4 points BLEU score improvement with Byte Pair Encoding (BPE)

Raw source	Offering a restaurant with WiFi, Hodor Ecolodge is located in Winterfell.
Tokenized source	offering^C a^L restaurant^L with^L wi ■^{C} fi^C ■,^{N} ho ■^{C} dor^L ecolodge^L is^L located^L in^L winter ■^{C} fell^L ■.^{N}
Tokenized output	die^C ho ■^{C} dor^L ecolodge^C in^L winter ■^{C} fell^L bietet^L ein^L restaurant^C mit^L wlan^U ■.^{N}
De-tokenized output	Die Hodor Ecolodge in Winterfell bietet ein Restaurant mit WLAN.

BLEU	50K-Vocab baseline	Joint BPE				Separate BPE			
		30K	**50K**	**70K**	**90K**	**30K**	**50K**	**70K**	**90K**
Epoch 5	39.54	**43.75**	43.46	43.40	41.23	42.81	42.35	39.73	N/A
Epoch 10	40.95	**44.55**	44.52	43.81	43.81	43.39	43.48	43.51	
Epoch 15	42.01	45.08	45.91	**46.14**	45.75	43.58	43.23	45.17	
Epoch 20	42.15	46.31	46.43	**46.61**	45.62	45.22	46.00	45.90	

Translation of informal language of customer reviews and partner-(company)-user comms

Examples

- The stuff
- The night guy aund the girl in the morning who looks like manage the hotel
- They keep your luggage for free if you for some days to Sapa
- And as well the offered us a breakfast in the morning asap
- Thans for the detail

Approach

Correct typos which are easy to fix → Adapt to the UGC domain → Translate → Iterate

Results

Adequacy score	Positive reviews	Negative reviews
Baseline	80 %	27 %
+typos correction+DA	95 %	96 %

Our challenges

Real-world content
- Named entities
- Rare words

Customer facing output
- Human loop
- BLEU & human evaluation correlation
- Business sensitive issues

Lack of parallel training data
- Use and sources of data
- Domain adaptation

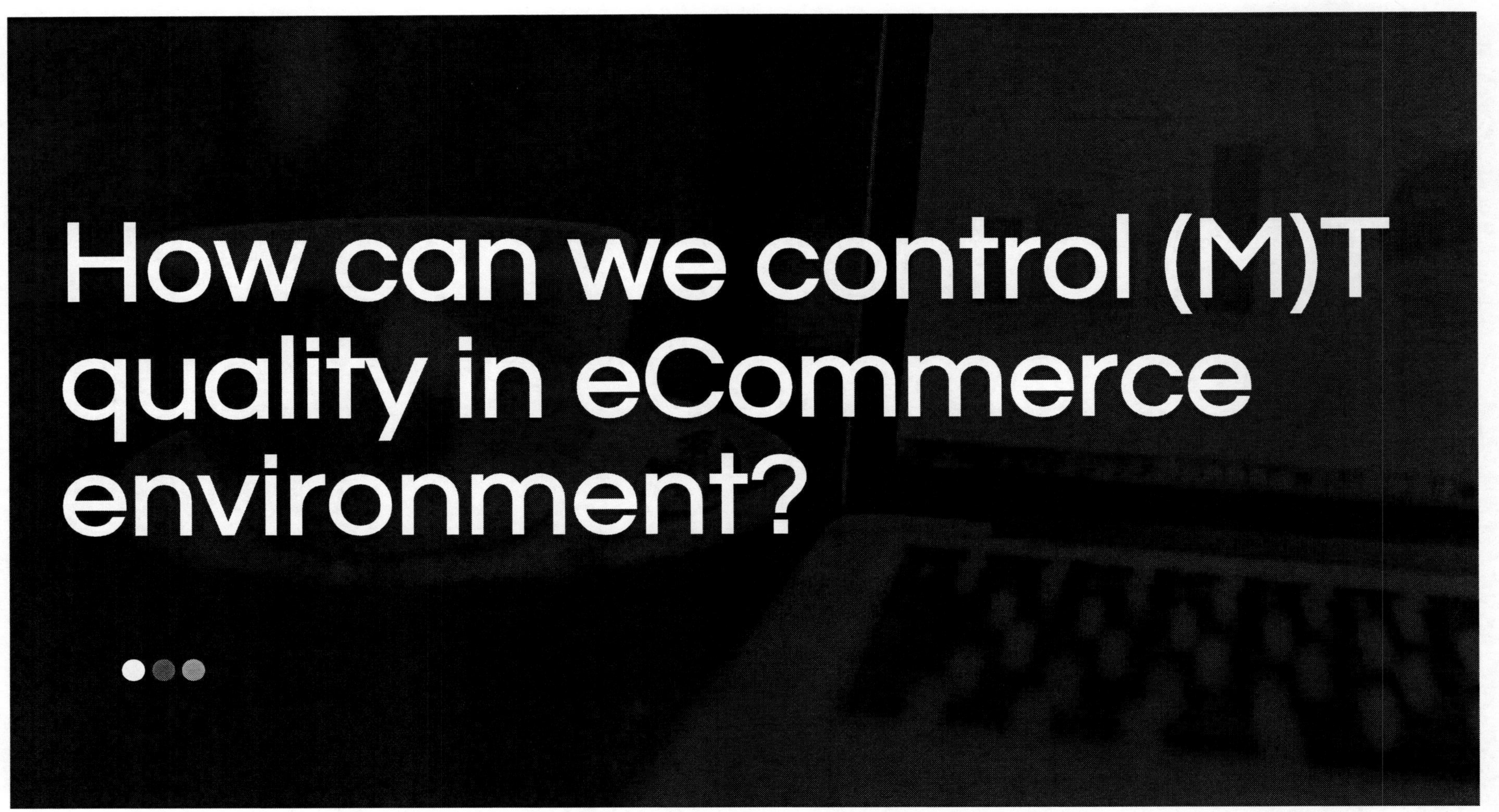

How can we control (M)T quality in eCommerce environment?

Integrated approach to MT evaluation.

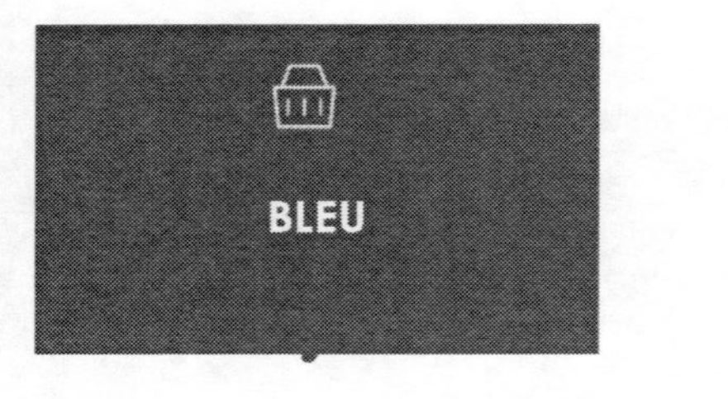

Applicable to make sure there are no new bugs introduced as the result of the MT engine retraining and some experiments.

Scoring the quality of entity handling.

Rough assessment of the MT-ed content in terms of its publishability

Links MT quality with potential threats for the business

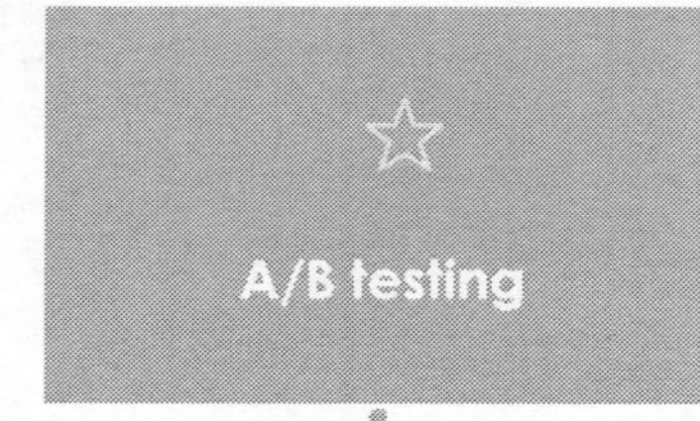

Two-sample hypothesis testing where business metrics are to be optimized

Improvement with more data is better seen from human evaluation...

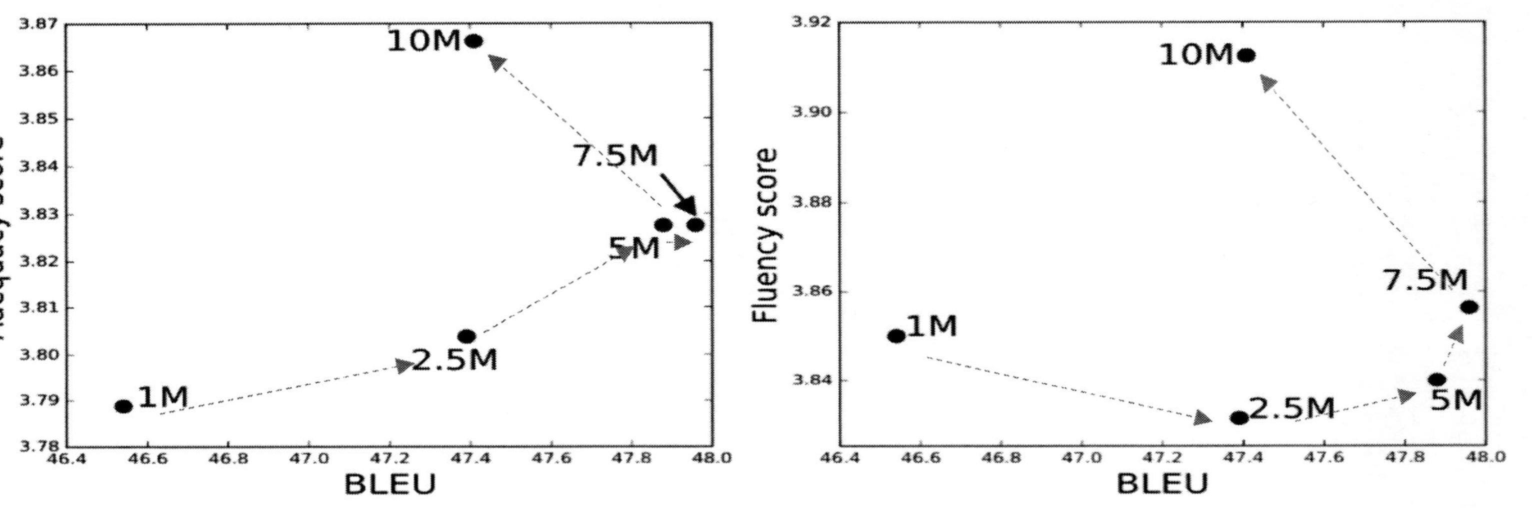

...which doesn't seem to be completely aligned with BLEU

Business Sensitivity Framework to detect if aspects and sub-aspects match between source & translated content

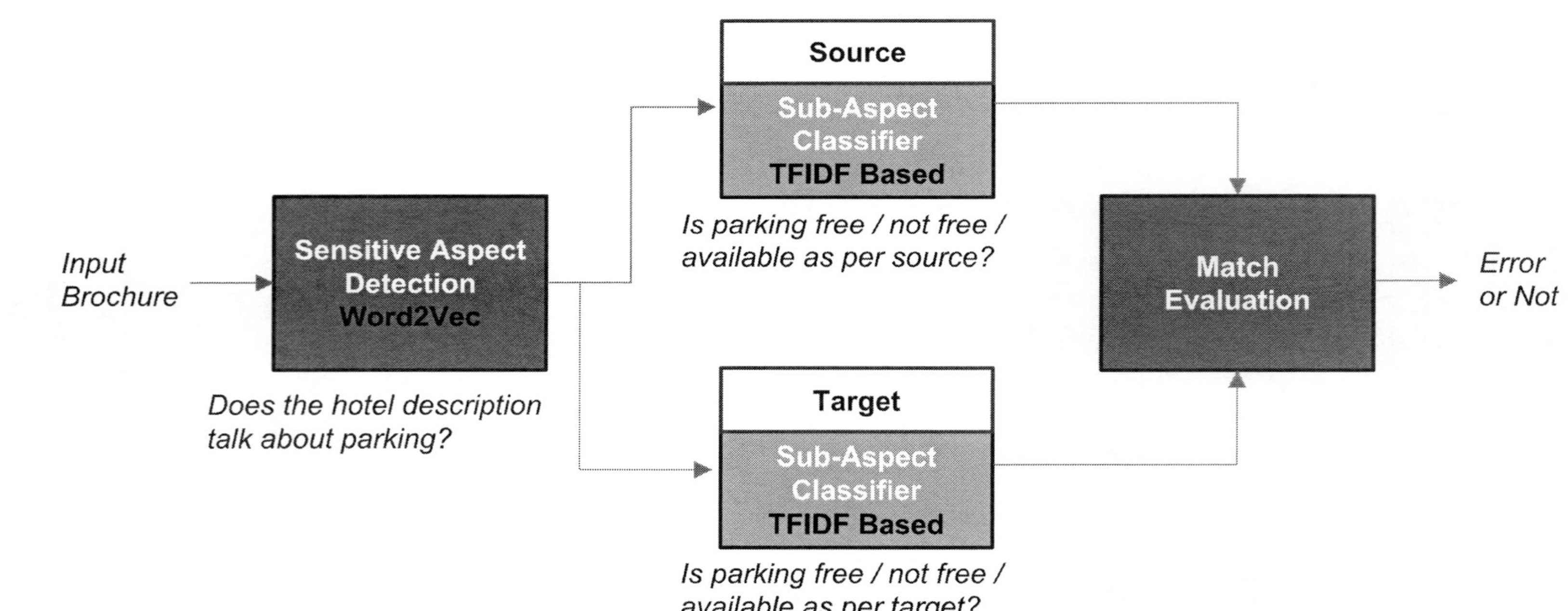

Business Sensitivity Framework: results

FREE/NOT FREE PARKING		translation		
		free parking	not free parking	not about parking
source	free parking	99.4%	0.5%	0.1%
	not free parking	5.1%	94.6%	0.3%
	not about parking	<0.1%	<0.1%	99.9%

Our challenges

Real-world content

- Named entities
- Rare words

Customer facing output

- Human loop
- BLEU & human evaluation correlation
- Business sensitive issues

Lack of parallel training data

- Use and sources of data
- Domain adaptation

-   A few thousand of in domain sentences.

-In addition to the hotel descriptions data, available external open data is used including data from:
- *Movie subtitles*
- *Wikipedia*
- *TED talks*
- *New commentary*
- *EuroParl*

-Synthetic Data

-Gradual downsampling (Wees et al., 2017)

Booking.com

Data generation for customer reviews based on mono - lingual / non-parallel bilingual data

Data	Idea	Methodology
External Corpus	Use in-domain language model to select most relevant sentences from external corpus	**Bilingual Cross Entropy Difference** (Axelrod et al) - To select sentences that are most similar to in-domain but different to out-of-domain.
Synthetic Data	Use large amount of mono-lingual data to create some synthetic in-domain data	**Rico Sennrich et al**. – Back translate target language in-domain data into source by reversing our MT model.
In-domain Data	Create a small amount of in-domain corpus as well, to test for additional impact	**Human Translation**

Domain Adaptation using gradual downsampling to most relevant data selected by in-domain language model

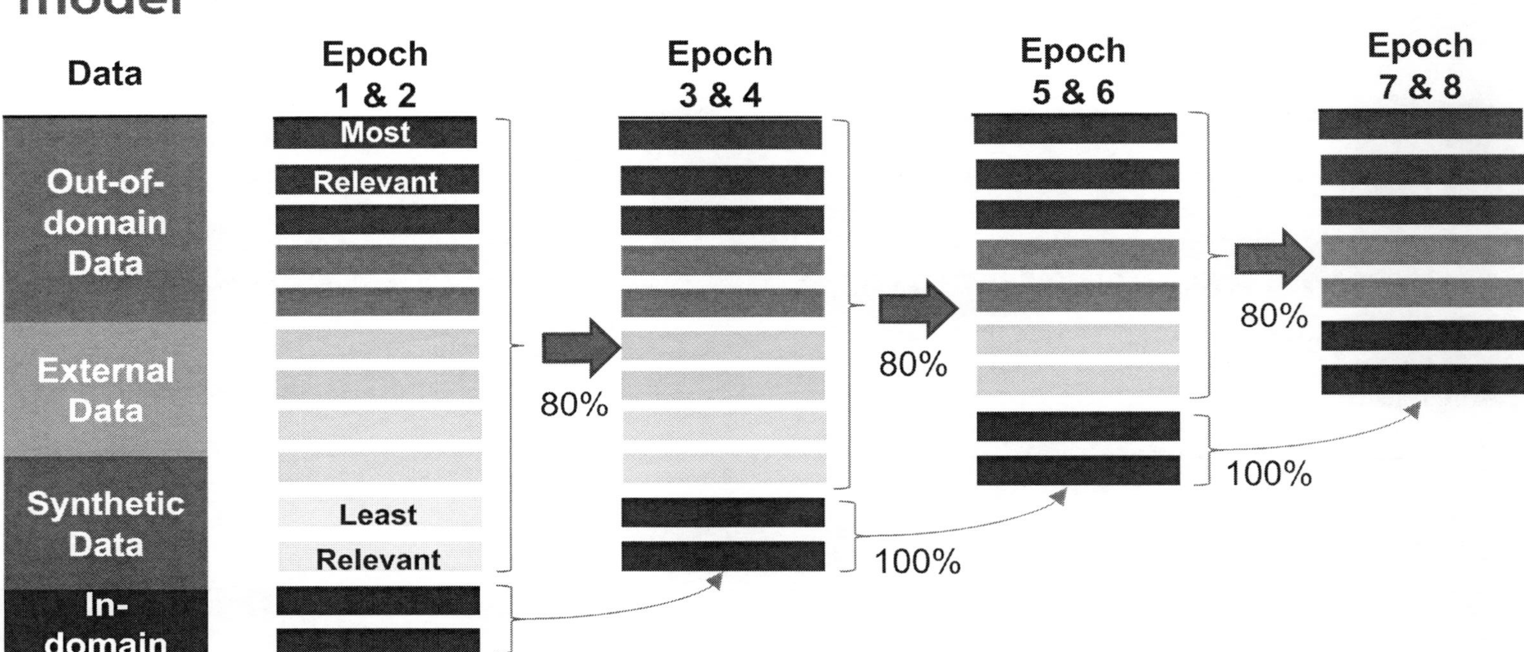

Gradual downsampling vs fine tuning

Gradual downsampling	Fine tuning
Faster iteration	Takes time to get the General Model trained
Trained for specific use case from the beginning	Can be adapted to multiple use cases
Applicable without In-domain parallel data	Needs In-domain parallel data
Less accurate	More accurate

No answer yet

Human Evaluation Results for Domain Adapted Model to translate customer reviews (gradual downsampling)

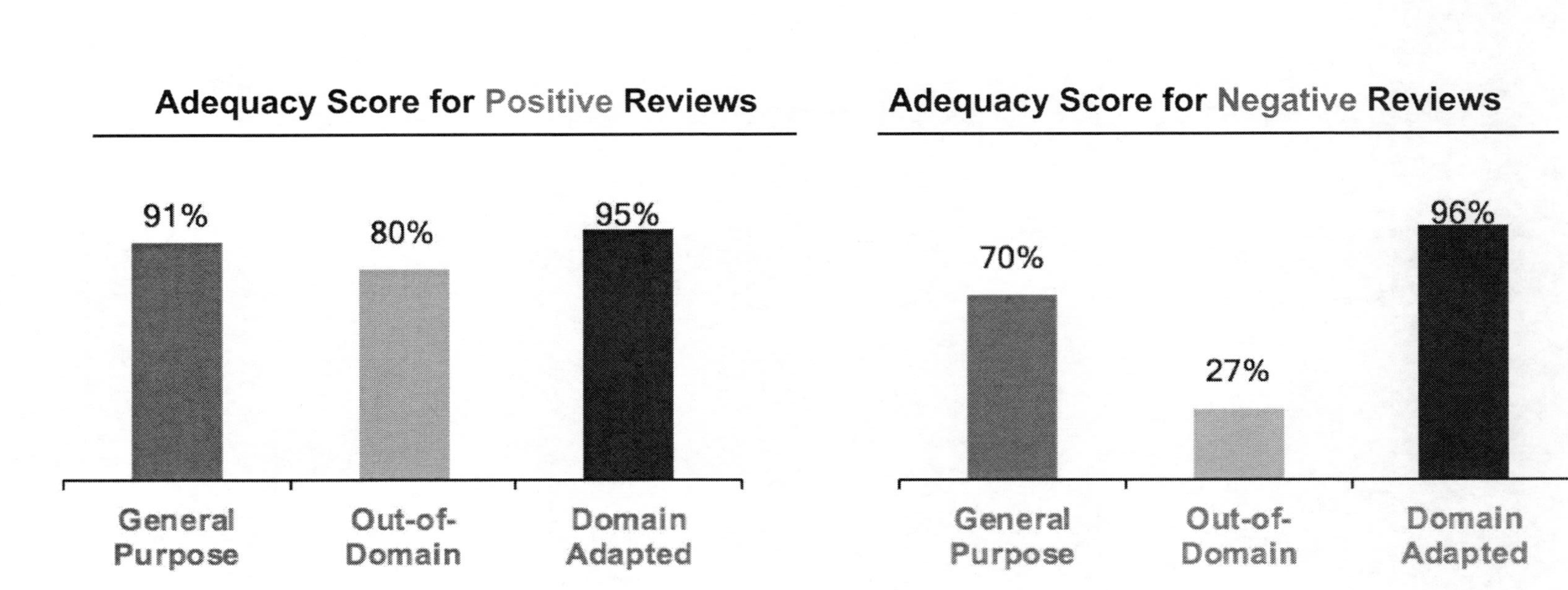

Want to know more?

Machine Translation at Booking.com:
Journey and Lessons Learned
EAMT (User Track)
Prague, May 2017
Best Paper Award

Toward a full-scale neural machine
translation in production: the
Booking.com use case
MT Summit XVI (Commercial Track)
Nagoya, Sep 2017

Automatic post-editing and Quality Estimation

What is the business rationale?

The Whys:

- Reduce monetary and legal risks
- Increase user trust
- Increase traction with partners and customers (B2B and B2C)
- As a part of the better integrated MT system, improve user experience

Complete MT-QE-APE architecture

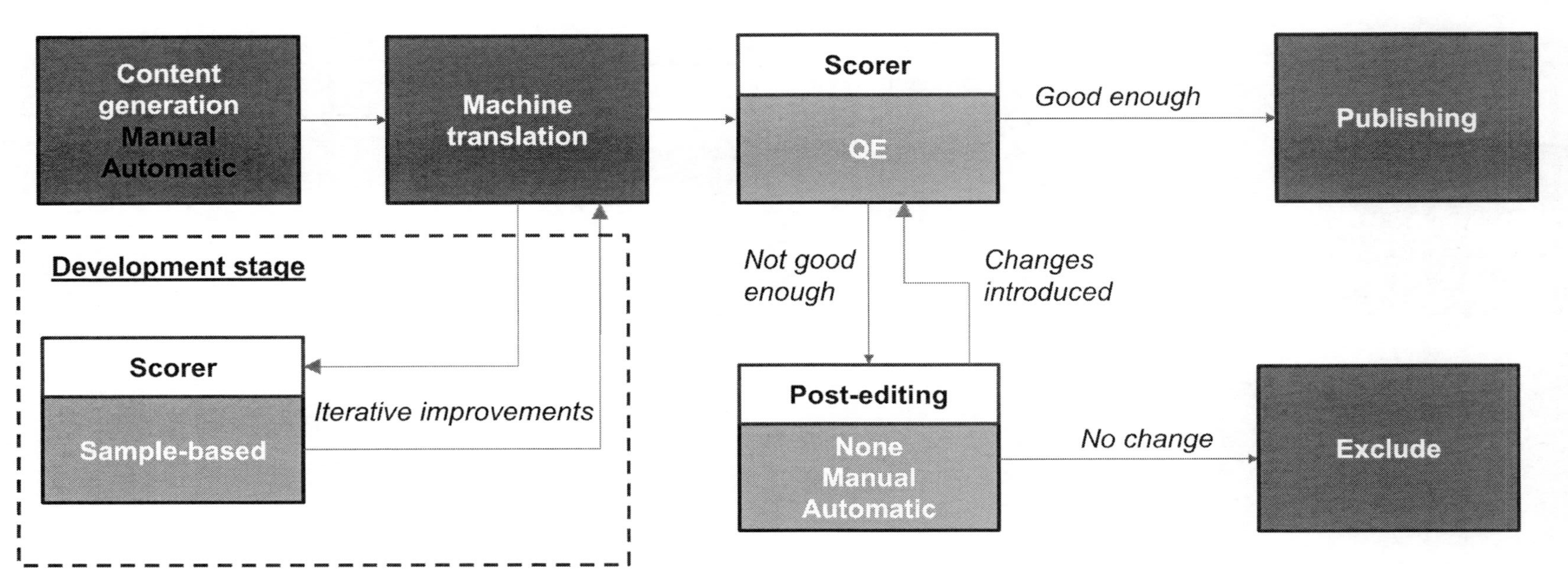

How can we validate?

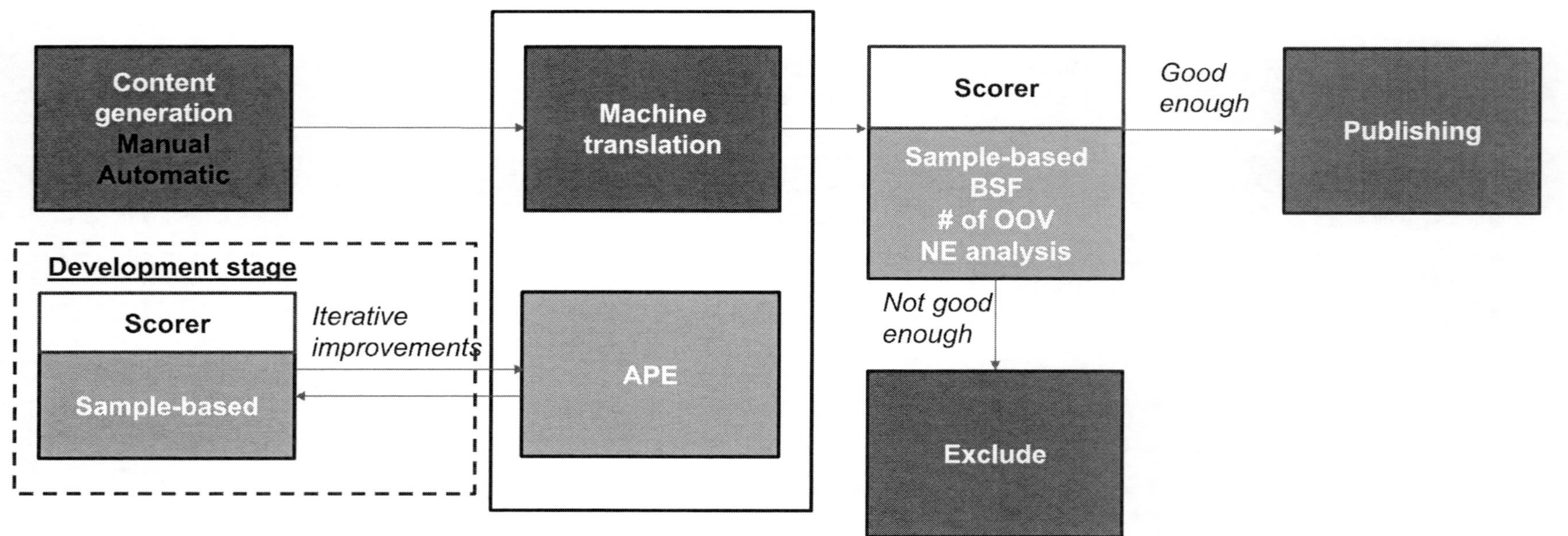

How can we design an APE system, which would address the most important problems?

Sentence level APE

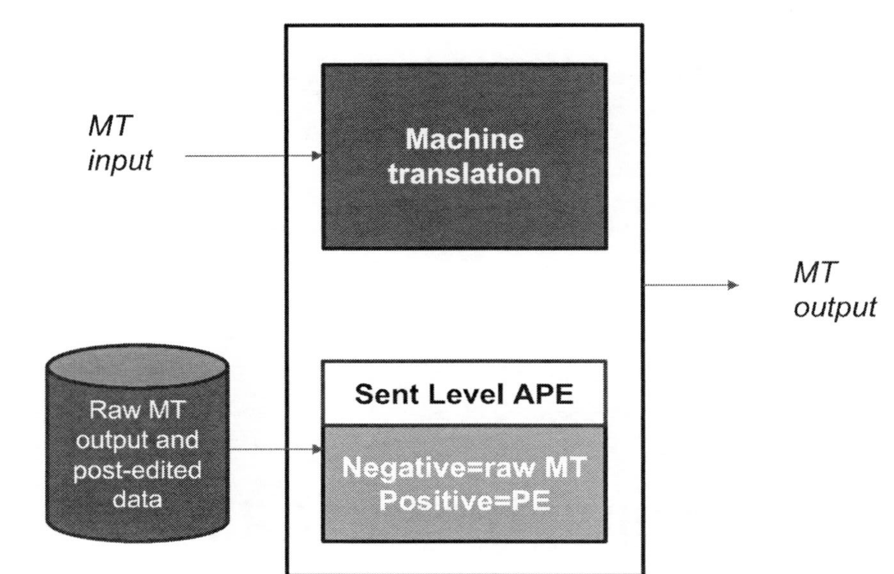

Credit: MT research group at the University of Edinburgh

Negative and Positive training examples

Source

Offering a restaurant with WiFi, Hodor Ecolodge is located in Winterfell. On-site **parking is free**.

Raw MT

Die Hodor Ecolodge in Winterfell bietet ein Restaurant mit WLAN. **Parkplatz vor Ort ist verfügbar**.

Post-edited MT

Die Hodor Ecolodge in Winterfell bietet ein Restaurant mit WLAN. **Parkplatz vor Ort ist kostenlos**.

How can we design an APE system, which would address the most important problems?

Word level

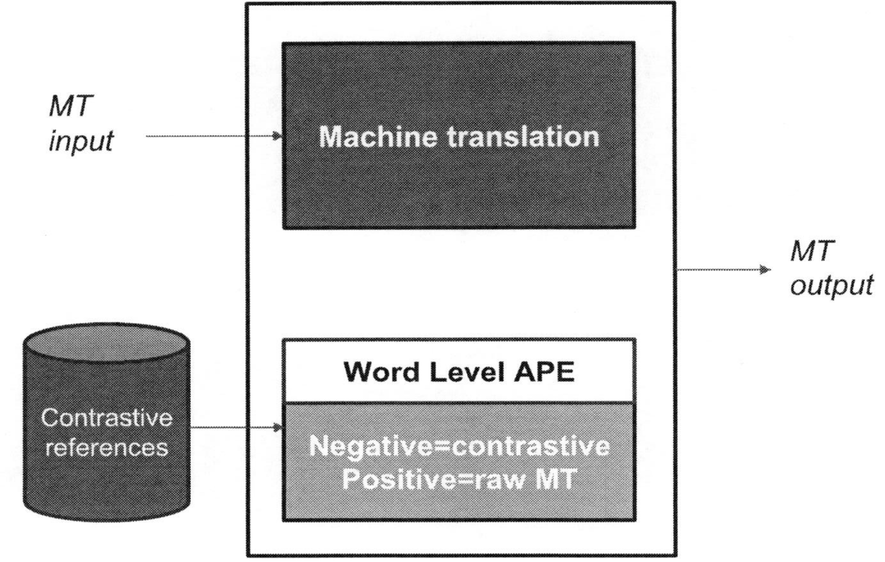

Credit: MT research group at the University of Edinburgh

Contrastive references

Source

On-site **parking is free**.

Translation

Parkplatz vor Ort ist verfügbar.

Contrastive

Parkplatz vor Ort ist nicht **verfügbar**
or
Parkplatz vor Ort ist kostenlos.

Future Directions (applied research and technology)

Explore alternative NMT technologies
- "Transformer" by (Vaswani et al., 2017)

Ensure high quality of translations
- Named Entities
- NMT with reconstruction (Tu et al., 2017)
- Optimization for UGC
- Conditioning MT output on structured data

Reinforcement learning (Nguyen et al., 2017)

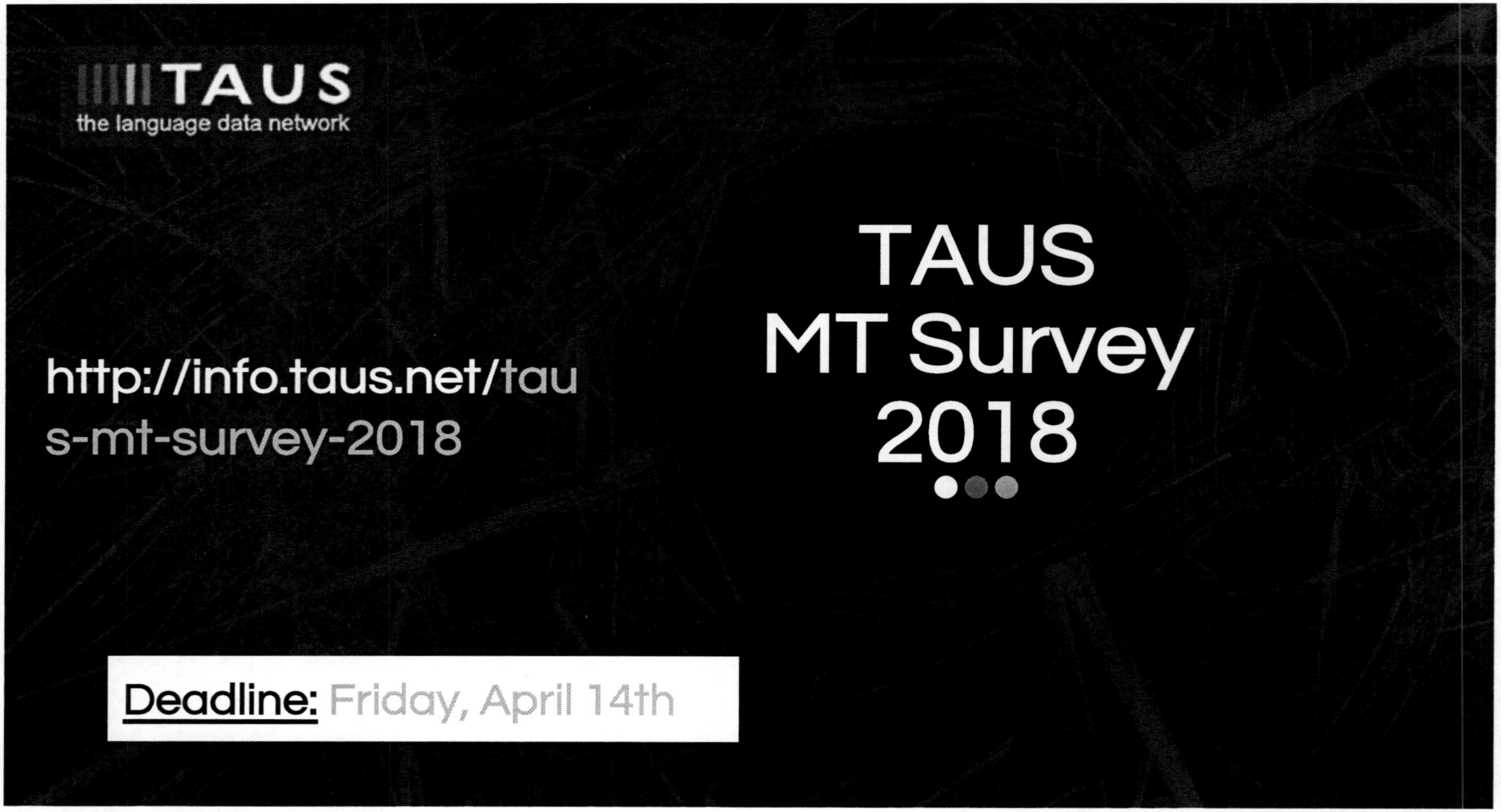

TAUS
the language data network
http://info.taus.net/tau
s-mt-survey-2018
TAUS
MT Survey
2018
Deadline: Friday, April 14th

Thank You
Questions?

Maxim Khalilov

maxim.khalilov@booking.com
www.linkedin.com/nl/maximkhalilov

Are we experiencing the
Golden Age of Automatic Post-Editing?

Marcin Junczys-Dowmunt
Microsoft AI and Research

Translation Quality Estimation and Automatic Post-Editing
AMTA 2018

Why automatic post-editing?

Proceedings for AMTA 2018 Workshop: Translation Quality Estimation and Automatic Post-Editing

Why automatic post-editing?

Can't we just retrain the original system?

Proceedings for AMTA 2018 Workshop: Translation Quality Estimation and Automatic Post-Editing

Why automatic post-editing?

Can't we just retrain the original system?

Not always:

- black-box scenario
- specialized system make better use of PE data (?)
- synergy effects (RB-MT + SMT, SMT + NMT)

Proceedings for AMTA 2018 Workshop: Translation Quality Estimation and Automatic Post-Editing

Popular metrics:
TER (Translation Error Rate) and BLEU

Proceedings for AMTA 2018 Workshop: Translation Quality Estimation and Automatic Post-Editing

Historic APE systems:

Simard et. al (2007). Statistical Phrase-based Post-editing. NAACL.

- Automatic Post-editing of a rule-based system with a phrase-based SMT system;
- About 30,000 paragraphs of triples per language pair (En-Fr/Fr-En);
- Train PB-SMT system on RB-MT output and PE data;
- Chain systems together;
- Impressive gains over the baselines.

Proceedings for AMTA 2018 Workshop: Translation Quality Estimation and Automatic Post-Editing

Historic APE systems:

Bechara et. al (2011). Statistical Post-Editing for a Statistical MT System. MT-Summit.

- ► Automatic Post-editing of a phrase-based SMT with another phrase-based SMT system.
- ► Barely any gains over the baselines.
- ► But interesting idea: Contextual Statistical APE

Proceedings for AMTA 2018 Workshop: Translation Quality Estimation and Automatic Post-Editing

Contextual Statistical APE

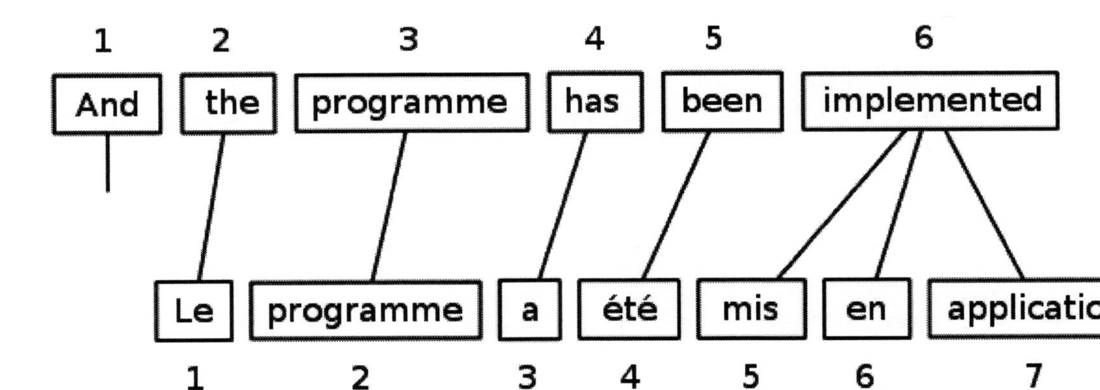

le#the

Proceedings for AMTA 2018 Workshop: Translation Quality Estimation and Automatic Post-Editing

Contextual Statistical APE

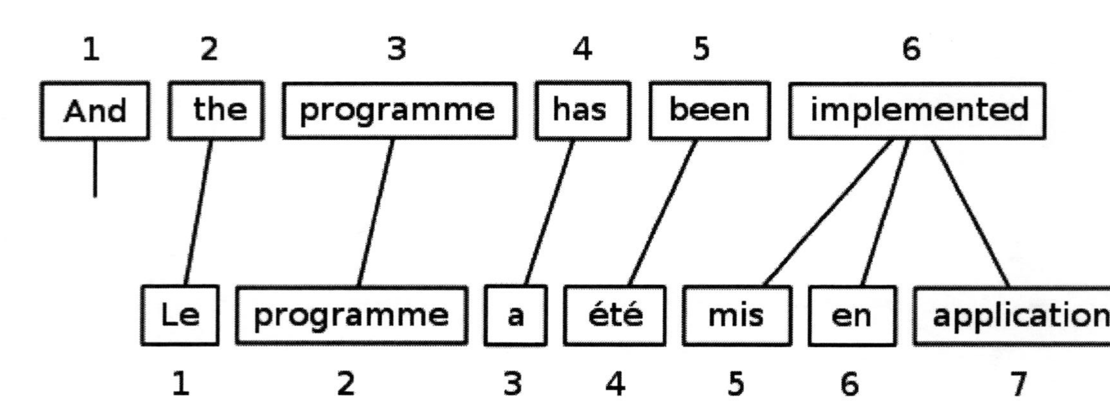

le#the programme#programme

Proceedings for AMTA 2018 Workshop: Translation Quality Estimation and Automatic Post-Editing

Contextual Statistical APE

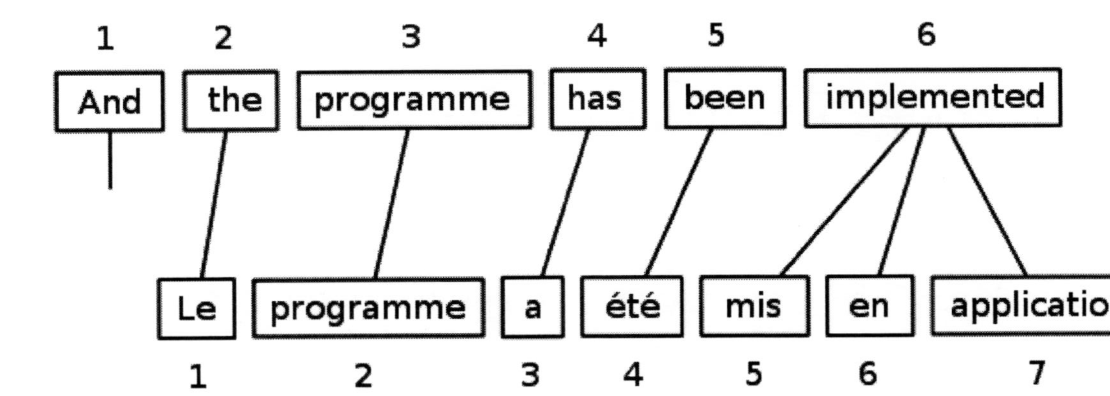

le#the programme#programme a#has

Contextual Statistical APE

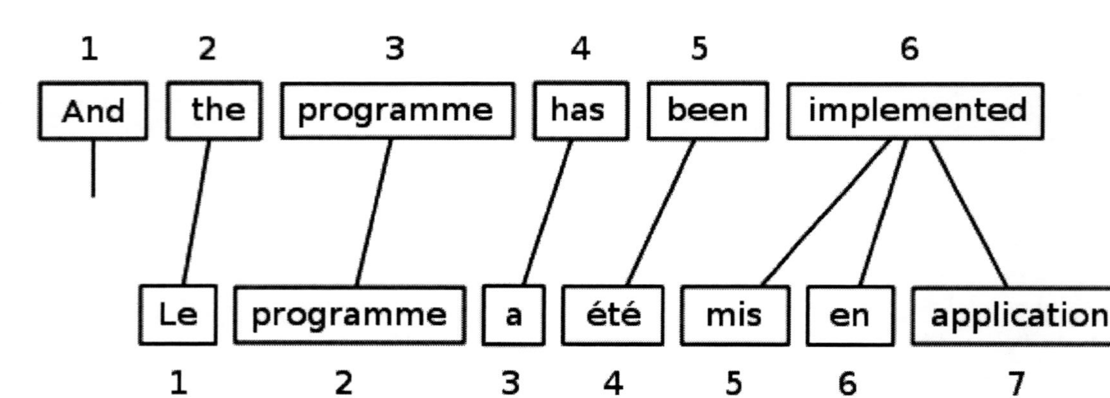

le#the programme#programme a#has été#been

154

Contextual Statistical APE

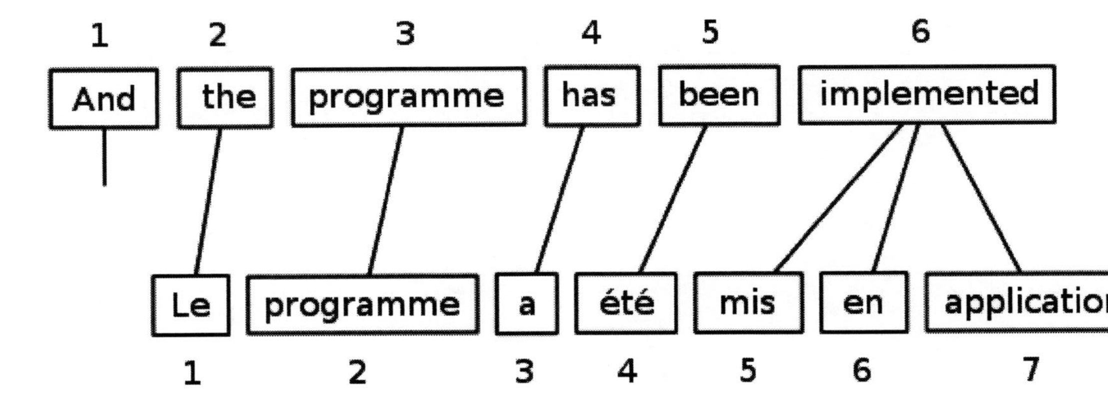

le#the programme#programme a#has été#been mis#implemented

Proceedings for AMTA 2018 Workshop: Translation Quality Estimation and Automatic Post-Editing

Contextual Statistical APE

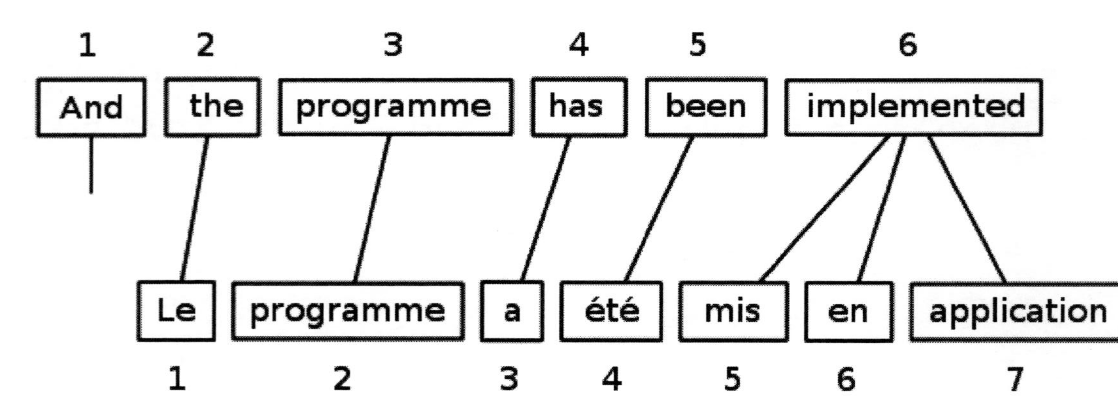

le#the programme#programme a#has été#been
mis#implemented en#implemented

Proceedings for AMTA 2018 Workshop: Translation Quality Estimation and Automatic Post-Editing

Contextual Statistical APE

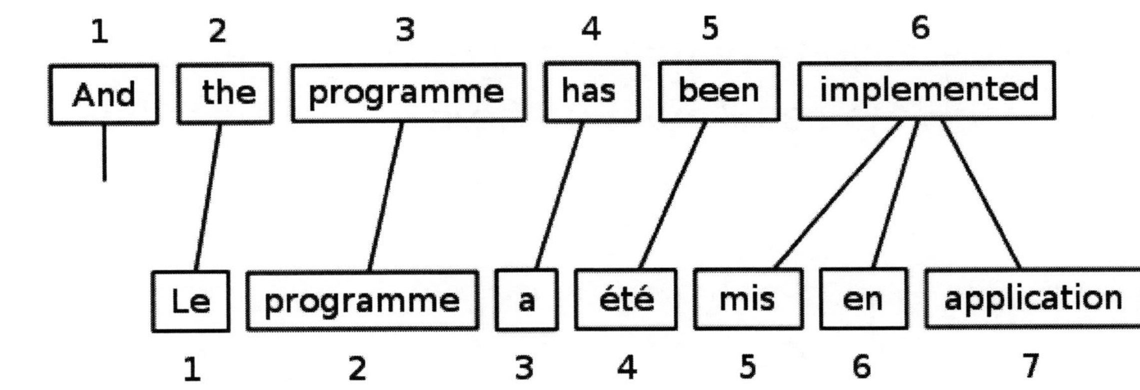

le#the programme#programme a#has été#been
mis#implemented en#implemented application#implemented

Proceedings for AMTA 2018 Workshop: Translation Quality Estimation and Automatic Post-Editing

Contextual Statistical APE

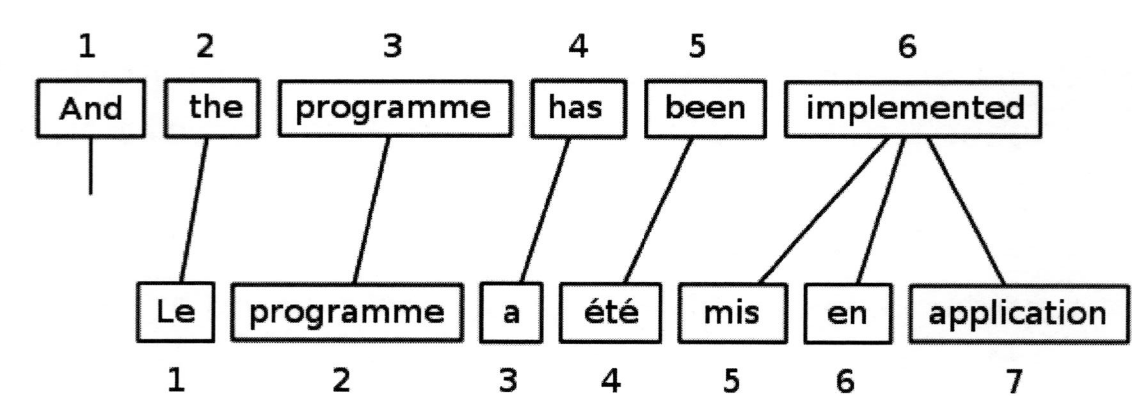

le#the programme#programme a#has été#been
mis#implemented en#implemented application#implemented

Problems?

Proceedings for AMTA 2018 Workshop: Translation Quality Estimation and Automatic Post-Editing

WMT 2015 Shared Task on Automatic post-editing (The Stone Age of Automatic post-editing)

ID	Avg. TER
Baseline	22.91
FBK Primary	23.23
LIMSI Primary	23.33
USAAR-SAPE	23.43
LIMSI Contrastive	23.57
Abu-MaTran Primary	23.64
FBK Contrastive	23.65
(Simard et al., 2007)	23.84
Abu-MaTran Contrastive	24.72

Proceedings for AMTA 2018 Workshop: Translation Quality Estimation and Automatic Post-Editing

WMT 2015 Shared Task on Automatic post-editing (The Stone Age of Automatic post-editing)

ID	Avg. TER
Baseline	22.91
FBK Primary	23.23
LIMSI Primary	23.33
USAAR-SAPE	23.43
LIMSI Contrastive	23.57
Abu-MaTran Primary	23.64
FBK Contrastive	23.65
(Simard et al., 2007)	23.84
Abu-MaTran Contrastive	24.72
WMT2016-best	23.29
WMT2017-best	??

Proceedings for AMTA 2018 Workshop: Translation Quality Estimation and Automatic Post-Editing

WMT 2016 Shared Task on Automatic post-editing

Create an APE system that returns automatic post-edition of an English-German black-box MT system. 10,000 training triplets of the following form were provided:

SRC *These files are encoded as UTF-8 or ASCII , which is a subset of UTF-8 .*

MT *Diese Dateien werden als UTF-8 oder ASCII , bei der es sich um eine Untergruppe von UTF-8 kodiert .*

PE *Diese Dateien werden als UTF-8 oder ASCII , eine Teilmenge von UTF-8 , kodiert .*

Problem: very little publicly available PE data

BLEU Scores with Varying Amounts of Training Data

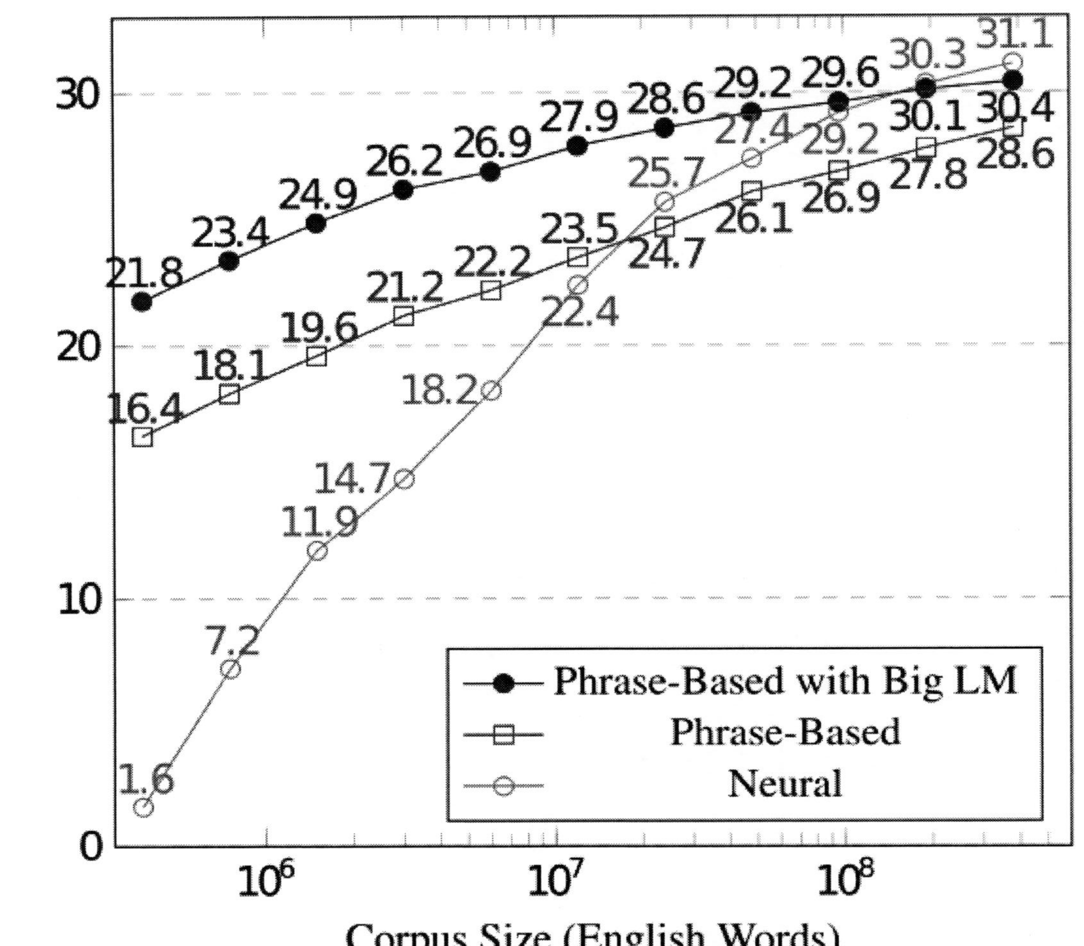

Source: Koehn and Knowles (2017). Six Challenges for Neural Machine Translation. 1st Neural Machine Translation Workshop. Vancouver.

Solution: create your own PE data using:

- Official APE training and develsopment data sets.
- EN-DE bilingual data from the WMT-16 shared tasks on IT and news translation.
- German monolingual Common Crawl (CC) corpus.

Proceedings for AMTA 2018 Workshop: Translation Quality Estimation and Automatic Post-Editing

Round-trip translation

*gibt die Prozesskennung des aktuellen Prozesses zurück . (= **PE**)*

DE-EN↓Moses

*the process ID of the current process . (= **SRC**)*

EN-DE↓Moses

*die Prozess-ID des aktuellen Prozesses . (= **MT**)*

Proceedings for AMTA 2018 Workshop: Translation Quality Estimation and Automatic Post-Editing

Selecting in-domain data

- Cross-entropy filtering of German CC corpus based on in-domain post-editing and IT-domain data.
- We keep 10M sentences with the best cross-entropy scores.

Filtering for TER statistics:

Data set	Sent.	NumWd	WdSh	NumEr	TER
training set	12K	17.89	0.72	4.69	26.22
development set	1K	19.76	0.71	4.90	24.81
round-trip.full	9,960K	13.50	0.58	5,72	42.02
round-trip.n10	4,335K	15.86	0.66	5.93	36.63
round-trip.n1	531K	20.92	0.55	5.20	25.28

Proceedings for AMTA 2018 Workshop: Translation Quality Estimation and Automatic Post-Editing

Experiments with neural models

- Attentional encoded-decoder models trained with Nematus:
  `https://github.com/rsennrich/nematus`
- C++/CUDA AmuNMT decoder:
  `https://github.com/emjotde/amunmt`

MT-PE and SRC-PE systems

- Trained on round-trip.n10 data (4M triplets).
- Fine-tuned on round-trip.n1 and 20x oversampled official training data (700K triplets).

Proceedings for AMTA 2018 Workshop: Translation Quality Estimation and Automatic Post-Editing

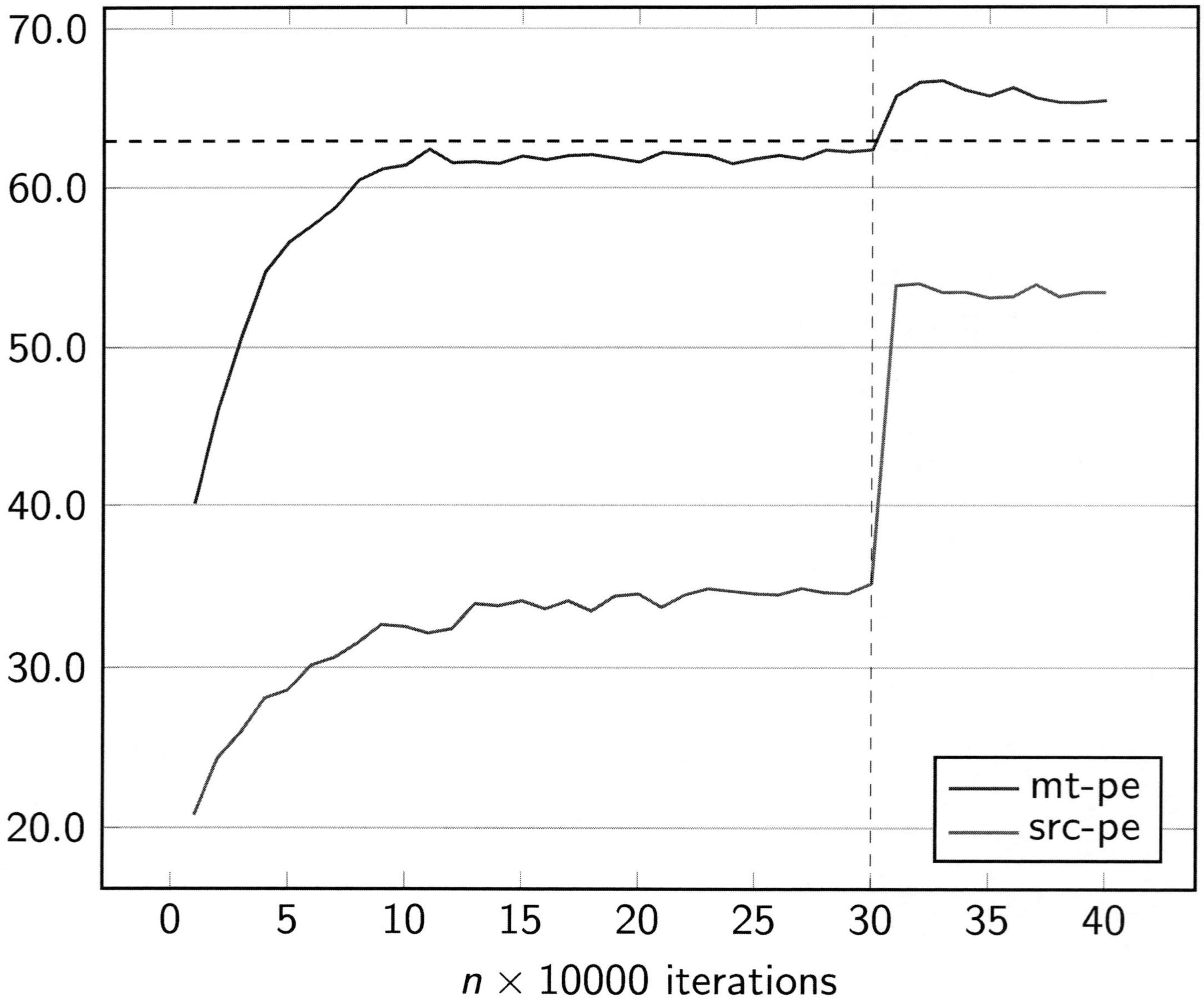

70.0
60.0
50.0
40.0
30.0
20.0
0
5
10
15
20
25
30
35
40
$n \times 10000$ iterations
mt-pe
src-pe

Log-linear combination

- Log-linear combination of two models with different input languages.

- Weights determined by MERT for two models: ca. 0.8 for mt-pe and 0.2 for src-pe model.

- Post-Editing Penalty (PEP) to control the faithfulness of the APE results.

Progress on the dev set

System	TER	BLEU
Baseline (mt)	25.14	62.92
mt→pe	23.37	66.71
mt→pe×4	23.23	66.88
src→pe	32.31	53.89
src→pe×4	31.42	55.41
mt→pe×4 / src→pe×4	22.38	68.07
mt→pe×4 / src→pe×4 / pep	**21.46**	**68.94**

Proceedings for AMTA 2018 Workshop: Translation Quality Estimation and Automatic Post-Editing

Automatic evaluation on unseen test set

- AMU (primary) = mt$\rightarrow$pe$\times$4 / src$\rightarrow$pe$\times$4 / pe
- AMU (contrastive) = mt$\rightarrow$pe$\times$4

System	TER	BLEU
AMU (primary)	**21.52**	**67.65**
AMU (contrastive)	**23.06**	**66.09**
FBK	23.92	64.75
USAAR	24.14	64.10
CUNI	24.31	63.32
Baseline (Moses)	24.64	63.47
Baseline (mt)	24.76	62.11
DCU	26.79	58.60
JUSAAR	26.92	59.44

Proceedings for AMTA 2018 Workshop: Translation Quality Estimation and Automatic Post-Editing

Results of human evaluation

#	Score	Range	System
1	**1.967**	1	**AMU (primary)**
2	0.033	2	FBK
3	-0.108	3-4	CUNI
	-0.191	3-5	USSAR
	-0.211	3-5	Baseline (mt)
4	-0.712	6-7	JUSAAR
	-0.778	6-7	DCU

Table: With post-edited sentence shown as reference

Source: WMT2016 overview paper.

Proceedings for AMTA 2018 Workshop: Translation Quality Estimation and Automatic Post-Editing

Results of human evaluation

#	Score	Range	System
1	2.058	1	Human
2	**0.867**	2	**AMU (primary)**
3	-0.213	3-4	CUNI
	-0.348	3-6	FBK
	-0.374	3-6	USSAR
	-0.499	5-7	Baseline (mt)
	-0.675	6-8	JUSAAR
	-0.816	7-8	DCU

Table: With post-edited sentence included as system

Source: WMT2016 overview paper.

Proceedings for AMTA 2018 Workshop: Translation Quality Estimation and Automatic Post-Editing

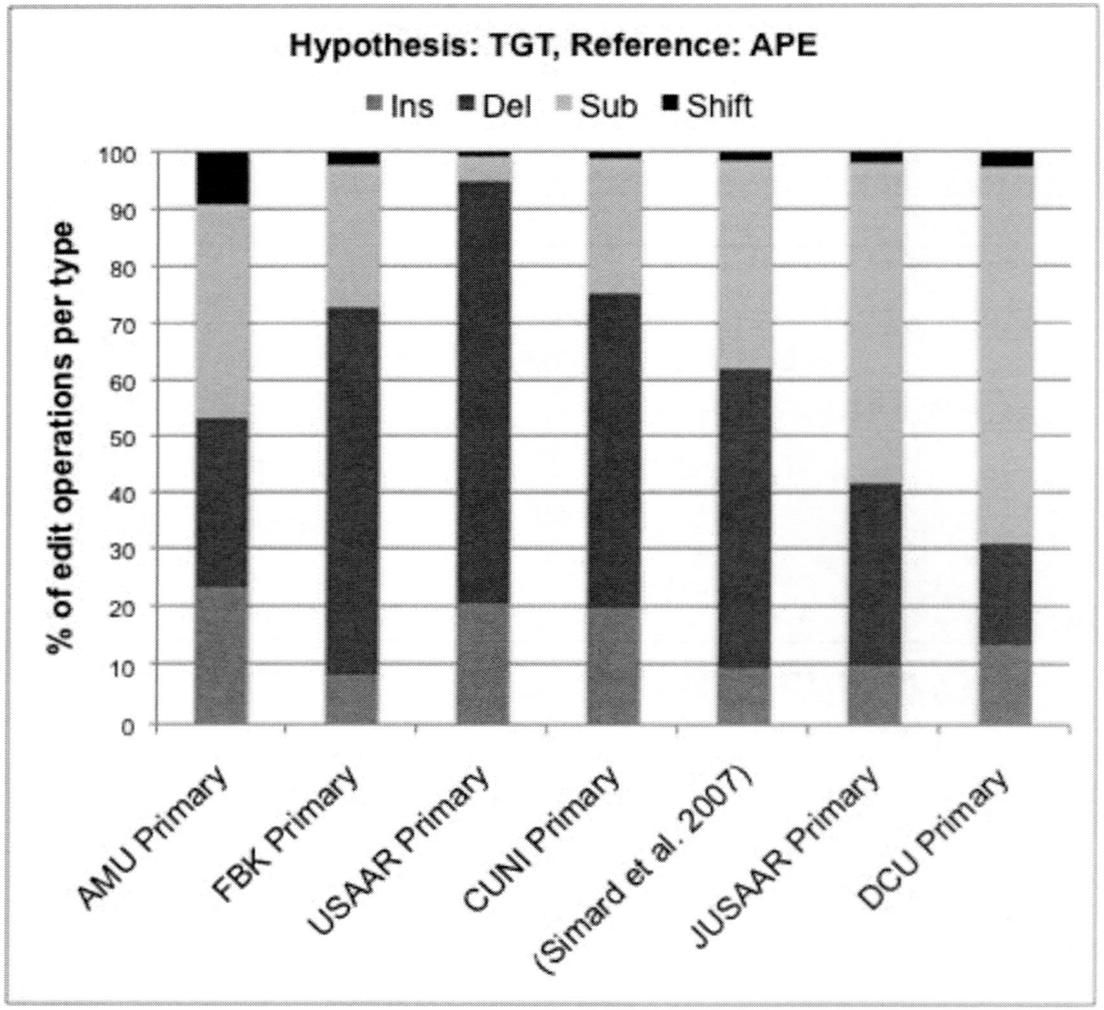

Source: WMT 2016 overview paper

Some conclusions

- One of the first successful applications of NMT models to APE
- Artificial APE triplets allow training of NMT models with little original training data and help against overfitting.
- Positive effects of log-linear combinations of NMT models with multiple input languages.
- Tuning with MERT to assign model component weights

Proceedings for AMTA 2018 Workshop: Translation Quality Estimation and Automatic Post-Editing

WMT 2017 Shared Task on Automatic post-editing

- The same setting;
- Additional 12,500 sentences of PE data;
- Still no post-editing of NMT system

Proceedings for AMTA 2018 Workshop: Translation Quality Estimation and Automatic Post-Editing

Our submission to the WMT 2017 Shared Task on Automatic Post-editing

- We explore the interaction of hard-attention and multi-encoder models.
- All models trained and available in Marian (http://marian-nmt.github.io)
- We use the same data as last year.
- This time proper regularization and no need for fine-tuning.

Proceedings for AMTA 2018 Workshop: Translation Quality Estimation and Automatic Post-Editing

Soft vs. hard monotonic attention

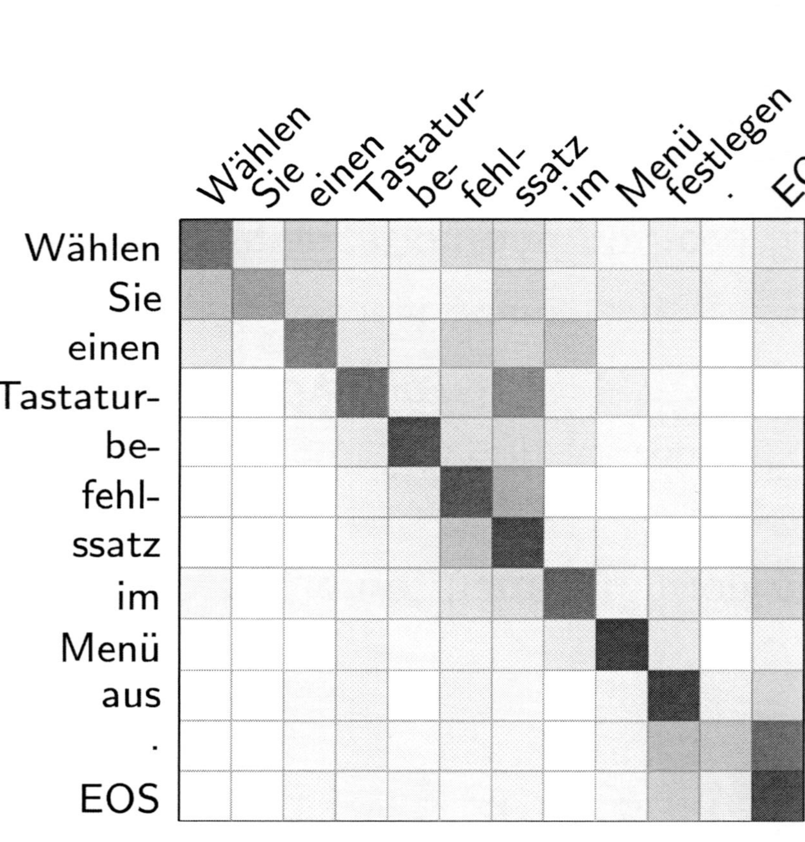

Proceedings for AMTA 2018 Workshop: Translation Quality Estimation and Automatic Post-Editing

Soft vs. hard monotonic attention

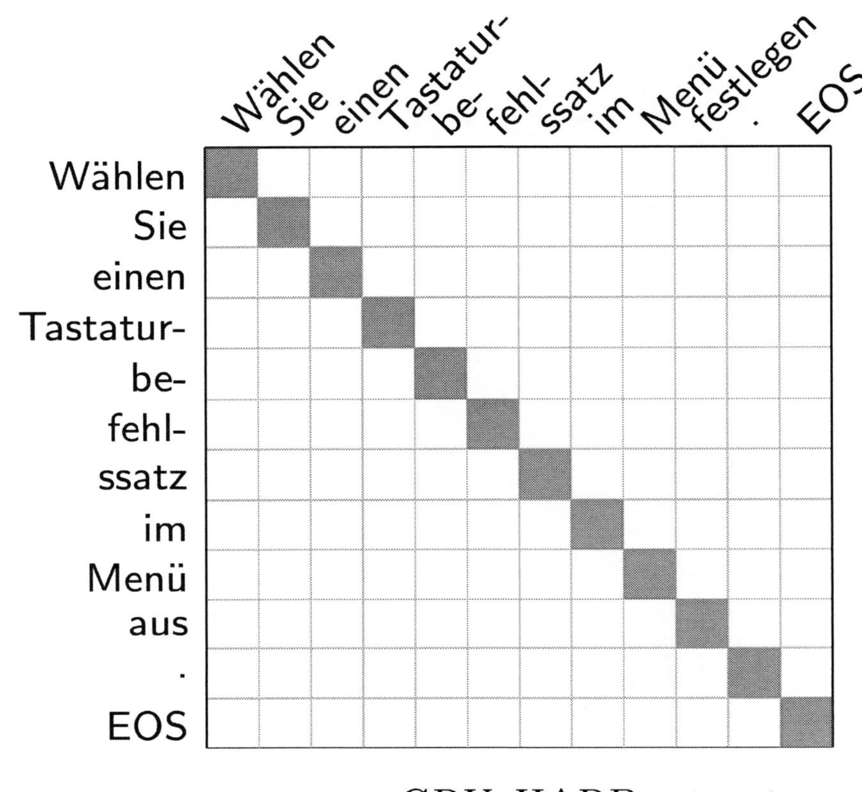

Proceedings for AMTA 2018 Workshop: Translation Quality Estimation and Automatic Post-Editing

Soft vs. hard monotonic attention

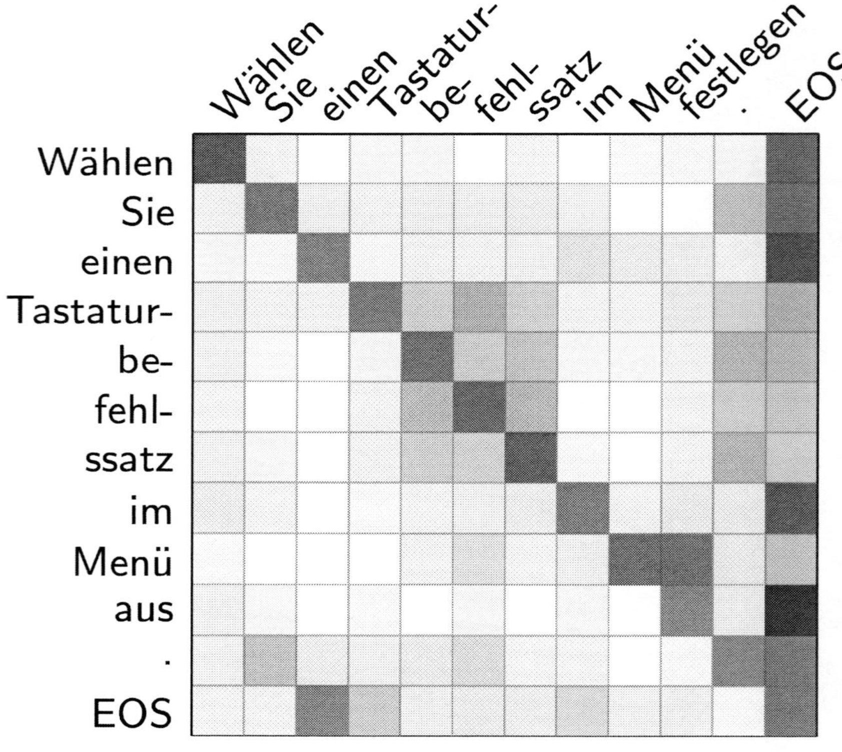

Proceedings for AMTA 2018 Workshop: Translation Quality Estimation and Automatic Post-Editing

Reminder: Gated Recurrent Unit

$$\begin{aligned}
\mathrm{GRU}\,(\mathbf{s},\mathbf{x}) &= (1-\mathbf{z}) \odot \underline{\mathbf{s}} + \mathbf{z} \odot \mathbf{s}, \\
\underline{\mathbf{s}} &= \tanh\,(\mathbf{W}\mathbf{x} + \mathbf{r} \odot \mathbf{U}\mathbf{s}), \\
\mathbf{r} &= \sigma\,(\mathbf{W}_r\mathbf{x} + \mathbf{U}_r\mathbf{s}), \\
\mathbf{z} &= \sigma\,(\mathbf{W}_z\mathbf{x} + \mathbf{U}_z\mathbf{s}),
\end{aligned} \tag{1}$$

where $\mathbf{x}$ is the cell input; $\mathbf{s}$ is the previous recurrent state; $\mathbf{W}$, $\mathbf{U}$, $\mathbf{W}_r$, $\mathbf{U}_r$, $\mathbf{W}_z$, $\mathbf{U}_z$ are trained model parameters[1]; σ is the logistic sigmoid activation function.

---

[1]Biases have been omitted.

Conditional GRU (cgru)

$$C = \{\mathbf{h}_1, \ldots, \mathbf{h}_n\}$$

$$\mathbf{s}_j = \text{cGRU}_{\text{att}}\left(\mathbf{s}_{j-1}, \mathbf{E}[y_{j-1}], C\right) \tag{2}$$

$$\mathbf{s}j' = \text{GRU}_1\left(\mathbf{s}_{j-1}, \mathbf{E}[y_{j-1}]\right)$$
$$\mathbf{c}_j = \text{ATT}\left(C, \mathbf{s}'_j\right)$$
$$\mathbf{s}_j = \text{GRU}_2\left(\mathbf{s}'_j, \mathbf{c}_j\right)$$

Proceedings for AMTA 2018 Workshop: Translation Quality Estimation and Automatic Post-Editing

Hard monotonic attention (gru-hard)

- Aharoni and Goldberg (2016) introduce a simple model for monolingual morphological re-inflection with hard monotonic attention.

- The target word vocabulary V_y is extended with a special step symbol $\langle \text{STEP} \rangle$

- Whenever $\langle \text{STEP} \rangle$ is predicted as the output symbol, the hard attention is moved to the next encoder state.

- We calculate the hard attention indices as follows:

$$a_1 = 1,$$

$$a_j = \begin{cases} a_{j-1} + 1 & \text{if } y_{j-1} = \langle \text{STEP} \rangle \\ a_{j-1} & \text{otherwise.} \end{cases}$$

$$\mathbf{s}_j = \text{GRU}\left(\mathbf{s}_{j-1}, \left[\mathbf{E}[y_{j-1}]; \mathbf{h}_{a_j}\right]\right), \tag{3}$$

Proceedings for AMTA 2018 Workshop: Translation Quality Estimation and Automatic Post-Editing

Mixing hard and soft attention (cgru-hard)

$$\mathbf{s}_j = \text{cGRU}_{\text{att}}\left(\mathbf{s}_{j-1}, \left[\mathbf{E}[y_{j-1}]; \mathbf{h}_{a_j}\right], C\right) \tag{4}$$

Proceedings for AMTA 2018 Workshop: Translation Quality Estimation and Automatic Post-Editing

Example sentence and corrections

mt	Wählen Sie einen Tastaturbefehlssatz im Menü festlegen .
src	Select a shortcut set in the Set menu .
CGRU	Wählen Sie einen Tastaturbefehlssatz im Menü aus .
GRU-HARD	Wählen Sie einen Tastaturbefehlssatz im Menü aus .
CGRU-HARD	Wählen Sie einen Tastaturbefehlssatz im Menü aus .
M-CGRU	Wählen Sie einen Tastaturbefehlssatz im Menü ” Satz ” aus .
M-CGRU-HARD	Wählen Sie einen Tastaturbefehlssatz im Menü ” Satz . ”
pe	Wählen Sie einen Tastaturbefehlssatz im Menü ” Satz . ”

Proceedings for AMTA 2018 Workshop: Translation Quality Estimation and Automatic Post-Editing

Dual attention

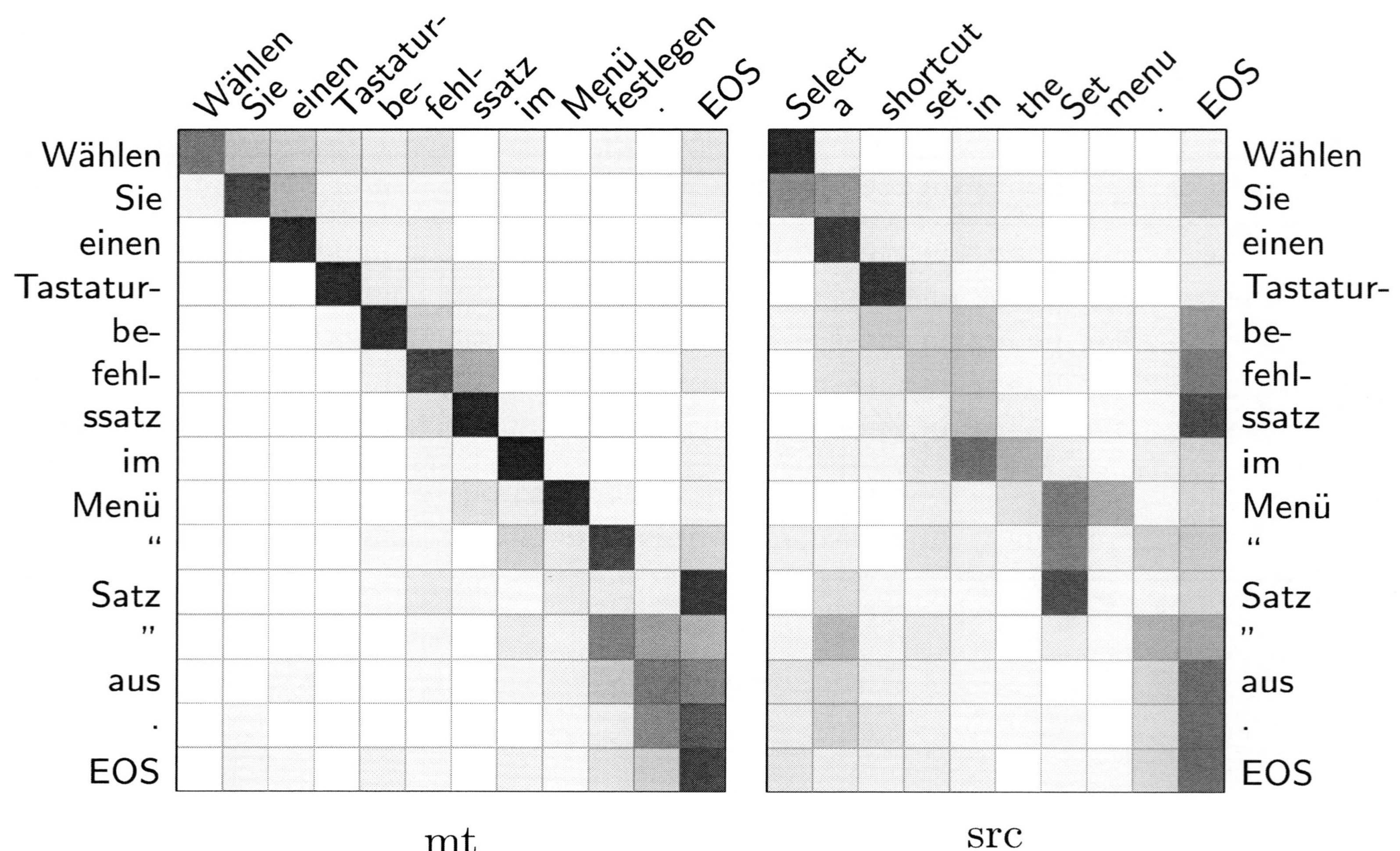

Proceedings for AMTA 2018 Workshop: Translation Quality Estimation and Automatic Post-Editing

Dual attention

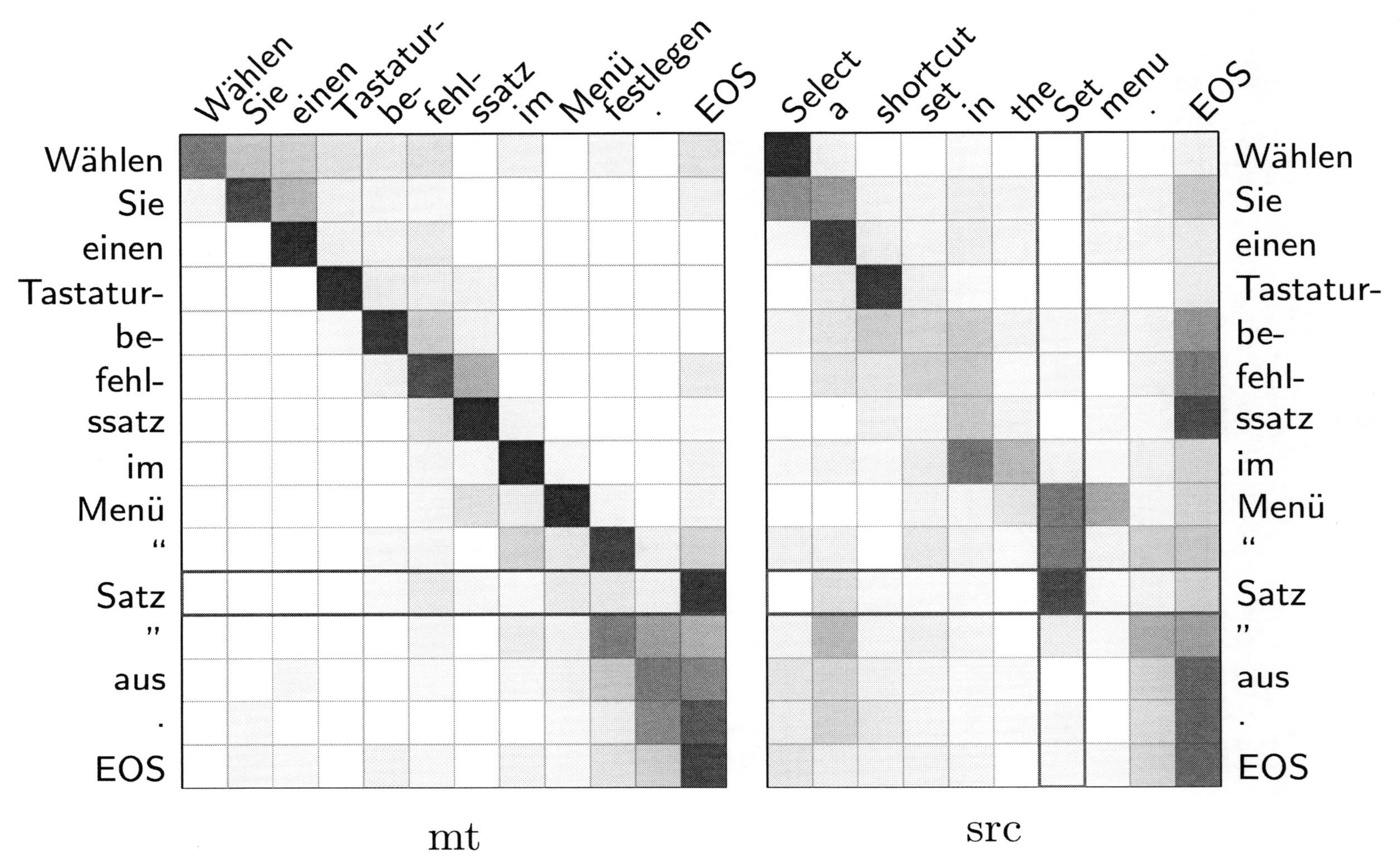

Dual soft attention (m-cgru)

$$C^{mt} = \{\mathbf{h}_1^{mt}, \ldots, \mathbf{h}_{T_{mt}}^{mt}\}$$

$$C^{src} = \{\mathbf{h}_1^{src}, \ldots, \mathbf{h}_{T_{src}}^{src}\}$$

$$\mathbf{s}_0 = \tanh\left(\mathbf{W}_{init}\left[\frac{\sum_{i=1}^{T_{mt}} \mathbf{h}_i^{mt}}{T_{mt}} ; \frac{\sum_{i=1}^{T_{src}} \mathbf{h}_i^{src}}{T_{src}}\right]\right).$$

$$\mathbf{s}_j = \text{cGRU}_{2\text{-att}}\left(\mathbf{s}_{j-1}, \mathbf{E}[y_{j-1}], C^{mt}, C^{src}\right). \tag{5}$$

Proceedings for AMTA 2018 Workshop: Translation Quality Estimation and Automatic Post-Editing

Dual soft attention (m-cgru)

$$\mathbf{s}_j = \text{cGRU}_{2\text{-att}}\left(\mathbf{s}_{j-1}, \mathbf{E}[y_{j-1}], C^{mt}, C^{src}\right). \tag{6}$$

$$\mathbf{s}'_j = \text{GRU}_1\left(\mathbf{s}_{j-1}, \mathbf{E}[y_{j-1}]\right),$$

$$\mathbf{c}^{mt}_j = \text{ATT}\left(C^{mt}, \mathbf{s}'_j\right),$$

$$\mathbf{c}^{src}_j = \text{ATT}\left(C^{src}, \mathbf{s}'_j\right),$$

$$\mathbf{c}_j = \left[\mathbf{c}^{mt}_j; \mathbf{c}^{src}_j\right],$$

$$\mathbf{s}_j = \text{GRU}_2\left(\mathbf{s}'_j, \mathbf{c}_j\right).$$

Proceedings for AMTA 2018 Workshop: Translation Quality Estimation and Automatic Post-Editing

Dual soft attention with hard attention (m-cgru-hard)

$$\mathbf{s}_j = \text{cGRU}_{2\text{-att}}\left(\mathbf{s}_{j-1}, \left[\mathbf{E}[y_{j-1}]; \mathbf{h}_{a_j}^{mt}\right], C^{mt}, C^{src}\right).$$

Proceedings for AMTA 2018 Workshop: Translation Quality Estimation and Automatic Post-Editing

Results

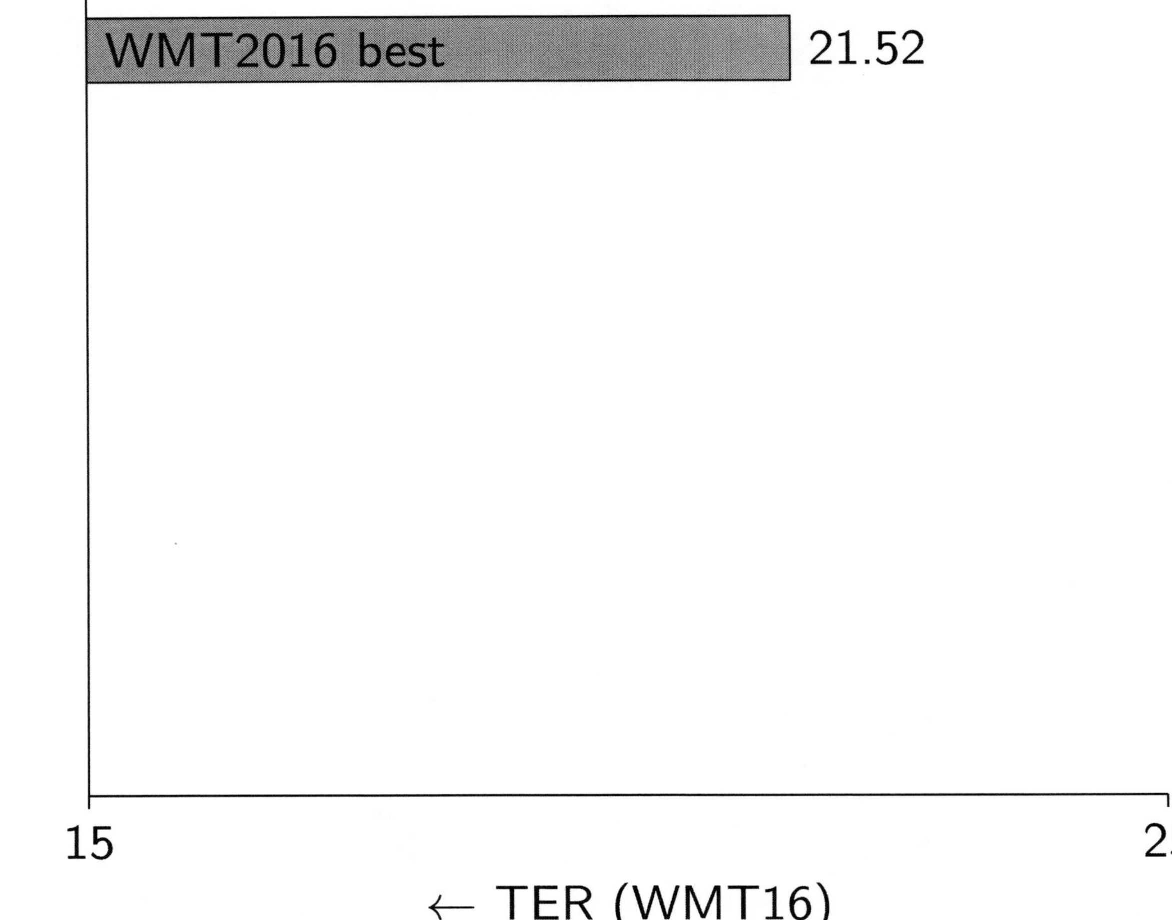

Results

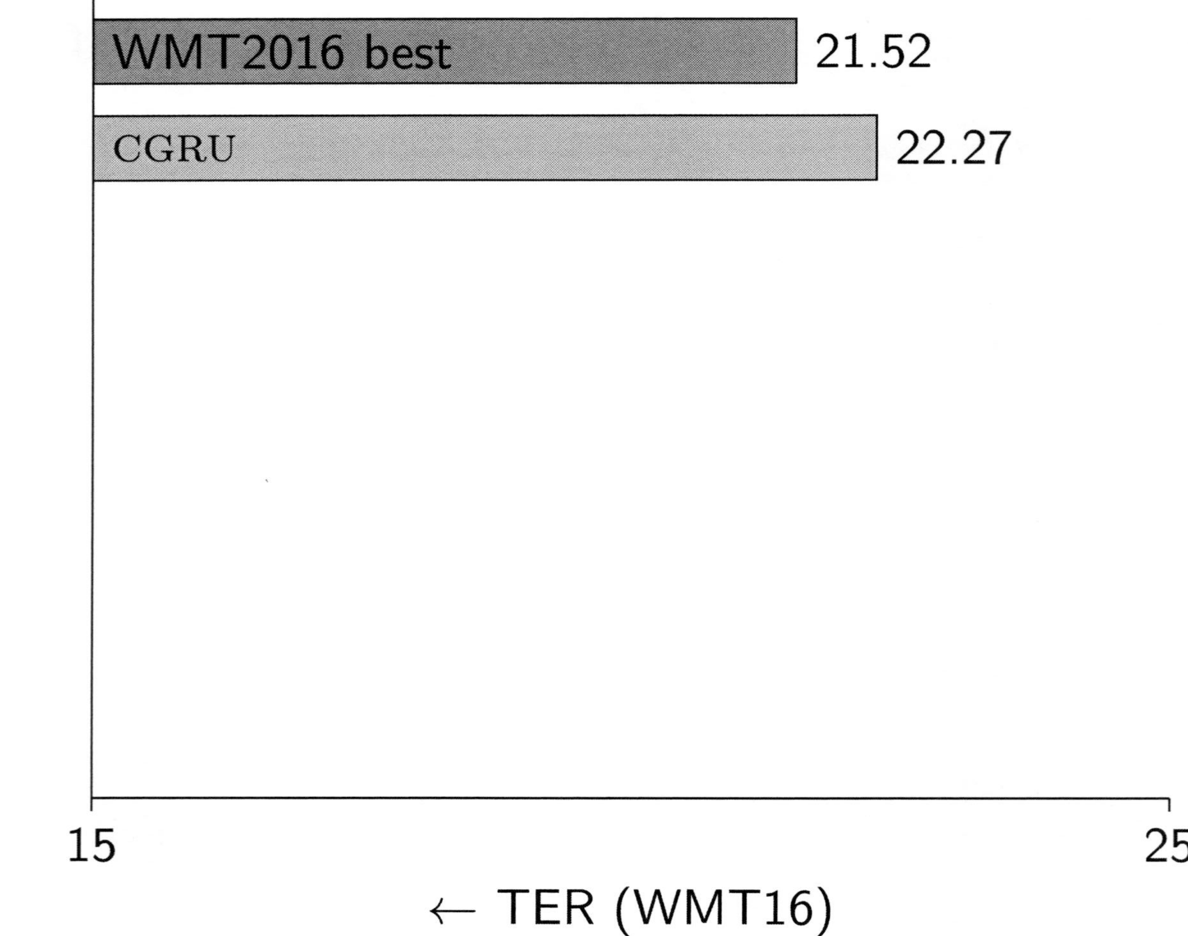

Proceedings for AMTA 2018 Workshop: Translation Quality Estimation and Automatic Post-Editing

Results

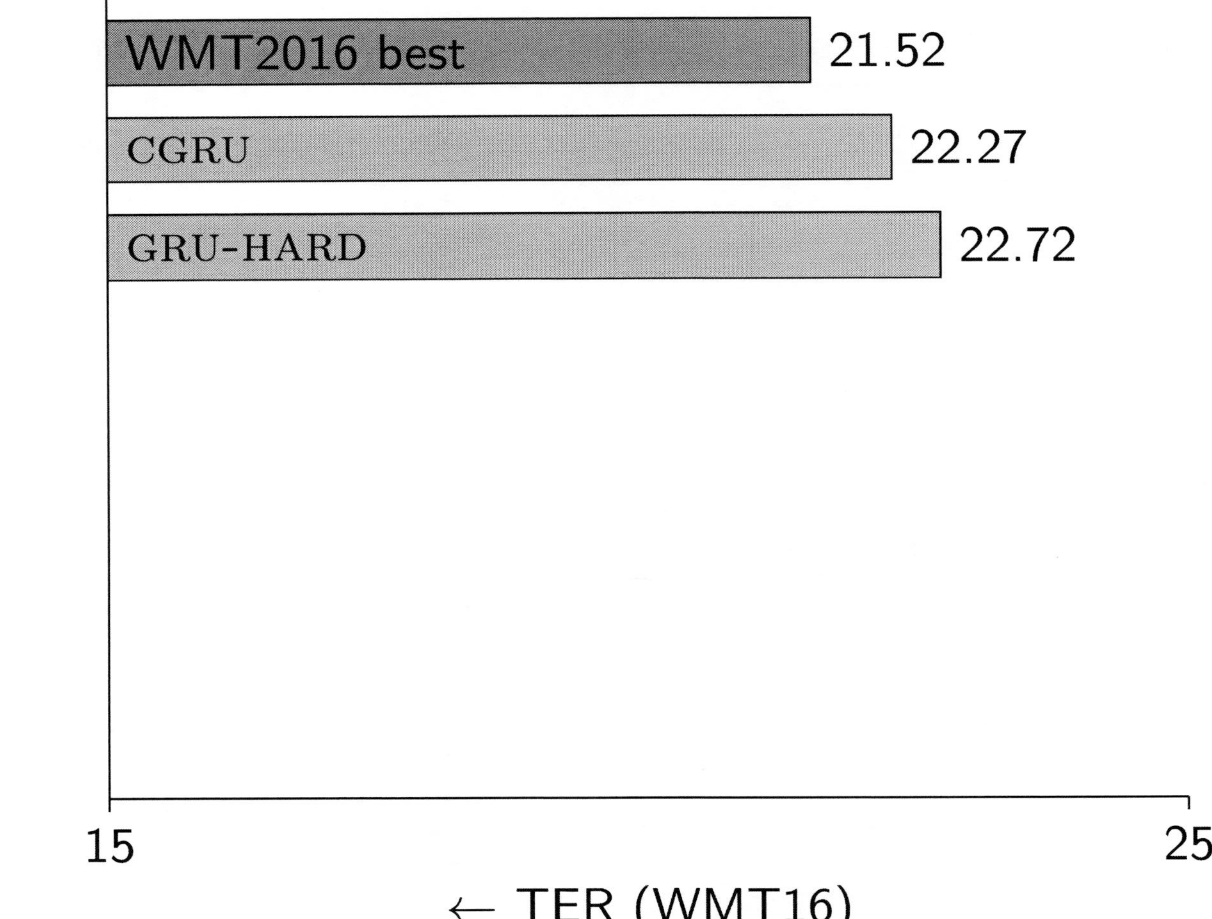

Proceedings for AMTA 2018 Workshop: Translation Quality Estimation and Automatic Post-Editing

Results

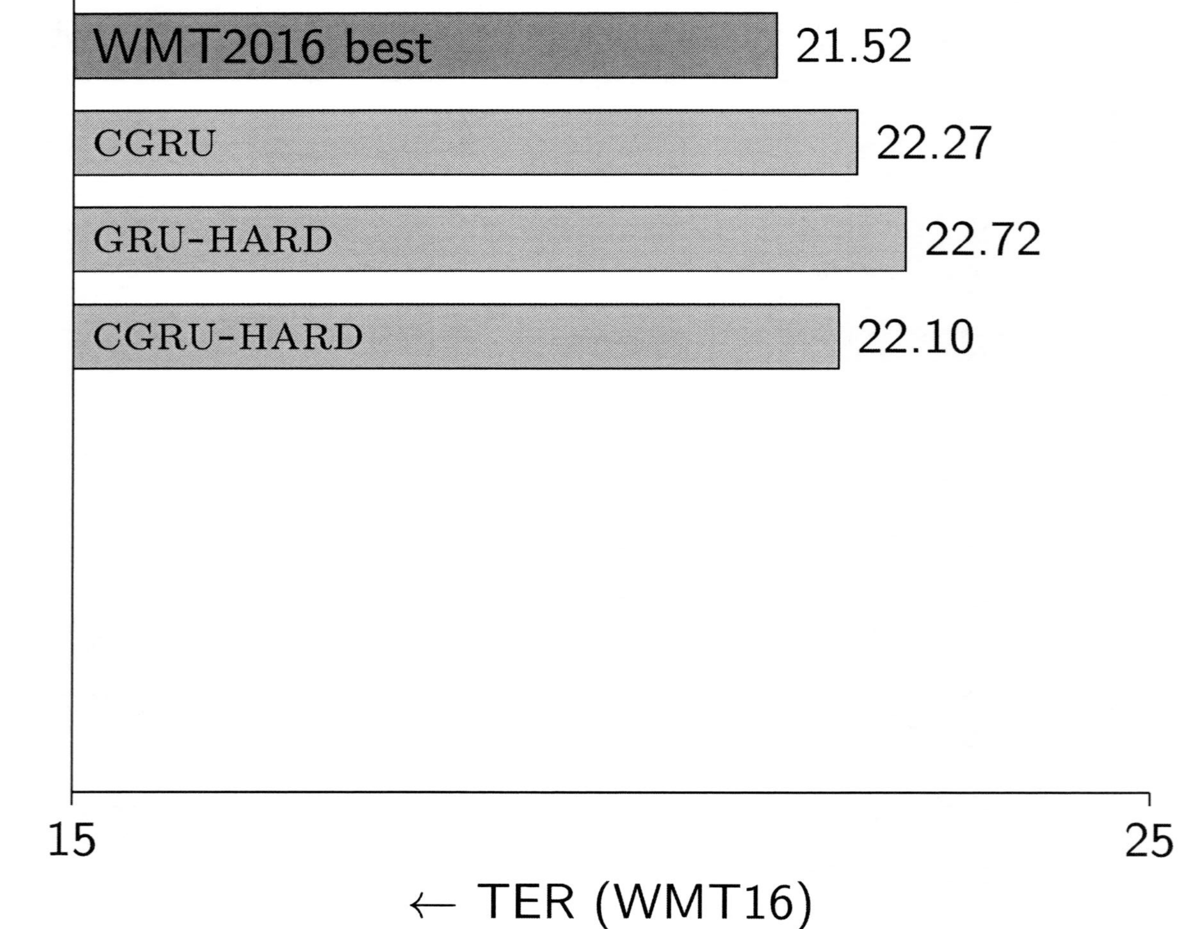

Proceedings for AMTA 2018 Workshop: Translation Quality Estimation and Automatic Post-Editing

Results

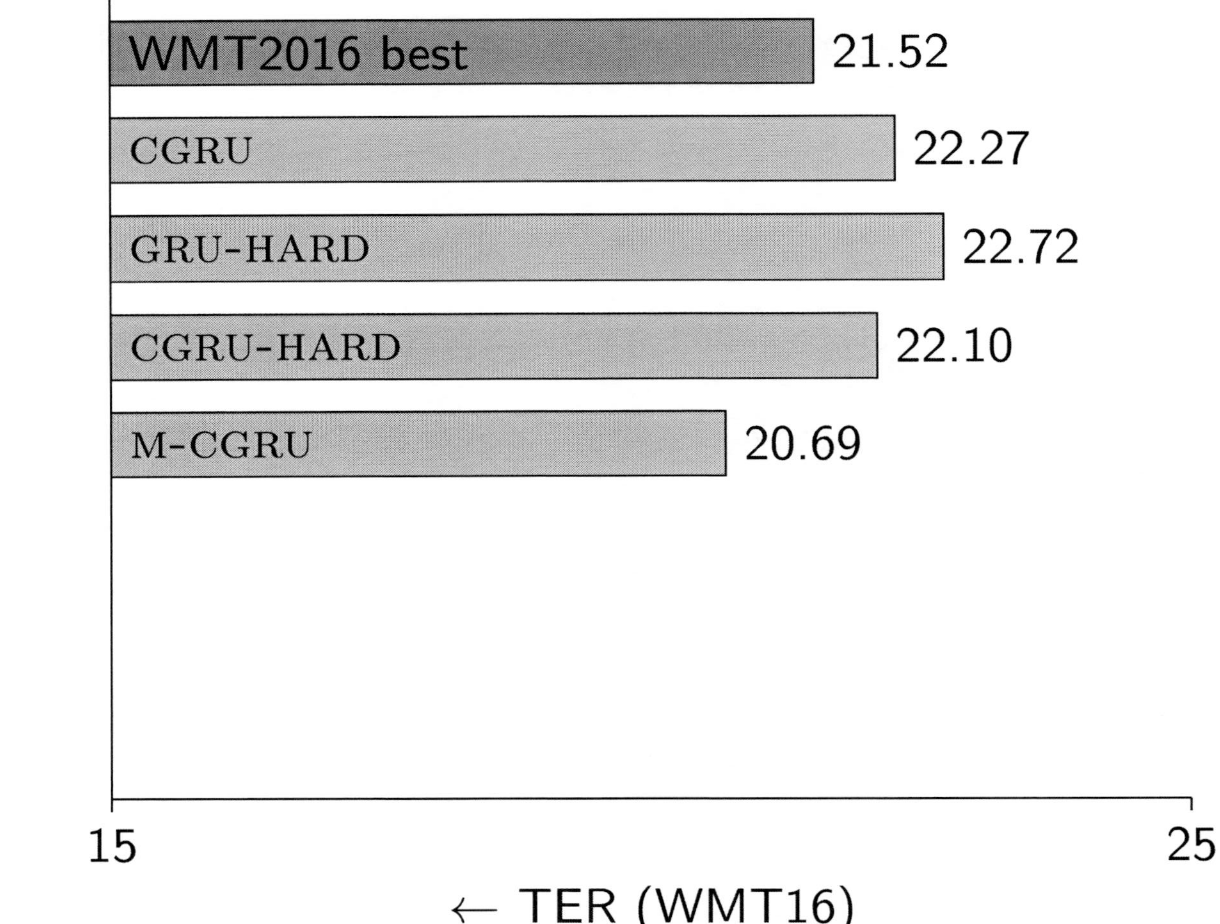

Proceedings for AMTA 2018 Workshop: Translation Quality Estimation and Automatic Post-Editing

Results

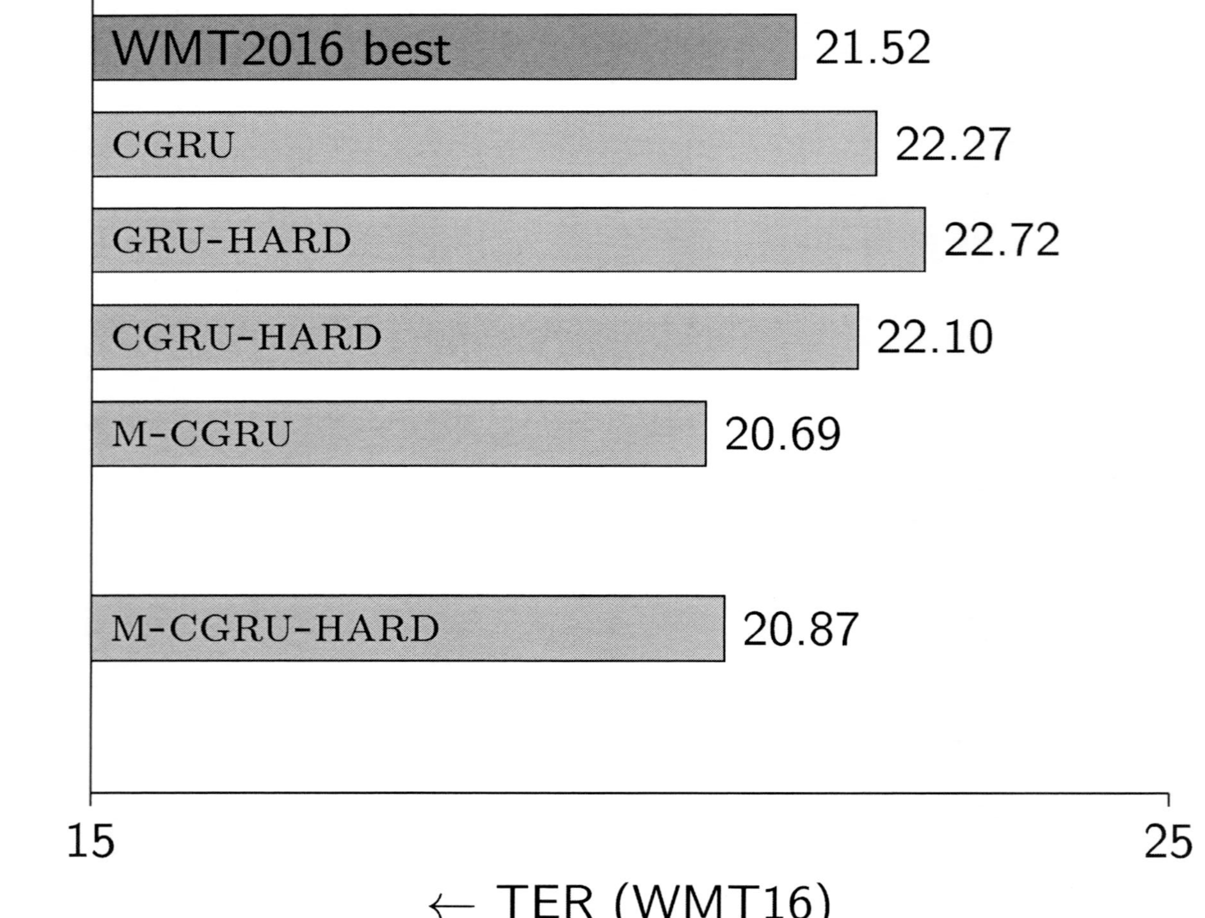

Proceedings for AMTA 2018 Workshop: Translation Quality Estimation and Automatic Post-Editing

Results

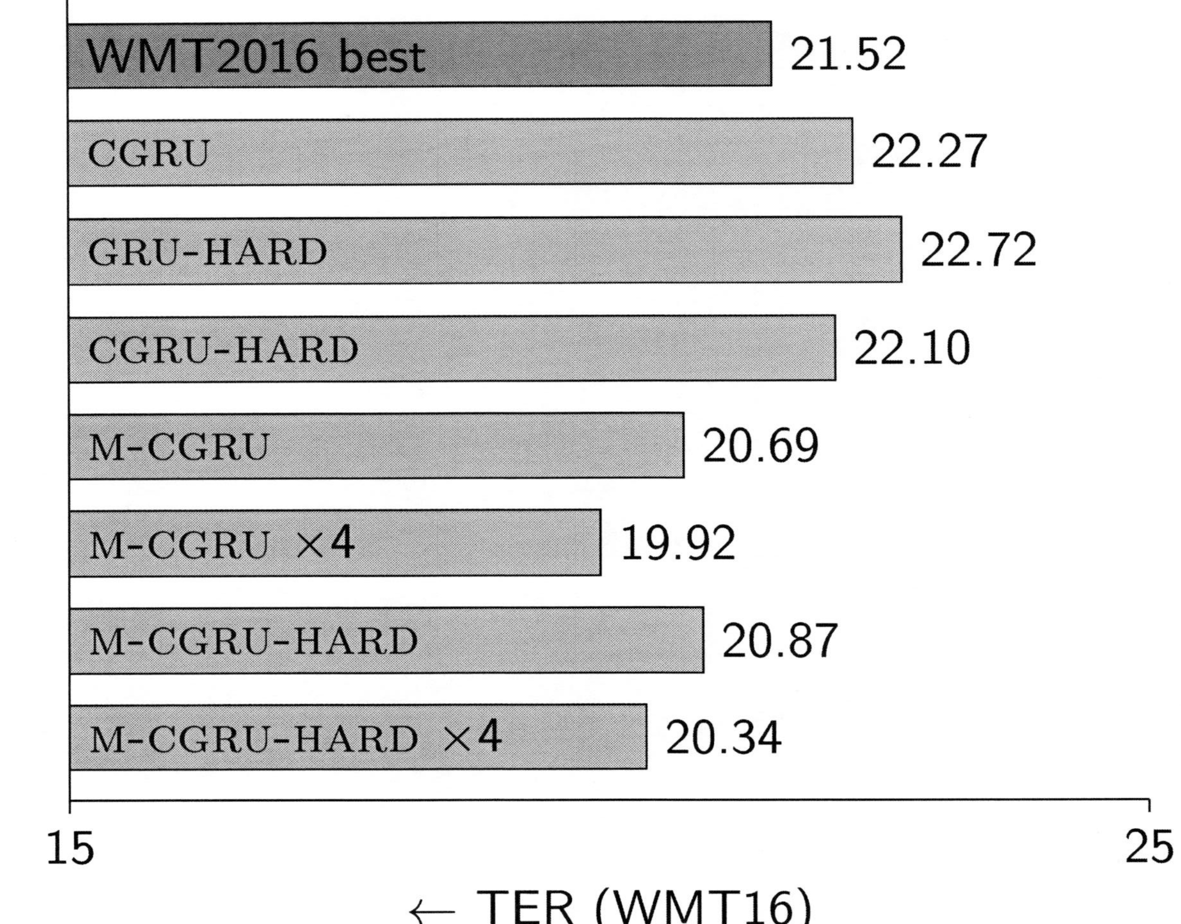

Proceedings for AMTA 2018 Workshop: Translation Quality Estimation and Automatic Post-Editing

Faithfulness

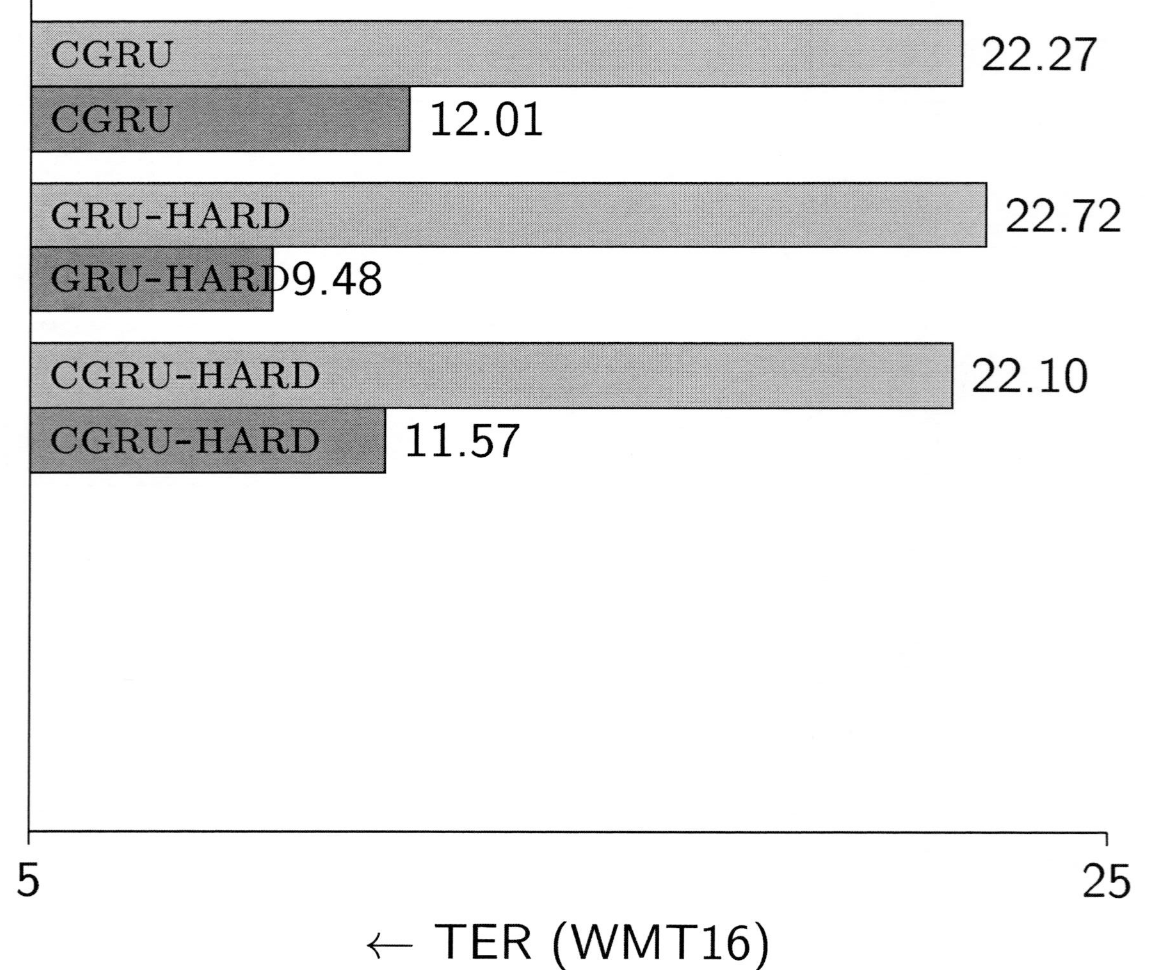

Proceedings for AMTA 2018 Workshop: Translation Quality Estimation and Automatic Post-Editing

Faithfulness

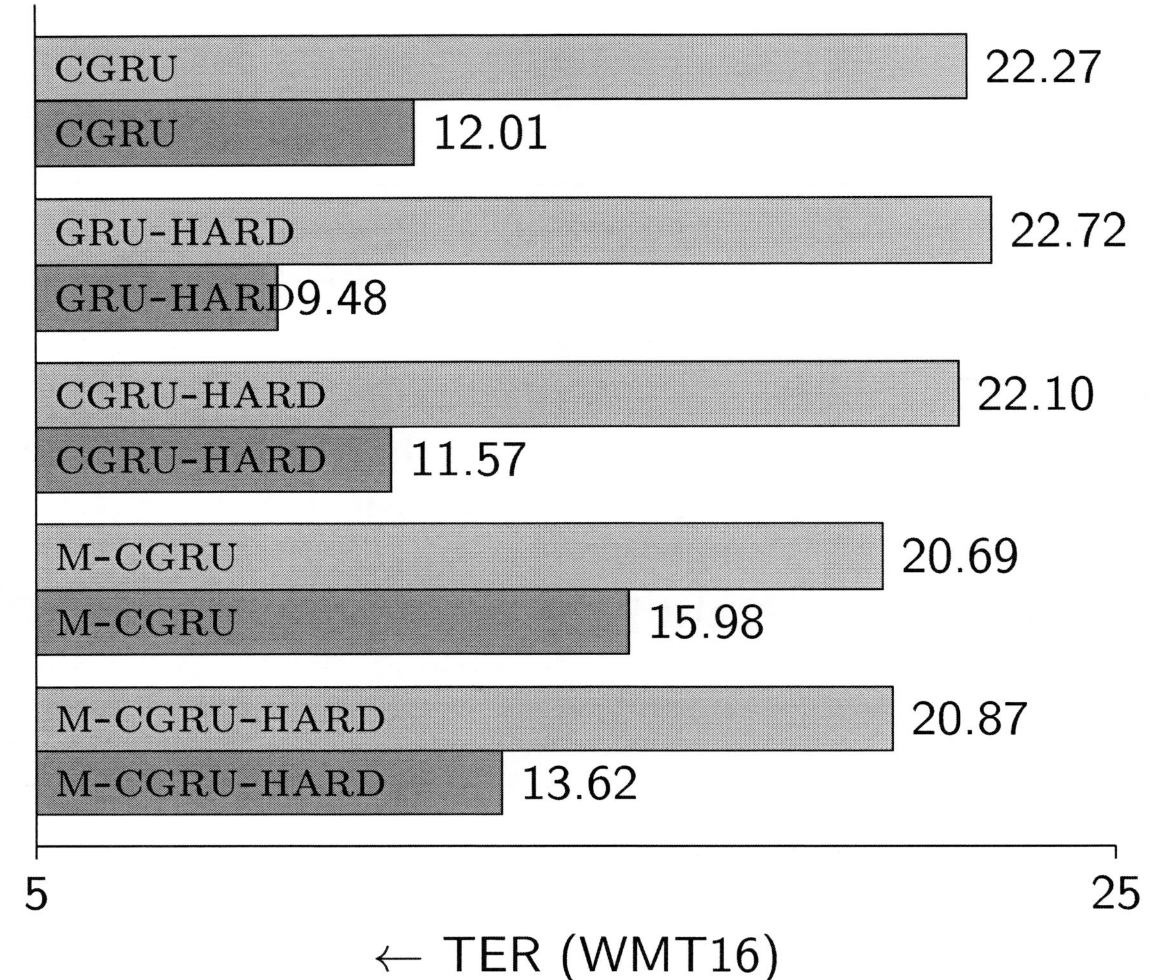

Proceedings for AMTA 2018 Workshop: Translation Quality Estimation and Automatic Post-Editing

Results for the WMT2017 shared task on APE

Systems	TER	BLEU
FBK EnsembleRerank Primary	19.60	70.07
AMU.multi-transducer-composed PRIMARY	**19.77**	**69.50**
DCU FRANKENAPE-TUNED PRIMARY	20.11	69.19
USAAR NMT-OSM PRIMARY	23.05	65.01
LIG chained syn PRIMARY	23.22	65.12
JXNU JXNU EDITFreq PRIMARY	23.31	65.66
CUNI char conv rnn beam PRIMARY	24.03	64.28
Official Baseline (MT)	24.48	62.49
Baseline 2 (Statistical phrase-based APE)	24.69	62.97

Proceedings for AMTA 2018 Workshop: Translation Quality Estimation and Automatic Post-Editing

Results for the WMT2017 shared task on APE

#	Ave %	Ave z	System
–	84.8	0.520	Human post edit
1	**78.2**	**0.261**	**AMU**
	77.9	0.261	FBK
	76.8	0.221	DCU
4	73.8	0.115	JXNU
5	71.9	0.038	USAAR
	71.1	0.014	CUNI
	70.2	-0.020	LIG
–	68.6	-0.083	No post edit

Source: WMT 2017 overview paper

Proceedings for AMTA 2018 Workshop: Translation Quality Estimation and Automatic Post-Editing

Results for the WMT2017 shared task on APE

Systems	Modified	Improved	Deteriorated
FBK Primary	1,607	1,035	334
AMU Primary	**1,583**	**1,040**	**322**
DCU Primary	1,592	1,014	361
...			

Source: WMT 2017 overview paper

Proceedings for AMTA 2018 Workshop: Translation Quality Estimation and Automatic Post-Editing

WMT 2018 Shared Task on Automatic post-editing

- First shared tasks to post-edit NMT output (exciting!)
- Still en-de and IT (not ideal!)
- Domain mis-match between artifical data and NMT (bad!)
- More artifical data (good!)

Proceedings for AMTA 2018 Workshop: Translation Quality Estimation and Automatic Post-Editing

More guesses

General MT is eating your lunch!

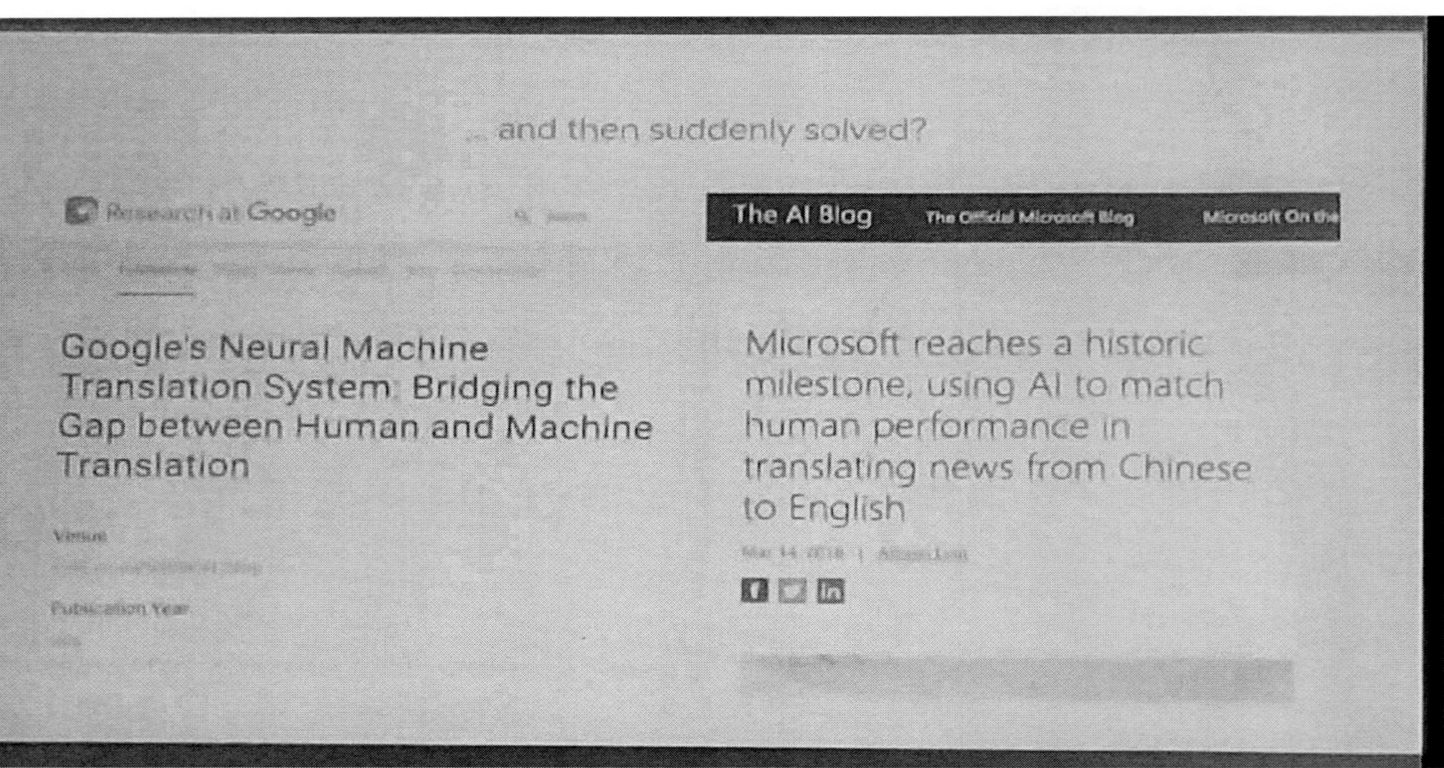

Justification

- ► General QE and APE will be gone before translators even need start worrying;
- ► QE and APE are bug-fixes that operate within very narrow error margin (too bad to exploit full error margin);
- ► This error margin might already be gone in many real-word applications.

Proceedings for AMTA 2018 Workshop: Translation Quality Estimation and Automatic Post-Editing

But ... but... it works, right?

Maybe, maybe not. I think we are mostly seeing:

- Favorably chosen test sets, domains and language pairs;
- Synergy effects (different approaches): SMT+NMT
- System combination effects (similar approches);
- Two-pass decoding effects (see MS results);
- Domain-adaptation or style-transfer effects (**the last hope!**)

Proceedings for AMTA 2018 Workshop: Translation Quality Estimation and Automatic Post-Editing

Challenges in Adaptive Neural Machine Translation

Marcello Federico
MMT Srl / FBK Trento, Italy

MODERN **MT**

Our Adventures with ModernMT
(2015-2017)

MODERN **MT**

Symbiotic Human and Machine Translation

MT seamlessly
- adapts to user data
- learns from post-editing

user enjoys
- enhanced productivity
- better user experience

MODERN MT

FONDAZIONE BRUNO KESSLER

3

Usable technology for the translation industry

- **easy** to install and deploy
- **fast** to set-up for a new project
- **effective**, also on small projects
- **scalable** with data and users
- works with commodity hardware

MODERN MT

FONDAZIONE BRUNO KESSLER

The Modern MT way

(1)   connect your CAT with a **plug-in**
(2)   drag & drop your **private** TMs
(3)   start translating!

Modern MT in a nutshell

zero training time
adapts to context
learns from user corrections
scales with data and users

Fast training

Training data is a **dynamic** collection of Translation Memories

At any time:

- new TMs are **added**
- existing TMs are **extended**

Training time comparable to uploading time!

MODERN MT

7

Context aware translation

SENTENCE

party

CONTEXT	**CONTEXT**
We are going out.	We approved the law

TRANSLATION	**TRANSLATION**
fête	parti

MODERN MT

Incremental learning

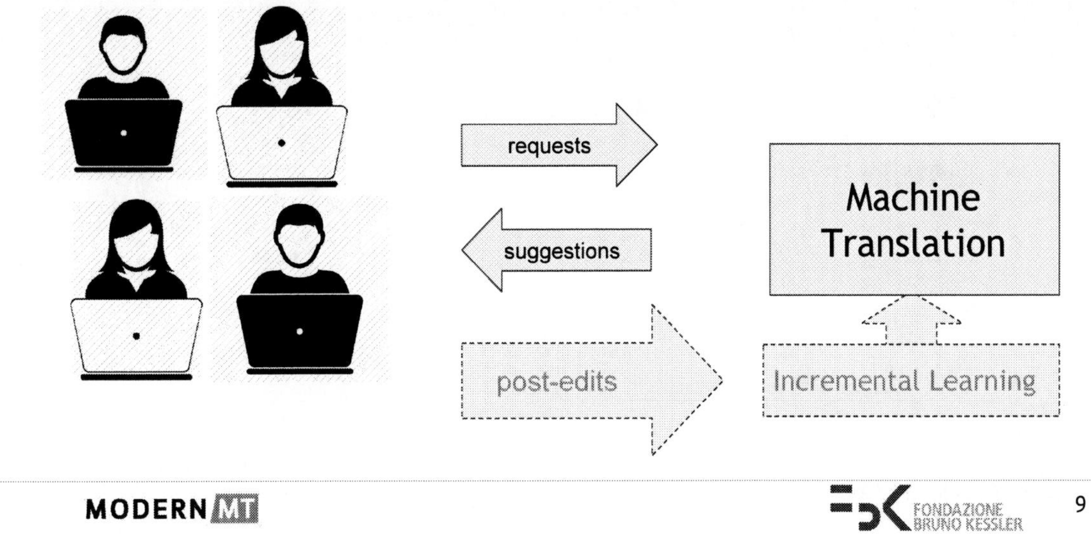

Core technology [original plan]

context analyser
phrase-based decoder
adaptive models
incremental structures
parallel processing

Simple. Adaptive. Neural.

Language support

- **45** languages
- **fast pre-/post-processing**
- **simple interfaces**
- **tags** and **XML** management
- localization of **expressions**
- TM **cleaning**

Context Analyzer

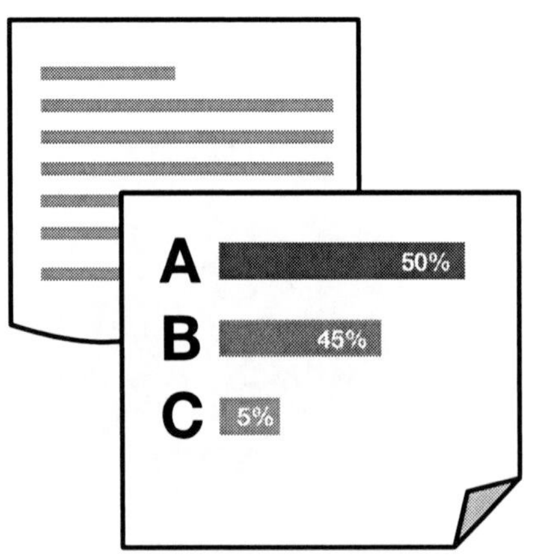

- analyze input text
- retrieve best matching TMs
- compute matching scores
- **dynamic structure**

Adaptive Phrase Table

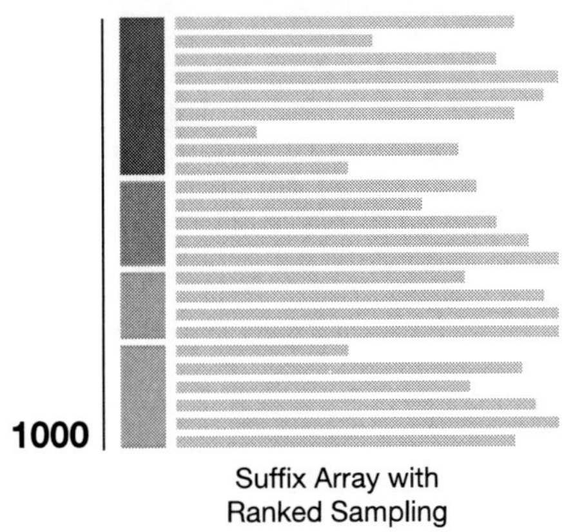

- suffix array indexed with TMs
- phrases sampled on demand
- priority sampling over TMs
- **dynamic structure**

Adaptive Language Model

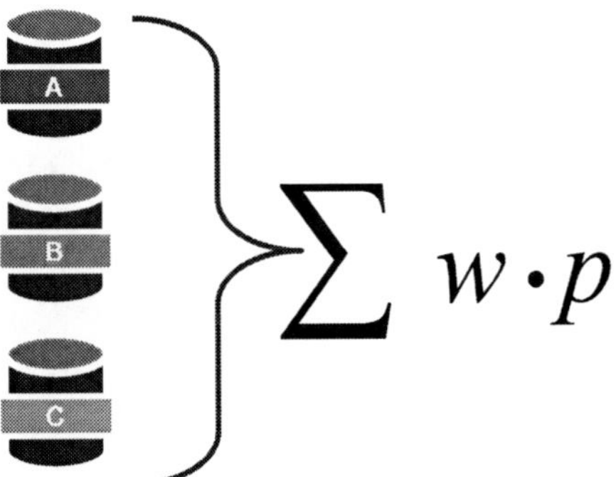

$$\sum w \cdot p$$

- large static background model
- n-grams stats indexed with TMs
- combination of *active* TM LMs
- TM LMs computed on the fly
- **dynamic structure**

Statistical vs. Neural MT

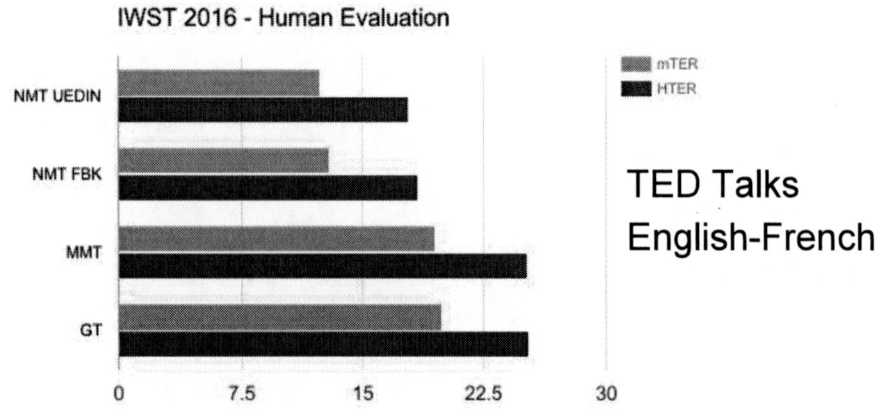

TED Talks
English-French

M. Cettolo, et al. (2016), *The IWSLT 2016 Evaluation Campaign*, IWSLT.

MODERN MT

FONDAZIONE BRUNO KESSLER   15

Second Prototype (0.14 January 2017)

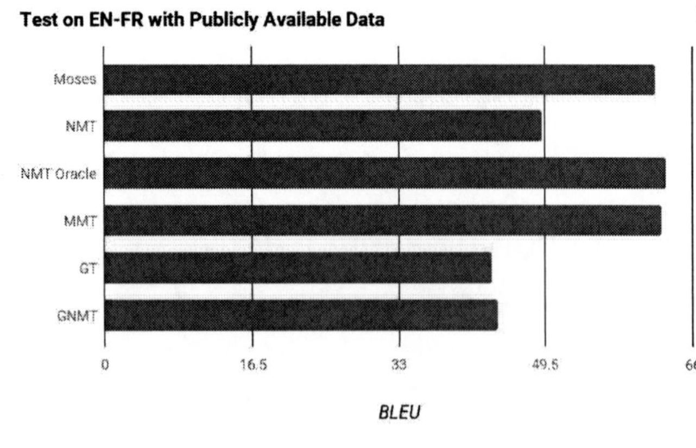

Open benchmark:

- Training speed:
  12x Moses - 100x NMT
- MT quality (BLEU):
  +1 vs Moses
  -0.5 vs NMT Ada

Domains: ECB, Gnome, JRC, KDE, OpenOffice, PHP, Ubuntu, UN-TM

MODERN MT   Simple. Adaptive. Neural.

What happened

Research on adaptive neural MT

Believed PBMT was competitive on technical translation

Finally realised superiority of NMT quality

Completed PBMT release and **switched to NMT**

Data collection for 14 translation directions

Roadmap from last review meeting

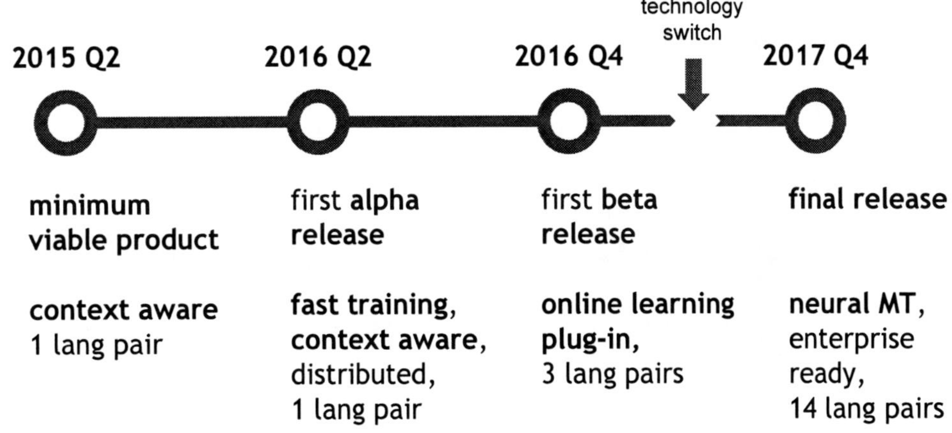

Multi-Domain Neural MT

Multi-user scenario

Multi-user scenario

Multi-user scenario

Adaptive Neural MT
(Adaptation *a priori*)

All we need is a memory

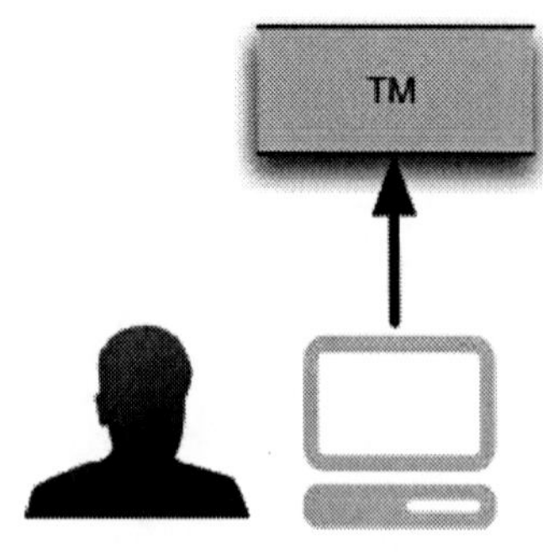

Proceedings for AMTA 2018 Workshop: Translation Quality Estimation and Automatic Post-Editing

All we need is a memory

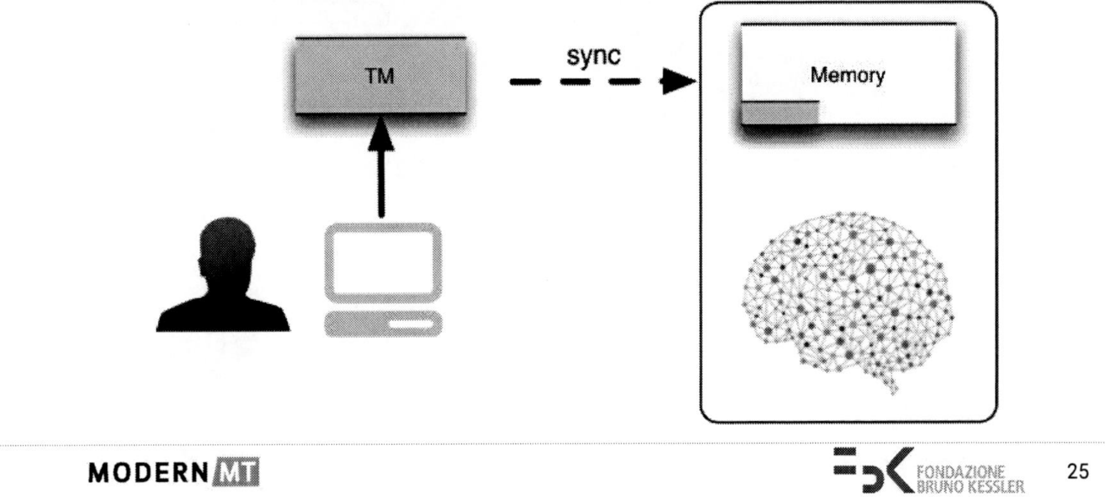

MODERN MT

FONDAZIONE
BRUNO KESSLER

25

All we need is a memory

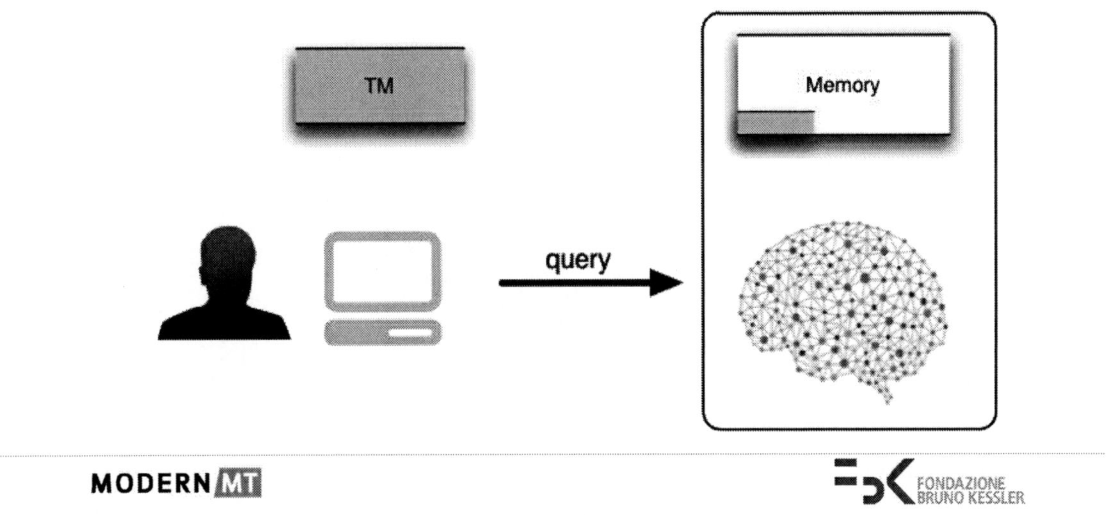

MODERN MT

FONDAZIONE
BRUNO KESSLER

All we need is a memory

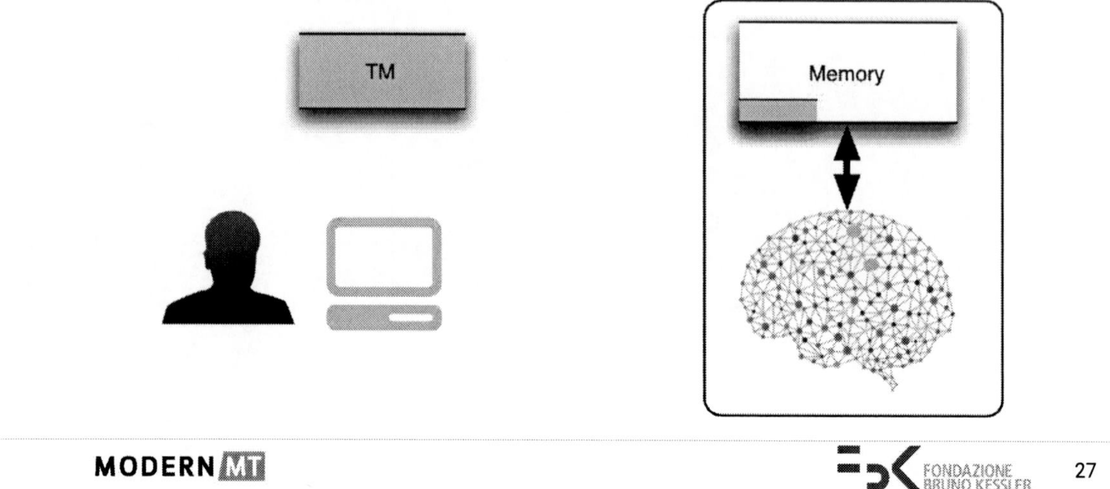

All we need is a memory

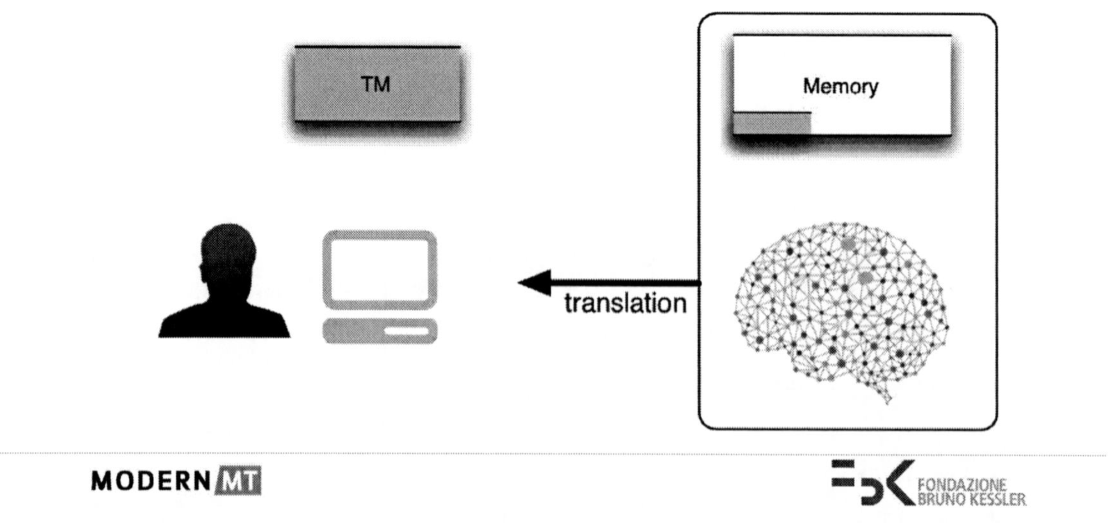

Multi-user adaptive NMT

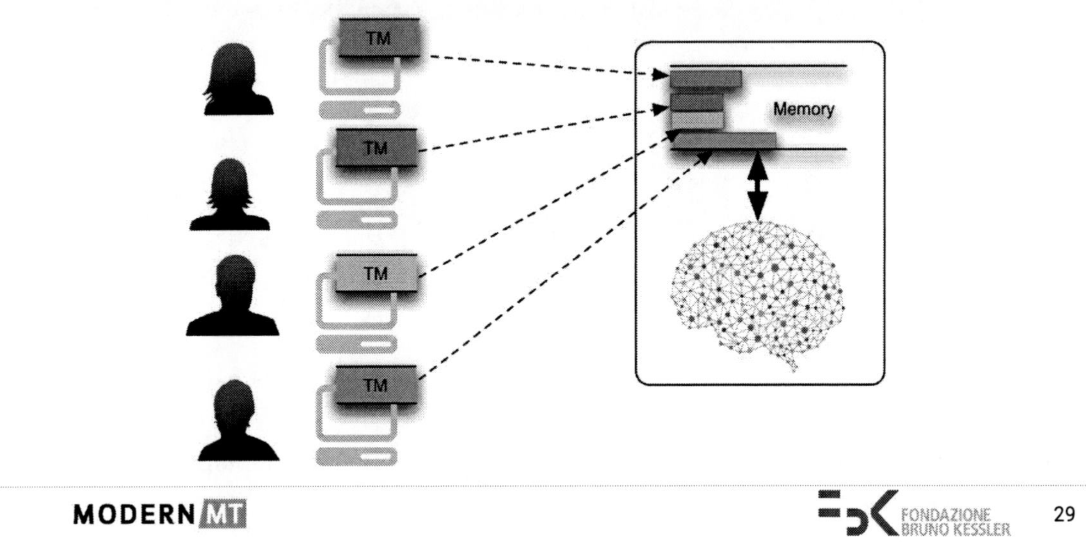

Multi-user adaptive NMT

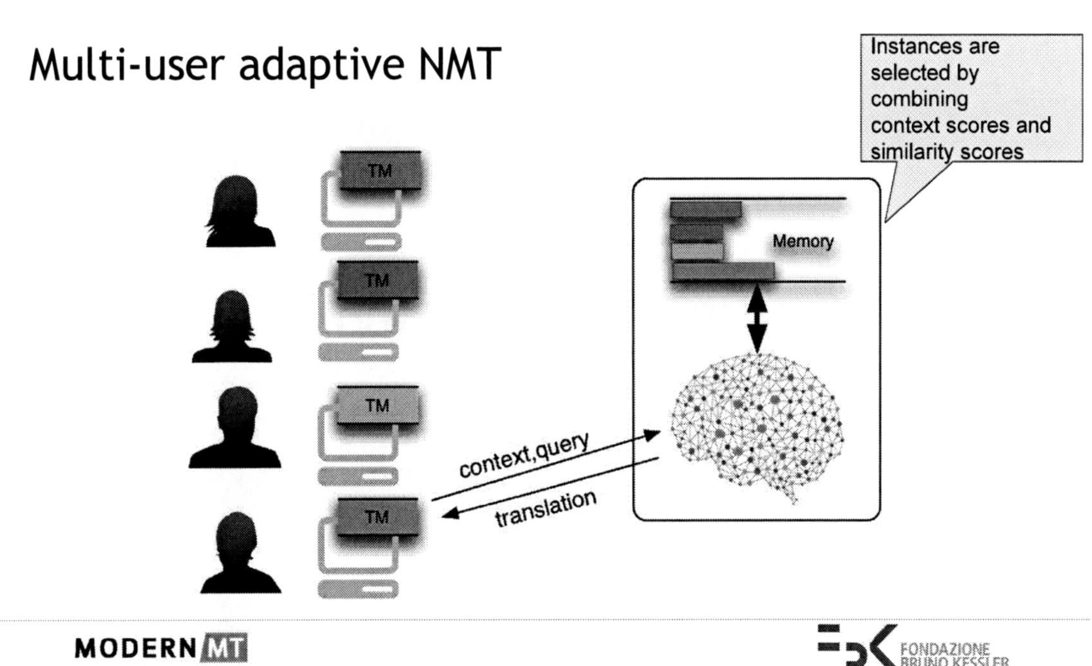

Proceedings for AMTA 2018 Workshop: Translation Quality Estimation and Automatic Post-Editing

221

Adaptation, too!

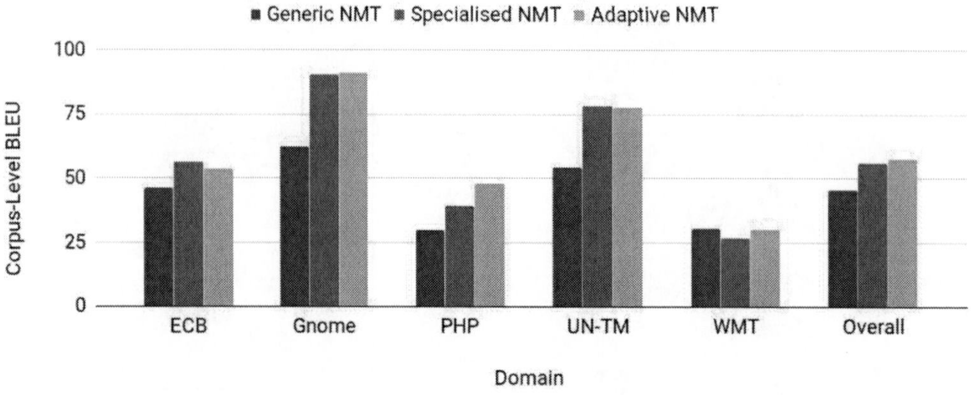

Farajian et al. (2017) "Multi-domain NMT through unsupervised adaptation", *WMT*.

Production Systems

Timeline 2017

Sep: integration of MateCat
Oct: NMT code released
Nov: co-development
      release of 14 engines
Dec: performance boost

Automatic Evaluations

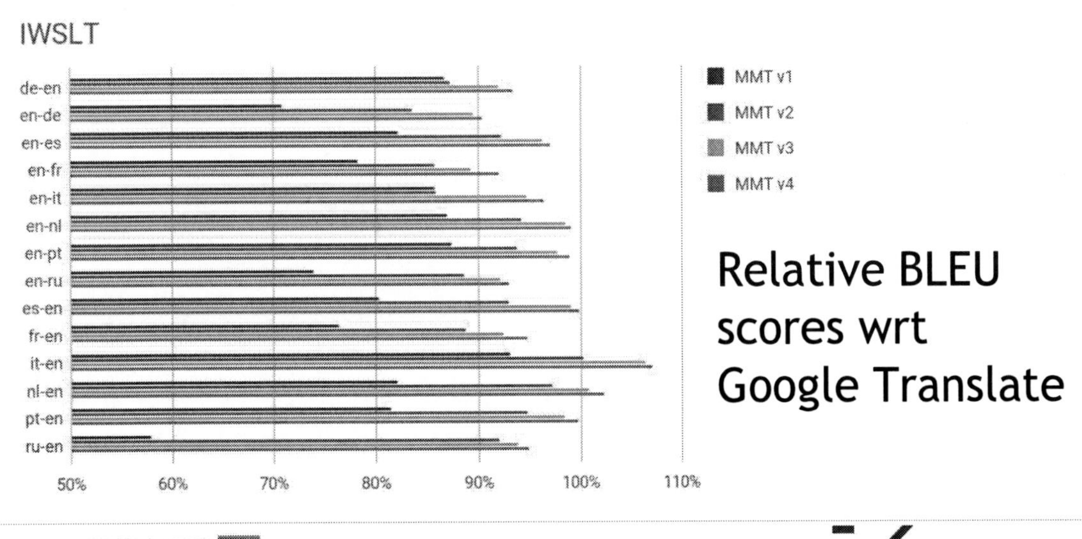

Relative BLEU scores wrt Google Translate

Micro HE Assessment

Progression in one month on English-Italian

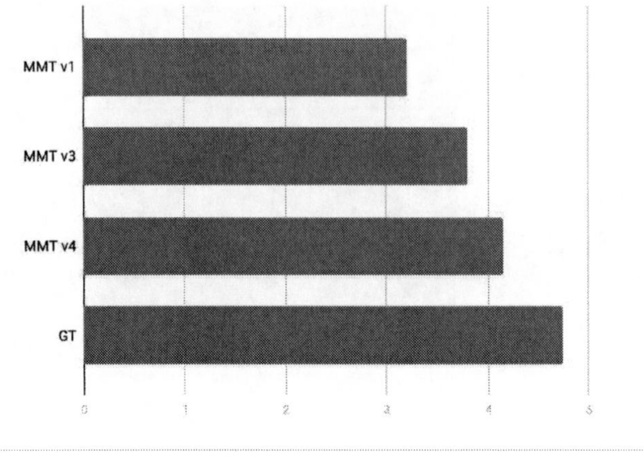

Performance of
generic MMT
1-6 scale
(w/o adaptation)

Quality Estimation

Quality Evaluation

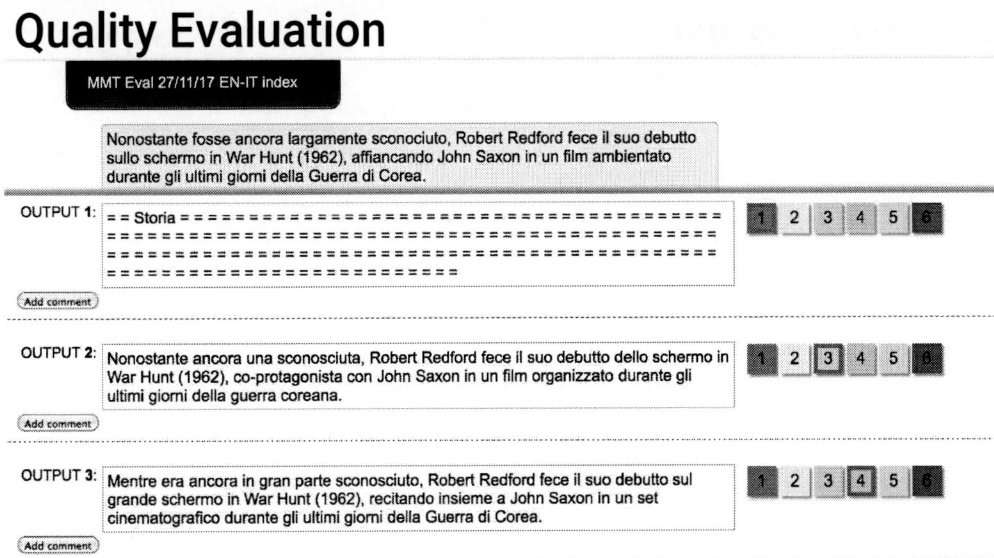

MODERN MT

37

Quality Evaluation

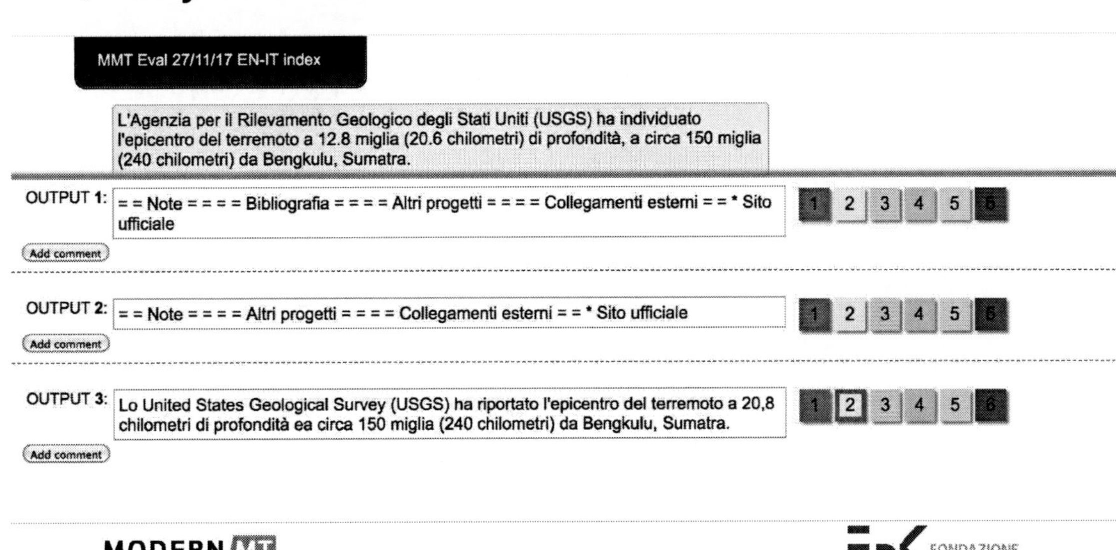

MODERN MT

Noisy training data

EN: What history teaches us

IT: === Storia ==================================

MODERN MT   Simple. Adaptive. Neural.

Data Cleaning

We added a simple QE module to filter out bad examples:

- Apply Fast-Align in two directions
- Compute Model 1 scores in two directions
- Combine and normalize scores
- Filter out on the distribution of scores

MODERN MT   Simple. Adaptive. Neural.

More Recent Adventures

MODERN **MT**

FONDAZIONE BRUNO KESSLER   41

Incremental Learning

MODERN **MT**

FONDAZIONE BRUNO KESSLER

Incremental Learning

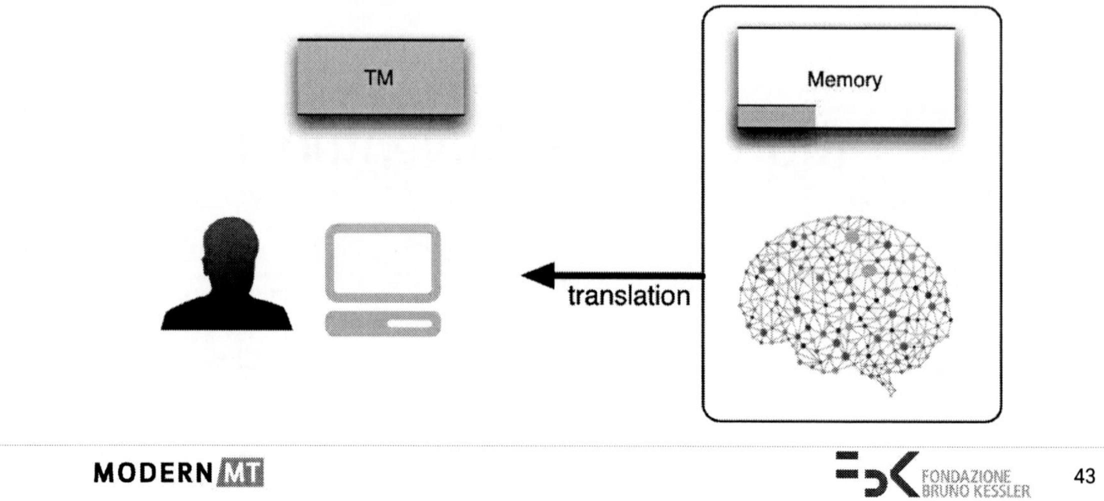

Incremental Learning

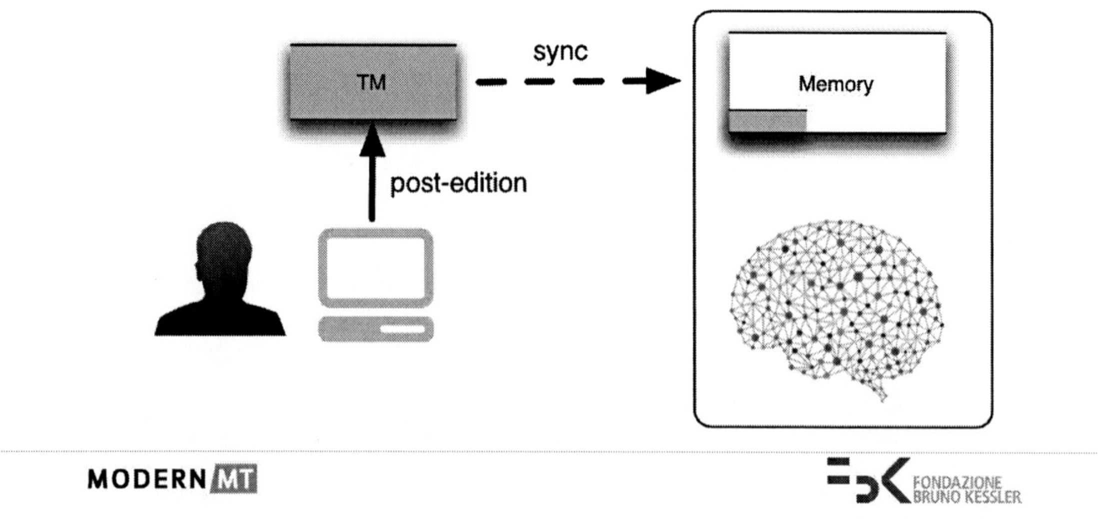

What happens when a new TM is uploaded?

We compare:

- Generic MT: production engine [En-It]
- Custom MT: Generic MT tuned on TM [takes hours]
- +Adaptive MT: Generic MT adapted on TM [real-time]
- +Incremental MT: TM updated with simulated PE

Incremental Learning

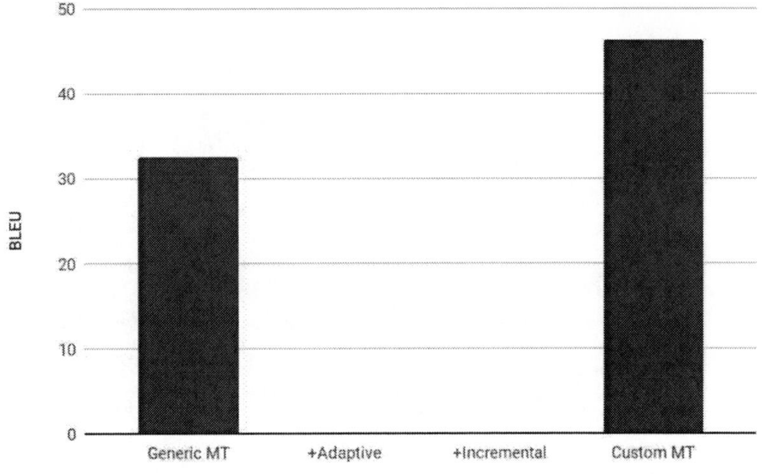

MODERN MT

Incremental Learning

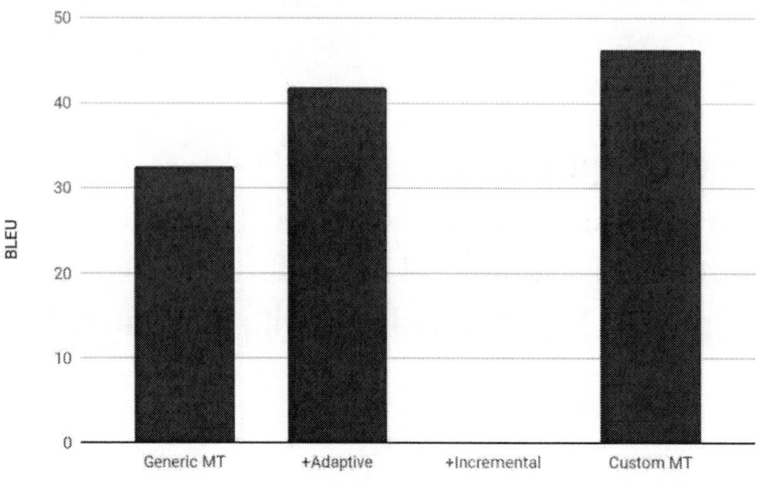

Incremental Learning

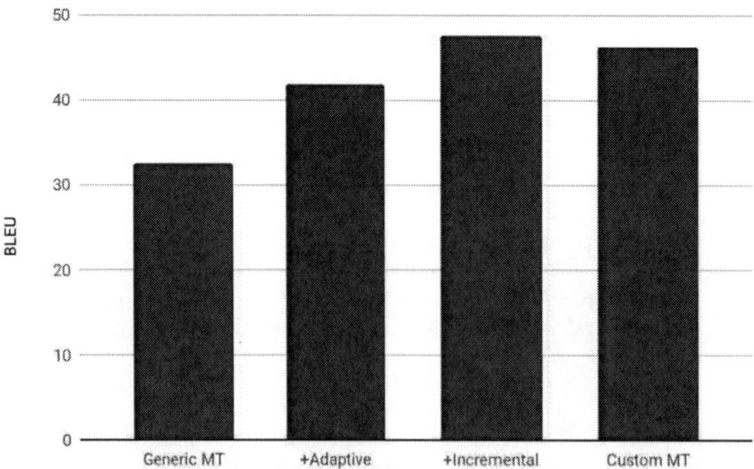

Proceedings for AMTA 2018 Workshop: Translation Quality Estimation and Automatic Post-Editing

230

Incremental Learning

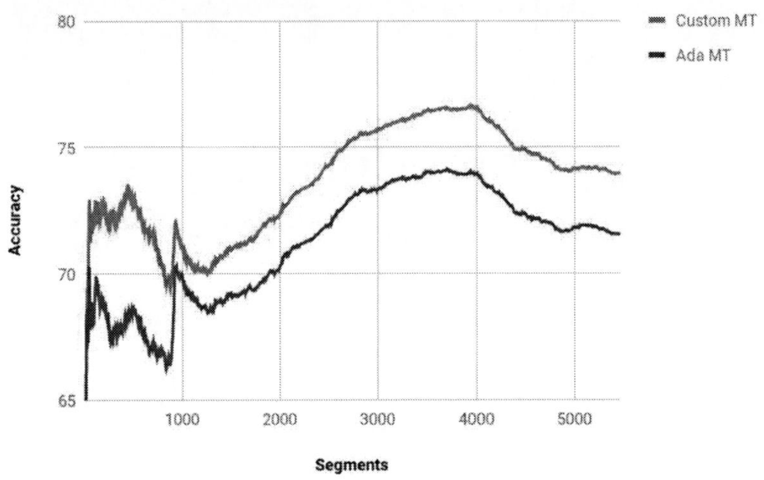

Incremental Learning

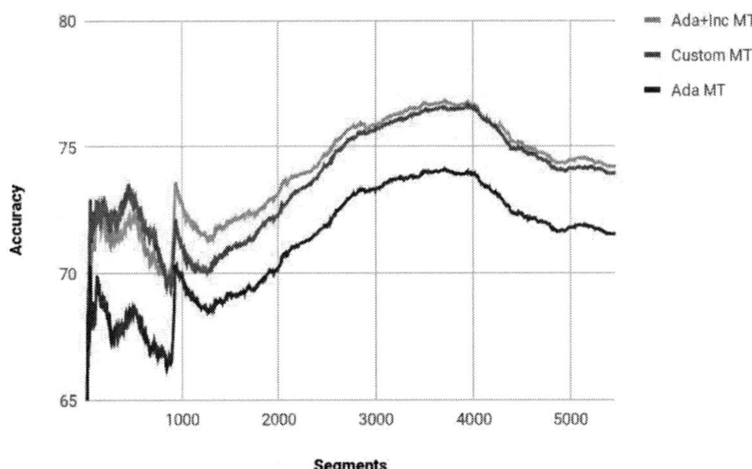

MODERN **MT**   FONDAZIONE BRUNO KESSLER

Online learning
(Adaptation *a posteriori*)

Online Learning

Use post-editing as new training instances

Perform one/more iterations

Can be combined with *a priori* adaptation

Updates generic or adapted model

Turchi et al. (2017), *Continuous learning from human post-edits for NMT, EAMT.*

Online Learning

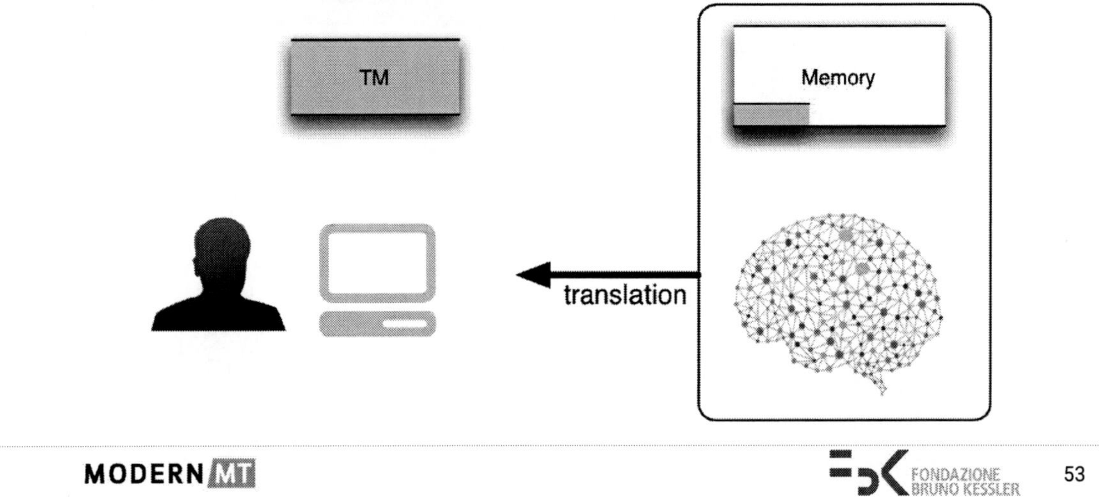

Online Learning

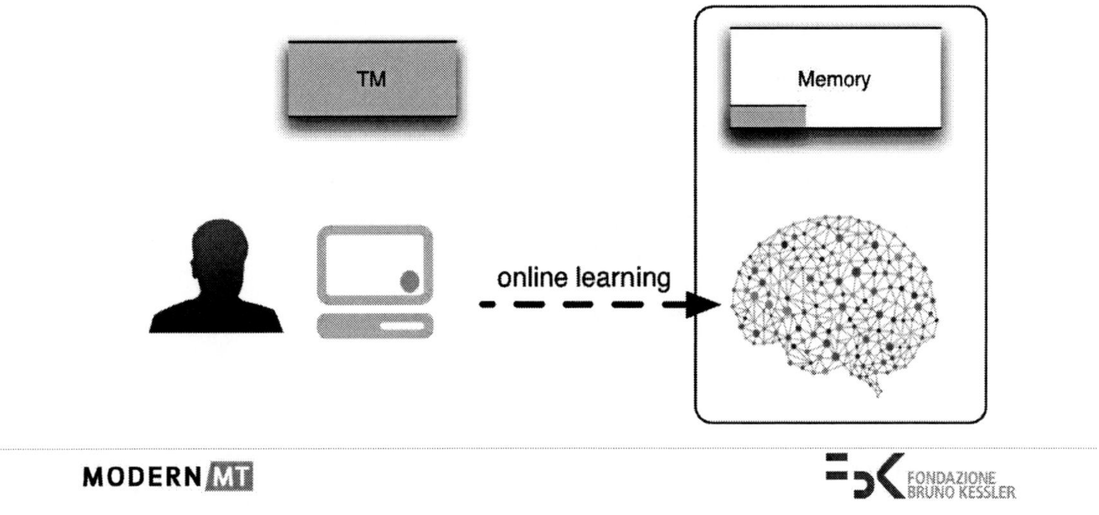

Incremental+Online Learning

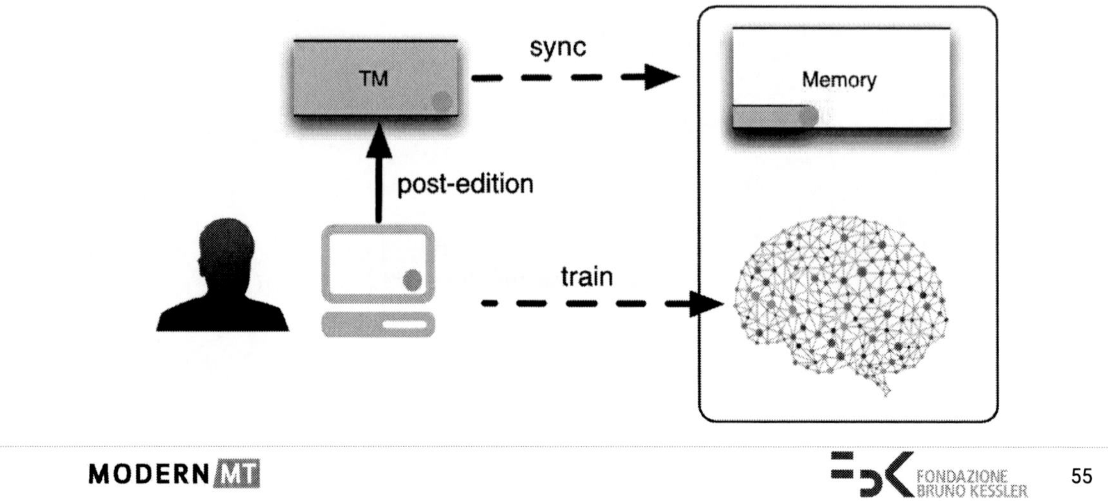

Incremental+Online Learning (single domains)

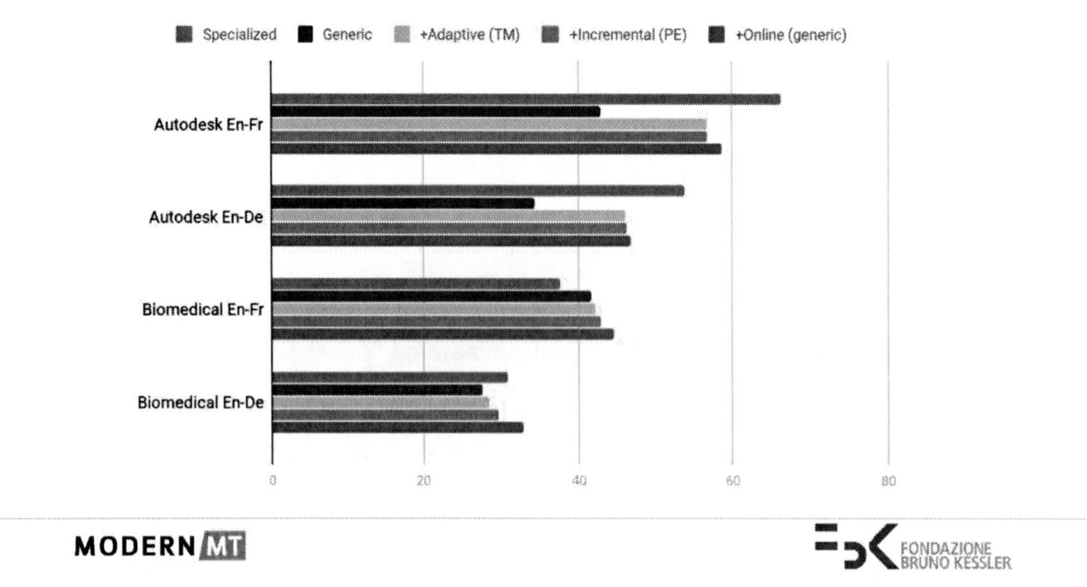

Incremental+Online Learning (two domains)

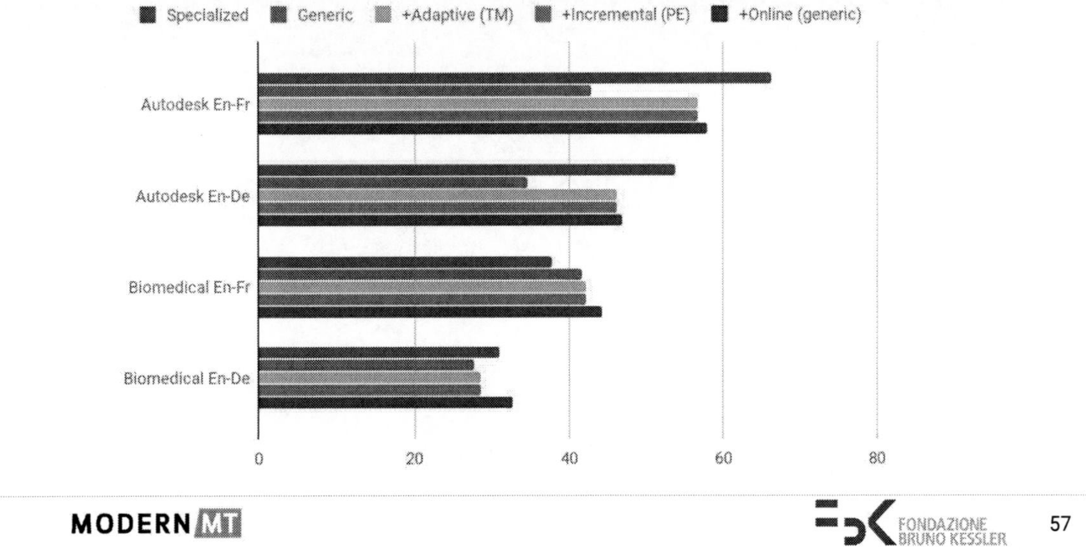

57

Challenges

Online-learning contribution is consistent

Does it scale with number of domains?

Incremental learning contributes marginally

Probably depends on test set size

We are not always able to beat specialized models

How to improve further adaptation ?

Automatic Post-Editing

Automatic Post-Editing

Can improve MT without touching it inside

We can adapt an "external" MT service!

Similar to NMT: two inputs (*src,mt*), one output (*ape*)

Can be trained with less data than NMT

We can deploy instance based adaptation

Chatterjee et al. (2017), *Multi-source Neural APE: FBK's participation …. , WMT.*

MODERN MT 

Automatic Post-Editing

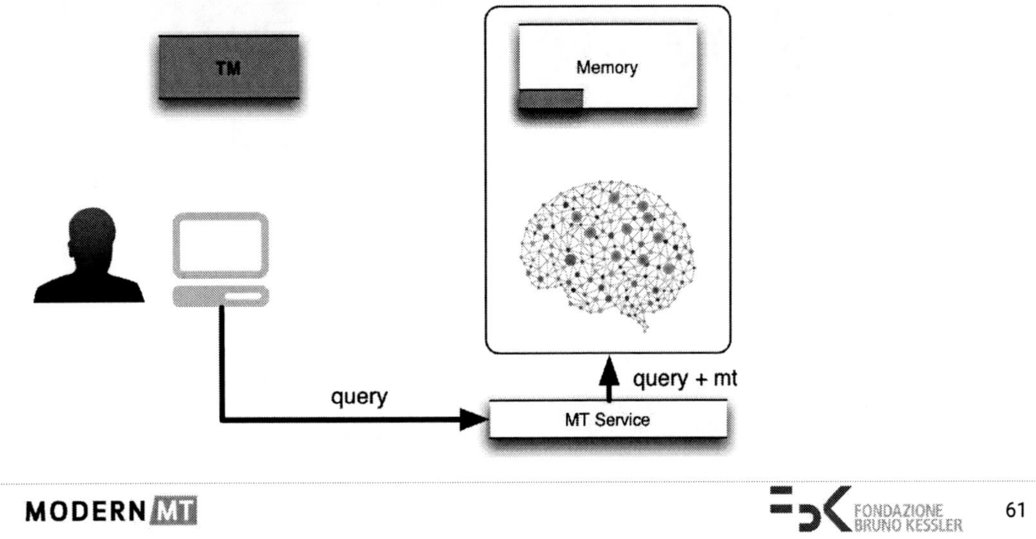

Automatic Post-Editing

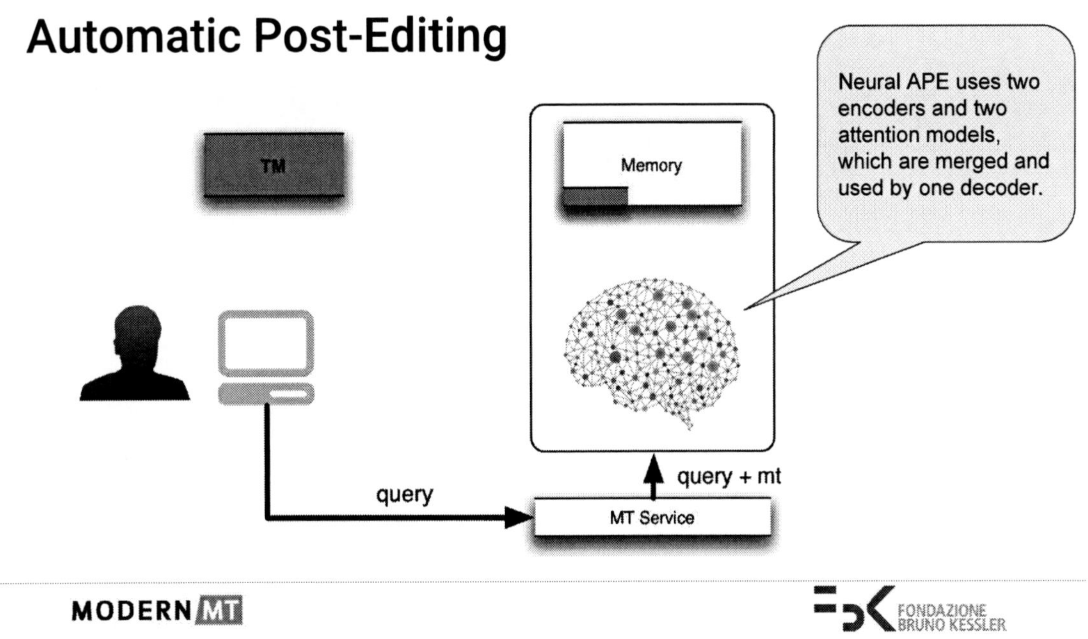

Automatic Post-Editing

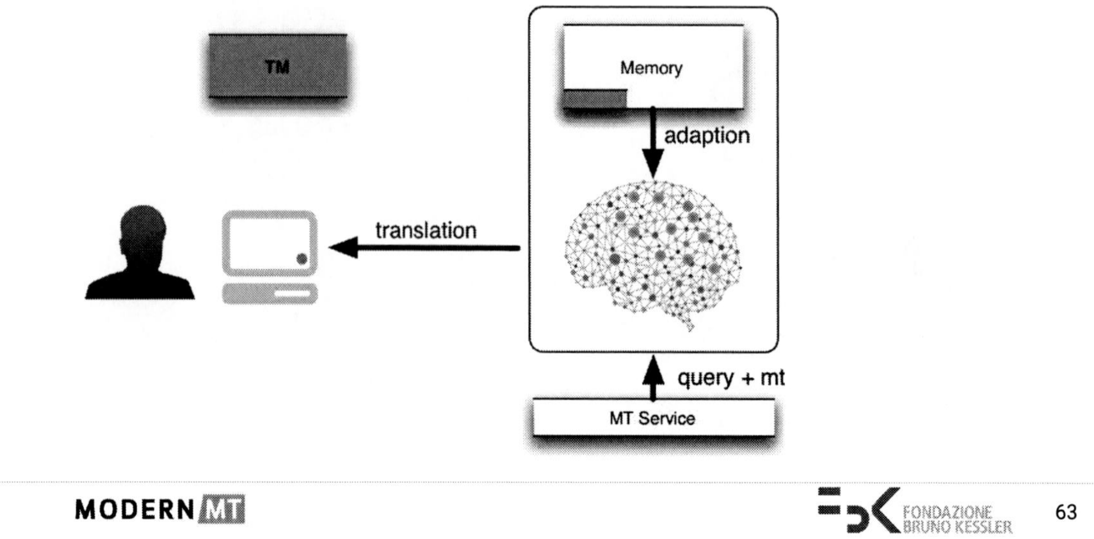

Automatic Post-Editing

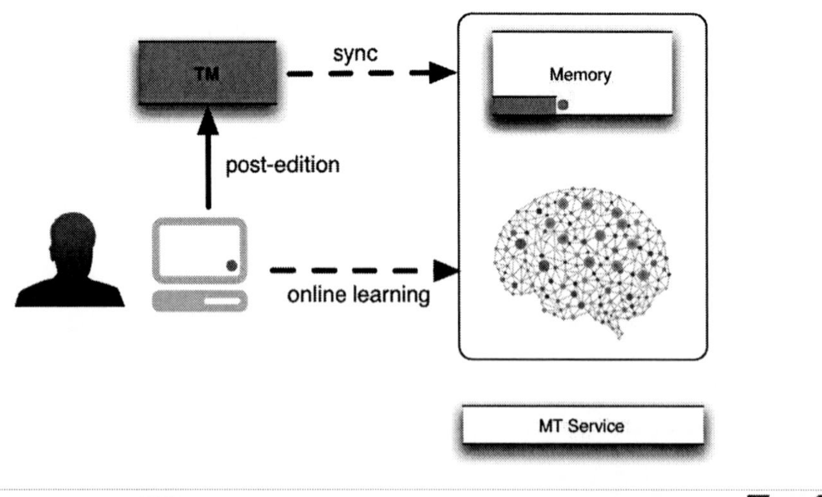

Automatic Post-Editing

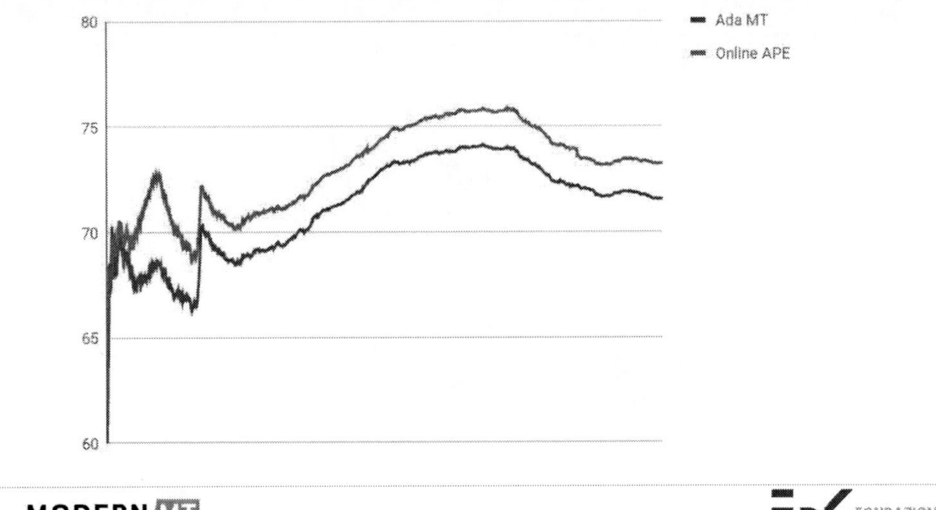

Automatic Post-Editing

Customer Domain EN-IT

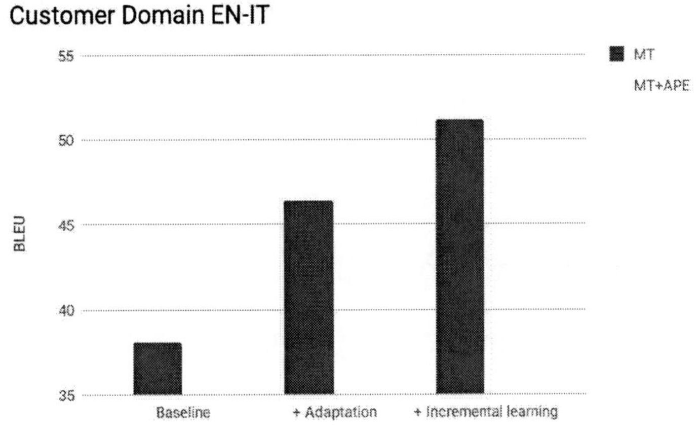

Automatic Post-Editing

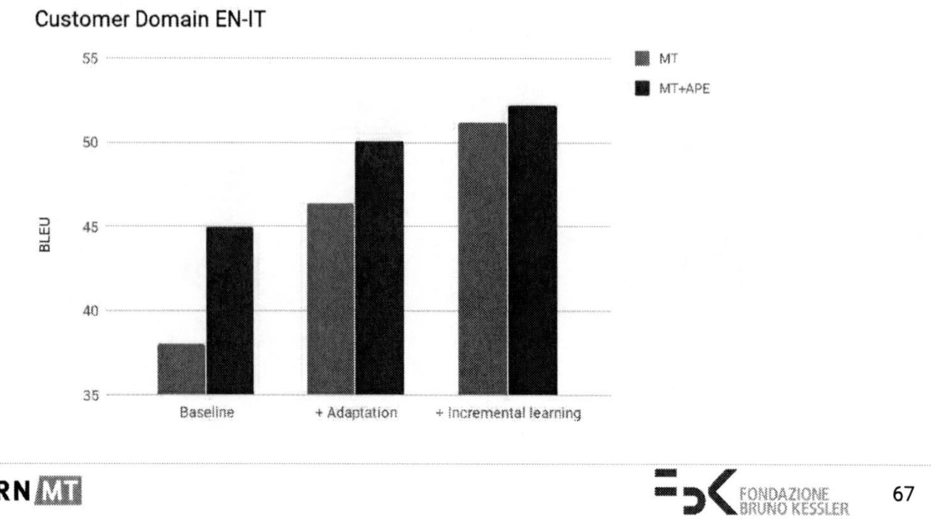

Automatic Post-Editing

Can improve on top of static and adaptive engine!

Uses incremental learning, adaptation and online learning

Portable (in principle) on the multi-domain setting

Limited gain on top of full-fledged adaptive NMT

Can be an extra component to manage

Conclusions

  69

Conclusions

Multi-user scenario goes beyond simple domain adaptation

We need to handle multiple evolving *domains*

Domain customization is not an option

Real-time adaptation/learning works!

But, there is still room for improvement!

MODERN MT 

Thank You

Website

www.ModernMT.eu

Github

github.com/ModernMT/MMT

Fine-grained evaluation of Quality Estimation for Machine translation based on a linguistically-motivated Test Suite

Eleftherios Avramidis[*], Vivien Macketanz[*], Arle Lommel[**] and Hans Uszkoreit[*]

[*]German Research Center for Artificial Intelligence (DFKI), Berlin, Germany
firstname.lastname@dfki.de
[**]Common Sense Advisory (CSA Research), Massachusetts, USA
alommel@csa-research.com

Abstract

We present an alternative method of evaluating Quality Estimation systems, which is based on a linguistically-motivated Test Suite. We create a test-set consisting of 14 linguistic error categories and we gather for each of them a set of samples with both correct and erroneous translations. Then, we measure the performance of 5 Quality Estimation systems by checking their ability to distinguish between the correct and the erroneous translations. The detailed results are much more informative about the ability of each system. The fact that different Quality Estimation systems perform differently at various phenomena confirms the usefulness of the Test Suite.

1 Introduction

The evaluation of empirical Natural Language Processing (NLP) systems is a necessary task during research for new methods and ideas. The evaluation task is the last one to come after the development process and aims to indicate the overall performance of the newly built system and compare it against previous versions or other systems. Additionally, it also allows for conclusions related to the decisions taken for the development parameters and provides hints for improvement. Defining evaluation methods that satisfy the original development requirements is an ongoing field of research.

Automatic evaluation in sub-fields of Machine Translation (MT) has been mostly performed on given textual hypothesis sets, where the performance of the system is measured against gold-standard reference sets with one or more metrics (Bojar et al., 2017). Despite the extensive research on various automatic metrics and scoring meth-

ods, little attention has been paid to the actual content of the test-sets and how these can be adequate for judging the output from a linguistic perspective. The text of most test-sets so far has been drawn from various random sources and the only characteristic that is controlled and reported is the generic domain of the text.

In this paper we make an effort to demonstrate the value of using a linguistically-motivated controlled test-set (also known as a *Test Suite*) for evaluation instead of generic test-sets. We will focus on the sub-field of sentence-level Quality Estimation (QE) on MT and see how the evaluation of QE on a Test Suite can provide useful information concerning particular linguistic phenomena.

2 Related work

There have been few efforts to use a broadly-defined Test Suite for the evaluation of MT, the first of them being during the early steps of the technology (King and Falkedal, 1990). Although the topic has been recently revived (Isabelle et al., 2017; Burchardt et al., 2017), all relevant research so far applies only to the evaluation of MT output and not of QE predictions.

Similar to MT output, predictions of sentence-level QE have also been evaluated on test-sets consisting of randomly drawn texts and a single metric has been used to measure the performance over the entire text (e.g. Bojar et al., 2017). There has been criticism on the way the test-sets of the shared tasks have been formed with regards to the distribution of inputs (Anil and Fran, 2013), e.g. when they demonstrate a dataset shift (Quionero-Candela et al., 2009). Additionally, although there has been a lot of effort to infuse linguistically motivated features in QE (Felice and Specia, 2012), there has been no effort to evaluate their predictions from a linguistic perspective. To the best of our knowledge there has been no use of a Test Suite in order to evaluate sentence-level QE, or to inspect the predictions with regards to linguistic categories or specific error types.

3 Method

The evaluation of QE presented in this paper is based on these steps: (1) construction of the Test Suite with respect to linguistic categories; (2) selection of suitable Test Suite sentences; and (3) analysis of the Test Suite by existing QE systems and statistical evaluation of the predictions. These steps are analysed below, whereas a simplified example is given in Figure 1.

3.1 Construction of the Test Suite

The Test Suite has been developed by a professional linguist, supported by professional translators. First, the linguist gathers or creates error-specific paradigms (Figure 1, stage a), i.e. sentences whose translation has demonstrated or is suspected to demonstrate systematic errors by known MT engines. The aim is to have a representative amount of paradigms per error type and the paradigms are as short as possible in order to focus solely on one phenomenon under examination. The error types are defined based on linguistic categories inspired by the MQM error typology (Lommel et al., 2014) and extend the error types presented in Burchardt et al. (2017), with additional fine-grained analysis of sub-categories. The main categories for German-English can be seen in Table 2.

Second, the paradigms are given to several MT systems (Figure 1, stage b) to check whether they are able to translate them properly , with the aim to acquire a "pass" or a "fail" label accordingly. In an effort to accelerate the acquisition of these labels, we follow a semi-automatic annotation method using regular expressions. The regular expressions allow a faster automatic labelling that focuses on particular tokens expected to demonstrate the issue, unaffected from alternative sentence formulations. For each gathered source sentence the linguist specifies regular expressions (Figure 1, stage c) that focus on the particular issue: one positive regular expression that matches a successful translation and gives a "pass" label and an optional negative regular expression that matches an erroneous translation and gives a "fail" (for phenomena such as ambiguity and false friends). The reg-

MT type	proportion
neural	64.7%
phrase-based	26.8%
both (same output)	8.5%

Table 1: MT type for the translations participating in the final pairwise test-set

ular expressions, developed and tested on the first translation outputs, are afterwards applied to all the alternative translation outputs (stage d) to acquire the automatic labels (stage e). Further modifications to the regular expressions were applied, if they did not properly match the new translation outputs. The automatically assigned labels were controlled in the end by a professional translator and native speaker of the target language (stage f). For the purposes of this analysis, we also assume that every sentence paradigm only demonstrates the error type that it has been chosen for and no other major errors occur.

3.2 Selection of suitable Test Suite sentences

The next step is to transform the results so that they can be evaluated by existing sentence-level QE methods, since the Test Suite provides binary pass/fail values for the errors, whereas most sentence-level QE methods predict a continuous score. For this purpose, we transform the problem to a problem of predicting comparisons. We deconstruct the alternative translations of every source sentence into pairwise comparisons, and we only keep the pairs that contain one successful and one failing translation (Figure 1, stage g). Sentence-level QE systems will be given every pair of MT outputs and requested to predict a comparison, i.e. which of the two outputs is better (stage h). Finally, the QE systems are evaluated based on their capability to properly compare the erroneous with the correct outputs (stage i). The performance of the QE systems will be therefore expressed in terms of the accuracy over the pairwise choices.

4 Experiment

4.1 Data and systems

The current Test Suite contains about 5,500 source sentences and their rules with regular expressions for translating German to English. These rules have been applied for evaluating 10,800 unique

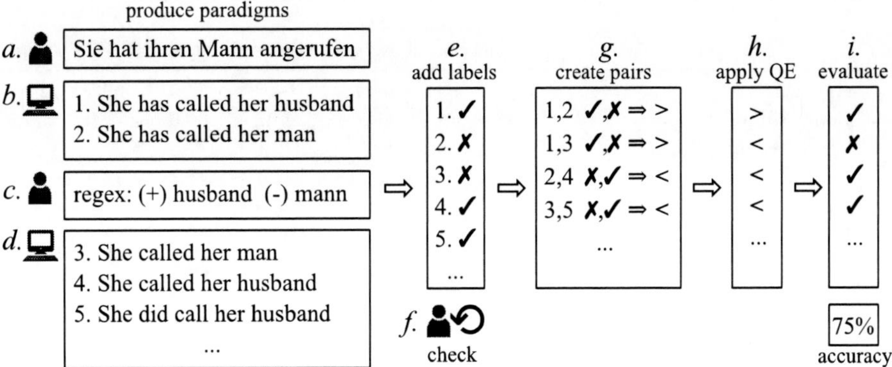

Figure 1: Example for the processing of test items for the lexical ambiguity of word "Mann"

MT outputs (MT outputs with the exact same text have been merged together). These outputs have been produced by three online commercial systems (2 state-of-the-art neural MT systems and one phrase-based), plus the open-source neural system by Sennrich et al. (2017). After creating pairs of alternative MT outputs that have a different label (Section 3.2) the final test-set contains 3,230 pairwise comparisons based on the translations of 1,582 source sentences. The MT types of the translations participating in the final test-set can be seen in Table 1.

For this comparative study we evaluate existing QE systems that were freely available to train and use. In particular we evaluate the baseline the following 6 systems:

- **B17:** The baseline of the shared task on sentence-level QE (Bojar et al., 2017) based on 17 black-box features and trained with Support Vector Regression (SVR) to predict continuous HTER values

- **B13:** the winning system of the shared task on QE ranking (Bojar et al., 2013; Avramidis and Popović, 2013) based on 10 features, trained with Logistic Regression with Stepwise Feature Selection in order to perform ranking. Despite being old, this system was chosen as it is the latest paradigm of Comparative QE that has been extensively compared with competitive methods in a shared task

- **A17:** three variations of the state-of-the-art research on Comparative QE (Avramidis, 2017), all three trained with a Gradient Boosting classifier. The *basic* system has the same feature set as B13, the *full* system contains a wide variety of 139 features and the *RFECV* contains the 25 highest ranked features from the full feature set, after running Recursive Feature Elimination with an SVR kernel.

The implementation was based on the open-source tools Quest (Shah et al., 2013) and Qualitative (Avramidis, 2016).

4.2 Results

Here we present the evaluation of the QE systems when applied on the Test Suite. The accuracy achieved by each of the 6 QE systems for the 14 error categories can be seen in Table 2.

First, it can be noted that the **quantity of evaluated samples** varies a lot and, although the original aim was to have about 100 samples per category, most of the neural outputs succeeded in the translations of the issues and therefore were not included in the test-set with the "pass/fail" comparisons. Obviously, conclusions for those error categories with few samples cannot be guaranteed.

Second, one can see that the **average scores** range between 52.1% and 57.5% (achieved by B13) which are nevertheless relatively low. This may be explained by the fact that all QE systems have been developed in the previous years with the focus on "real text" test-sets. The Test Suite on the contrary is not representative of a real scenario and has a different distribution than the one expected from real data. Additionally, many of the linguistic phenomena of the Test Suite may have few or no occurrences on the development data of the QE systems. Finally, all QE systems have been devel-

	amount	B17 baseline	B13 winning	basic	A17 RFECV	full
Ambiguity	89	58.4	64.0	**73.0**	69.7	62.9
Composition	75	58.7	77.3	**80.0**	72.0	77.3
Coordination & ellipsis	78	53.8	**73.1**	71.8	71.8	70.5
False friends	52	38.5	32.7	**48.1**	38.5	42.3
Function word	126	33.3	**38.9**	35.7	32.5	34.9
Long distance dep. & interrogatives	266	52.3	63.9	60.2	63.9	**65.8**
Multi-word expressions	43	32.6	**44.2**	32.6	39.5	39.5
Named entity & terminology	55	50.9	54.5	56.4	58.2	**60.0**
Negation	13	38.5	53.8	**76.9**	**76.9**	**76.9**
Non-verbal agreement	45	40.0	**57.8**	53.3	**57.8**	53.3
Punctuation	138	11.6	29.7	**32.6**	28.3	27.5
Subordination	46	41.3	43.5	**47.8**	45.7	**47.8**
Verb tense/aspect/mood/type	2137	56.6	**59.4**	55.5	57.3	57.7
Verb valency	67	50.7	55.2	50.7	58.2	**62.7**
Total	3230	52.1	**57.5**	55.0	56.1	56.7
weighed		44.1	53.4	55.3	55.0	**55.6**

Table 2: QE accuracy (%) per error category

oped in the previous years with the focus on rule-based or phrase-based statistical MT and therefore their performance on MT output primarily from neural systems is unpredictable.

We also report scores averaged not out of the total amount of the samples, but instead giving equal importance to each error category. These scores indicate a different winner: the full system of A17. However, due to the distributional shift of the Test Suite, there is limited value in drawing conclusions from average scores, since the aim of the Test Suite is to provide a qualitative overview of the particular linguistic phenomena.

When it comes to **particular error categories**, the three systems B13, A17-basic and A17-full seem to be complementary, achieving the highest score for 5 different error categories each. The systems B17 and A17-RFECV lack a lot in their performance. The highest category score is achieved for the phenomenon of *Composition* (compounds and phrasal verbs) by A17-basic, followed by *negation* (albeit with very few samples) at 76.9%. A17-basic is also very strong in *ambiguity*, achieving 73%. The 4 systems B13 and A17 perform much better concerning *long-distance relationships*, which may be attributed to the parsing and grammatical features they contain, as opposed to the B17 which does not include parsing. Finally, A17-full does better with *named entities* and

terminology, possibly because its features include alignment scores from IBM model 1.

We notice that **verb tenses, aspects, moods and types** comprise a major error category which contains more than 2,000 samples. This enables us to look into the subcategories related to the verbs. The performance of the systems for different tenses can be seen in Table 3, where B17 and B13 are the winning systems for 5 categories each. The tense with the best performance is the *future II subjunctive II* with a 78% accuracy by B13. Despite its success in the broad spectrum of error categories, A17-full performs relatively poorly on verb tenses.

Finally, Table 4 contains the accuracy scores for **verb types**. A17-full does much better on verb types, with the exception of the *negated modal* which gets a surprising 70.3% accuracy from B17.

5 Conclusion and further work

In this paper we demonstrated the possibility of performing evaluation of QE by testing its predictions on a fine-grained error typology from a Test Suite. In this way, rather than judging QE systems based on a single score, we were able to see how each QE system performs with respect to particular error categories. The results indicate that no system is a clear winner, with three out of the 5 QE systems to have complementary results for

	amount	B17 baseline	B13 winning	basic	A17 RFECV	full
future I	297	**58.9**	**58.9**	52.5	50.5	51.5
future I subjunctive II	249	**62.7**	52.6	45.0	51.4	53.0
future II	158	39.2	56.3	**60.1**	58.2	53.2
future II subjunctive II	168	32.7	**78.0**	74.4	68.5	75.6
perfect	294	55.4	**56.8**	49.3	55.8	54.8
pluperfect	282	**72.7**	65.6	64.9	69.9	68.1
pluperfect subjunctive II	159	52.2	53.5	**55.3**	52.8	**55.3**
present	286	**58.0**	54.9	51.4	51.0	52.8
preterite	105	61.0	**68.6**	53.3	67.6	**68.6**
preterite subjunctive II	88	**62.5**	61.4	58.0	53.4	55.7

Table 3: QE accuracy (%) on error types related to verb tenses

	amount	B17 baseline	B13 winning	basic	A17 RFECV	full
Ditransitive	275	46.9	57.8	55.6	56.4	**60.0**
Intransitive	171	42.1	**69.6**	57.3	59.1	64.3
Modal	473	63.4	67.2	57.9	66.6	**67.2**
Modal negated	657	**70.3**	49.9	47.2	46.0	46.3
Reflexive	376	44.7	61.2	61.2	**62.2**	58.5
Transitive	134	39.6	68.7	69.4	64.9	**68.7**

Table 4: QE accuracy (%) on error types related to verb types

all the error categories. The fact that different QE systems with similar overall scores perform differently at various phenomena confirms the usefulness of the Test Suite for understanding their comparative performance.

Such linguistically-motivated evaluation can be useful in many aspects. The development or improvement of QE systems may use the results about the found errors in order to introduce new related features. The development may also be aided by testing these improvements on an isolated development set.

Further work should include the expansion of the Test Suite with more samples in the less-populated categories and support for other language pairs. Finally, we would ideally like to broaden the comparison among QE systems, by including other state-of-the-art ones that unfortunately were not freely available to test.

Acknowledgments

Part of this work has received funding from the EU Horizon 2020 research and innovation program QT21 under grant agreement N° 645452.

References

Guillaume Wisniewski Anil and Kumar Singh Fran. 2013. Quality Estimation for Machine Translation: Some Lessons Learned. *Machine Translation* 27(3-4):213–238. https://link.springer.com/article/10.1007/s10590-013-9141-9.

Eleftherios Avramidis. 2016. Qualitative: Python Tool for MT Quality Estimation Supporting Server Mode and Hybrid MT. *The Prague Bulletin of Mathematical Linguistics (PBML)* 106:147–158. https://ufal.mff.cuni.cz/pbml/106/art-avramidis.pdf.

Eleftherios Avramidis. 2017. Comparative Quality Estimation for Machine Translation: Observations on machine learning and features. *Proceedings of the 20th Annual Conference of the European Association for Machine Translation, The Prague Bulletin of Mathematical Linguistics* (108):307–318. https://doi.org/10.1515/pralin-2017-0029.

Eleftherios Avramidis and Maja Popović. 2013. Machine learning methods for comparative and time-oriented Quality Estimation of Machine Translation output. In *Proceedings of the Eighth Workshop on Statistical Machine Translation*. Association for Computational Linguistics, Sofia, Bulgaria, pages 329–336. http://www.aclweb.org/anthology/W13-2240.

Ondej Bojar, Christian Buck, Chris Callison-Burch, Christian Federmann, Barry Haddow, Philipp Koehn, Christof Monz, Matt Post, Radu Soricut, and Lucia Specia. 2013. Findings of the 2013 Workshop on Statistical Machine Translation. In *Proceedings of the Eighth Workshop on Statistical Machine Translation*. Association for Computational Linguistics, Sofia, Bulgaria, pages 12–58. https://doi.org/10.3115/1626431.1626433.

Ondej Bojar, Rajen Chatterjee, Christian Federmann, Yvette Graham, Barry Haddow, Shujian Huang, Matthias Huck, Philipp Koehn, Qun Liu, Varvara Logacheva, Christof Monz, Matteo Negri, Matt Post, Raphael Rubino, Lucia Specia, and Marco Turchi. 2017. Findings of the 2017 Conference on Machine Translation (WMT17). In *Proceedings of the Second Conference on Machine Translation, Volume 2: Shared Task Papers*. Association for Computational Linguistics, Copenhagen, Denmark, pages 169–214. http://www.aclweb.org/anthology/W17-4717.

Aljoscha Burchardt, Vivien Macketanz, Jon Dehdari, Georg Heigold, Jan-Thorsten Peter, and Philip Williams. 2017. A Linguistic Evaluation of Rule-Based, Phrase-Based, and Neural MT Engines. *The Prague Bulletin of Mathematical Linguistics* 108:159–170. https://doi.org/10.1515/pralin-2017-0017.

Mariano Felice and Lucia Specia. 2012. Linguistic Features for Quality Estimation. In *Proceedings of the Seventh Workshop on Statistical Machine Translation*. Association for Computational Linguistics, Montréal, Canada, pages 96–103. http://www.aclweb.org/anthology/W12-3110.

Pierre Isabelle, Colin Cherry, and George Foster. 2017. A Challenge Set Approach to Evaluating Machine Translation. In *EMNLP 2017: Conference on Empirical Methods in Natural Language Processing*. http://arxiv.org/abs/1704.07431.

Margaret King and Kirsten Falkedal. 1990. Using test suites in evaluation of machine translation systems. *Proceedings of the 13th conference on Computational linguistics - 2*:211–216. https://doi.org/10.3115/997939.997976.

Arle Lommel, Aljoscha Burchardt, Maja Popović, Kim Harris, Eleftherios Avramidis, and Hans Uszkoreit. 2014. Using a new analytic measure for the annotation and analysis of MT errors on real data. In *Proceedings of the 17th Annual Conference of the European Association for Machine Translation (EAMT-14)*. Croatian Language Technologies Society, European Association for Machine Translation, pages 165–172. http://www.mt-archive.info/10/EAMT-2014-Lommel.pdf.

Joaquin Quionero-Candela, Masashi Sugiyama, Anton Schwaighofer, and Neil Lawrence. 2009. *Dataset shift in machine learning*. MIT Press.

Rico Sennrich, Alexandra Birch, Anna Currey, Ulrich Germann, Barry Haddow, Kenneth Heafield, Antonio Valerio Miceli Barone, and Philip Williams. 2017. The University of Edinburgh's Neural MT Systems for WMT17. In *Proceedings of the Second Conference on Machine Translation, Volume 2: Shared Task Papers*. Association for Computational Linguistics, Copenhagen, Denmark, pages 389–399. http://www.aclweb.org/anthology/W17-4739.

Kashif Shah, Eleftherios Avramidis, Ergun Biçici, and Lucia Specia. 2013. QuEst: Design, Implementation and Extensions of a Framework for Machine Translation Quality Estimation. *The Prague Bulletin of Mathematical Linguistics* 100:19–30. https://doi.org/10.2478/pralin-2013-0008.PBML.

A Comparison of Machine Translation Paradigms
for Use in Black-Box Fuzzy-Match Repair

Rebecca Knowles
Department of Computer Science
Johns Hopkins University
rknowles@jhu.edu

John E. Ortega
Dept. de Llenguatges
i Sistemes Informàtics
Universitat d'Alacant
jeo10@alu.ua.es

Philipp Koehn
Department of Computer Science
Johns Hopkins University
phi@jhu.edu

Abstract

Fuzzy-match repair (FMR), which combines a human-generated translation memory (TM) with the flexibility of machine translation (MT), is one way of using MT to augment resources available to translators. We evaluate rule-based, phrase-based, and neural MT systems as black-box sources of bilingual information for FMR. We show that FMR success varies based on both the quality of the MT system and the type of MT system being used.

1 Introduction

Translation memories (TM) play a key role in computer-aided translation (CAT) tools: helping translators to reuse past work (i.e. when translating highly-repetitive texts) by showing them parallel language resources similar to the text at hand (Bowker, 2002). A TM consists of pairs of segments in the source and target language that were produced by past human translation work. In this work, we focus on the *fuzzy-match repair* (FMR)[1] task: automatically modifying target-language TM text before providing it to the human translator, a task similar to automatic post-editing.

Given a new source segment s' to translate, a CAT tool can provide the translator with the best fuzzy-match segment s found in the TM and its corresponding validated translation segment t. The translator can modify mismatched sub-segments[2] of t to produce a correct translation of the new segment s', rather than translating it from scratch. The goal of FMR is to use a source of bilingual information (for example, a dictionary, MT system, phrase table, etc.) to translate the mismatched sub-segments and correctly combine them with the target segment prior to presenting it to the translator. Delivering a correctly repaired segment should save the human translator time, by decreasing the number of changes they need to make in order to complete the translation. A "perfectly" repaired segment would require no changes from the translator.

Ortega et al. (2014) and Ortega et al. (2016) present an algorithm for fuzzy-match repair (FMR) using any source of bilingual information (SBI) as a black-box. Using Apertium (Forcada et al., 2011) as their black-box machine translation (MT) system, they find that the best fuzzy-match repaired segments are closer to the reference translations than either MT or TM alone. We extend that work by comparing three types of MT systems (rule-based, phrase-based, and neural) as the source of bilingual information and by examining the way that both MT system quality and type impact performance.

We begin with a discussion of related work. In Sections 3 and 4, we describe the algorithm used in FMR and the MT systems we tested as sources of bilingual information, respectively. Then, in Section 5 we show that while phrase-based statistical machine translation (henceforth SMT) and neural MT (henceforth NMT) systems both outperform a rule-based (RB) system, these two types of systems perform in markedly different ways as black-box input to the FMR system.

2 Related Work

Attempting to "repair" and propose translations that are closer to the desired translation is a common approach to combining TMs and MT. Simard and Isabelle (2009); He et al. (2010); Koehn and Senellart (2010) all combine TMs and statistical MT in ways that require either a glass-box or explicitly modified MT.

Our work focuses on ways of applying *any* MT system to the task of FMR, without requiring knowledge of the system's inner workings. We use the approach from Ortega et al. (2016) (described in more detail in Section 3). That particular fuzzy-match repair system allows the CAT tool to use any source of bilingual information, but in their publications, they focus only on Apertium (Forcada et al., 2011) as the source of bilingual information. Their work, as well as ours in this paper, depends on an oracle evaluation. In order to be truly useful in a live system, FMR will require some form of quality estimation in order to select the best repaired segment. Research in that area is ongoing.

---

[1] Or fuzzy-match post-editing (Kranias and Samiotou, 2004). The use of the term "fuzzy-match" references the fuzzy-match score used to find similar source sentences.

[2] Throughout this work, we refer to a complete line of text as a *segment* (rather than a sentence, as a number of the lines of text in the data we use do not constitute full grammatical sentences, but may include things like titles). Sequences of one or more tokens within the segment are *sub-segments*.

In the trade-off between adequacy (translations with the same meaning as the source) and fluency (translations that sound fluid or natural), neural machine translation systems, tend towards greater fluency, while sometimes producing fluent-sounding but semantically inappropriate output (Bojar et al., 2016; Koehn and Knowles, 2017; Toral and Sánchez-Cartagena, 2017). In the FMR application, the full segment from the translation memory may already provide the (fluent) backbone for the translation, while only containing a few subsegment mismatches (such as numbers, names, noun phrases, and so on). This differs from automatic post-editing, where there may be structural issues to repair as a result of errors in the machine translation output. All of this naturally raises the question of how rule-based MT (which may provide greater adequacy for individual subsegments) will compare to neural MT systems (which may provide greater fluency) or phrase-based statistical MT systems (which may fall between the two) for the task of FMR. We also address the question of how NMT systems, which are particularly sensitive to changes in domain or style (Koehn and Knowles, 2017) will perform when used to translate sub-segments rather than full sentences.

Neural MT systems have recently produced state-of-the-art performance across a number of language pairs (Bojar et al., 2017). While NMT has been applied to other CAT applications, namely interactive translation prediction, (Knowles and Koehn, 2016; Wuebker et al., 2016) and neural approaches have been used for automatic post-editing (Pal et al., 2016; Junczys-Dowmunt and Grundkiewicz, 2016; Hokamp, 2017), this is the first work we are aware of that uses NMT for FMR.

3 Black-Box MT for FMR

Here we provide an overview of an algorithm for using black-box MT for FMR. For full details, see Ortega et al. (2016) (Sections 2 and 3), whose algorithm we follow. Black-box approaches allow one system to be used for many tasks, rather than requiring specially-tailored MT systems for every task.

Given a new source-language sentence s' to translate, the FMR system selects (by fuzzy-match score, or FMS) the source-target pair of segments (s, t) from the TM that most closely matches s'. The FMS takes on values between 0% (entire segment requires edits) to 100% (segments identical). A common definition of FMS[3] is given by:

$$\text{FMS}(s, s') = \left(1 - \frac{\text{ED}(s, s')}{\max(|s|, |s'|)}\right) \times 100\% \quad (1)$$

where $\text{ED}(s, s')$ is the (word-based) *edit distance* or Levenshtein distance (Wagner and Fischer, 1974) and $|s|$ and $|s'|$ are the lengths (in tokens) of s and s'. Edit distance is used to find mismatches between s' and s. Sub-segment pairs (σ, σ') containing at least a mismatched word are extracted (via phrase-pair extraction

---

[3]CAT providers often use proprietary variations of FMS.

(Koehn, 2009)) from s and s' respectively. The (σ, σ') are passed to the black-box MT system for translation, producing output translations (μ, μ'). To constrain the set which can be used for repairs, any pair (μ, μ') for which μ is not found in t is discarded. The remaining (μ, μ') pairs are then used to "patch" or repair t, by swapping the μ found in t for the new μ' in the hopes of editing t into an accurate translation of s'. More than one such patching action can be applied in the process of forming the final repaired segment, and the system may output multiple unique final repaired segments (using different subsets of the set of available (μ, μ') pairs).

4 Data and Machine Translation Systems

We compare representatives of three MT paradigms: Apertium (rule-based, or RB), Moses (phrase-based SMT) and Nematus (NMT with attention).[4] Test data for the FMR experiments is drawn from the 2015 DGT-TM data set which is composed of highly-repetitive and formal official legal acts and is lowercased in post-processing (Steinberger et al., 2012). We choose English to Spanish as the language pair and translation direction.[5]

4.1 Rule-Based MT (Apertium)

Apertium (Forcada et al., 2011) is a rule-based (RB) machine translation system, which performs translation using a pipeline of components: a morphological analyzer, a part of speech tagger, a lexical transfer module (which uses a bilingual dictionary to translate lexical forms from source language to target), and a structural transfer module (which performs syntactic operations). We use a recent version[6] as a baseline.

4.2 Neural MT (Nematus)

We use the attention-based encoder-decoder Nematus (Sennrich et al., 2017) and the compatible AmuNMT decoder[7] (Junczys-Dowmunt et al., 2016).

Initial model training is done using Europarl v7 (Koehn, 2005) and News Commentary v10 data[8] (WMT13 training data for English–Spanish), with 2012 News Test data for validation. Following the domain adaptation method described in Luong and Manning (2015) and Freitag and Al-Onaizan (2016), we continue training on DGT-TM 2011–2013, with 3000

---

[4]Due to limited space, we present the best system trained for each MT type. Other systems trained, which included ones trained on more directly comparable training data, showed the same trends.

[5] In Ortega et al. (2016), Apertium's Spanish–English was the lowest-performing language pair (as compared to Spanish–Portuguese and Spanish–French); we choose it here to demonstrate the range of improvement possible.

[6]http://apertium.org (en–es, SVN rev. 83165)

[7]Now part of Marian (https://github.com/marian-nmt/marian).

[8]http://www.casmacat.eu/corpus/news-commentary.html

lines from the 2014 release as validation data.[9]

We use these training parameters: vocabulary of size 50,000, word embedding layer size of 500, hidden layer size of 1000, batch size of 80, Adadelta (Zeiler, 2012) as the optimizer, maximum sentence length of 50, and default learning rate of 0.0001. All other parameters are set to Nematus defaults. Data is preproccessed with the standard preprocessing scripts: tokenization, truecasing, and byte pair encoding (Sennrich et al., 2016). We report scores with a beam size of 12.

4.3 Phrase-Based SMT (Moses)

We use Moses (Koehn et al., 2007) to train our phrase-based statistical MT (SMT) system using the same parallel text as the NMT model, with the addition of Common Crawl,[10] for phrase extraction. Europarl v7, News Commentary v10, monolingual News Crawl from 2007–2011, Spanish Gigaword v3 (Mendonça et al., 2011), and target side DGT-TM data were used to build a 5-gram interpolated language model.

We use an operation sequence model (Durrani et al., 2015) with order 5, Good-Turing discounting of phrase translation probabilities, binning of phrase pair counts, pruning of low-probability phrase pairs, and sparse features for target word insertion, deletion, and translation, and phrase length. Tuning is run on the same DGT-TM data used for NMT model validation.

5 Experiments and Results

5.1 MT System Quality

We first compare the MT systems in terms of both BLEU score and word error rate (WER)[11] on the task of translating the full segments from the 1993 segments of the 2015 DGT-TM test set used for evaluating FMR.[12] Results are shown in the right two columns of Table 1, under the heading "MT Output". Both the SMT and NMT systems report higher BLEU scores and lower WER than the RB system. The best performing system by these metrics is the SMT system, with a BLEU score of 57.2 and a WER of 35.2.

5.2 Oracle Fuzzy-Match Repair Results

At times the FMR system fails to repair a segment (e.g. if no set of sub-segment translations match the target-side TM segment) and at others it produces multiple patched segments. To handle the latter, we use the oracle evaluation approach from Ortega et al. (2016),

which, given a fuzzy-match score threshold θ (we use 60%, 70%, and 80% as values of θ), consists of:

1. For each segment s' in the test set, find the best segment pair (s, t) from the translation memory such that $\text{FMS}(s', s) \geq \theta$, if such a pair exists.[13]

2. If there exists such a pair (s, t), produce all possible FMR segments using that pair. Select the repaired segment with the lowest edit distance to the reference t' (oracle evaluation). If no repaired segment was produced through the FMR process (or no satisfactory pair (s, t) was found), produce a translation of s' using the MT system.

This would not be possible in a real use setting, as it requires access to the reference translation to determine which repaired segment has the lowest WER (with respect to the reference). Thus the oracle results represent the most optimistic case for fuzzy-match repair (the case where we can always select the optimal repaired segment when more than one is produced) possible within this fixed framework; quality estimation and ranking of hypotheses for a more real-world setting has been left for future work by Ortega et al. (2016). The challenge of combining several such CAT options is far from trivial (Forcada and Sánchez-Martínez, 2015); for example, we found that for high-quality MT systems, MT output can (under certain FMS thresholds) outperform the best FMR output upwards of 15% of the time.

Table 2 shows example segments: source and reference (s', t'), the best fuzzy-match from the TM (s, t), and the best output from the three MT systems. In this example, the SMT system produces the best repair, with a WER of 25.0% (as compared to the TM WER of 37.5%). The SMT system successfully inserts the desired translation (*formación*) of the mismatched word *training*, replacing *desarrollo*, but fails to add the token *los*, and doesn't change the translation of *promote*. This latter error is to be expected, since *promote* is a matching word across the source and TM source, so the system does not try to repair it.

Table 1 reports word error rate[14] over several subsets of the test set. In the *Match* columns, the score is computed based on a subset of the full data: for each fuzzy-match threshold θ (60%, 70%, and 80%) we select the segments for which a fuzzy-match could be found in the TM (such that fuzzy-match score $\geq \theta\%$), and apply FMR (in the event that FMR does not successfully produce a repair, we instead back off to the unmodified

---

[9]As the fuzzy-match repair scenario assumes that no sentences from that test set have been observed in the TM, we remove exact test set matches from DGT-TM training data.

[10]Available at `http://www.statmt.org/wmt13/translation-task.html`

[11]Computed over the full corpus as $\frac{\sum_i ED(t_i, r_i)}{\sum_i |r_i|}$, where ED is the Levenshtein edit distance and r_i is the ith reference in the corpus.

[12]The initial set consisted of 2000 segments, of which 7 were discarded for being longer than 100 tokens.

[13]Note that we use the fuzzy-match score solely on the source side. Esplà-Gomis et al. (2015) propose using an additional threshold of $|FMS(s', s) - FMS(t', t)| < \phi$ to lessen the incidence of correct repairs being marked as incorrect due to inconsistencies resulting from free translations (e.g. two different but equally appropriate translations of the same phrase appearing in s and s', respectively).

[14]The WER is again computed at the document level, as before, over the particular set of sentences as defined by the column of the table.

	60% FMT		70% FMT		80% FMT		MT Output	
Sys.	*Match*	*Full*	*Match*	*Full*	*Match*	*Full*	*WER, Full*	*BLEU, Full*
TM	20.8	-	16.7	-	13.4	-	-	-
RB	18.5	37.5	15.0	39.6	12.2	43.7	60.8	19.2
SMT	15.6	26.7	12.7	27.3	10.4	27.9	35.2	57.2
NMT	15.2	27.1	12.0	26.8	9.4	28.5	36.8	52.6

Table 1: The left section of the table contains word error rates for fuzzy-match repair. In the *Match* columns, the score is computed based on a subset of the full data: 60% Fuzzy-Match Threshold (1184 segments for which a fuzzy-match could be found in the TM with fuzzy-match score $\geq$ 60%), 70% Fuzzy-Match Threshold (828 segments), and 80% Fuzzy-Match Threshold (660 segments), with the oracle best fuzzy-match repaired segment scored, backing off to the TM if no repair was successful. In the *Full* column, the data from the corresponding *Match* column backs off to MT output when no TM segment with a sufficiently high FMS is available.The rightmost sections (MT Output) contain BLEU scores and WER for machine translation output of the full data set.

s':src	promote human resources training;
t':ref	promover la formación de los recursos humanos;
s:TM	promote human resources development;
t:TM	fomentar el desarrollo de los recursos humanos;
RB	fomentar el desarrollo de los los recursos humanos que entrenan;
SMT	fomentar la formación de recursos humanos;
NMT	fomentar los recursos humanos;

Table 2: Example segments, showing the best fuzzy-match repaired segments for three MT systems.

TM segment). In the *Full* column, the data from the corresponding *Match* column backs off to MT output when no TM segment with a sufficiently high FMS is available. The *WER, Full* column under the MT Output heading in Table 1 can be compared directly to any of the *Full* columns. We see that FMR with either SMT or NMT outperforms all pure MT utput (across all three system types). The worst FMR performance between those two systems is the NMT at the 80% fuzzy-match threshold with a WER of 28.5 on *Full* data, yet this still outperforms even the best MT output with its WER of 35.2. This underscores the potential usefulness of FMR.

Interestingly, despite having worse BLEU scores and WER on full-sentence translations, the NMT system actually outperformed the SMT system as a source of bilingual information for FMR on the subsets of data for which TM matches were found. The better full-data performance of the SMT system can be attributed to backing off to (better) MT output when no TM best-match was available. All of the MT systems outperform the no-repair TM baseline WER (in which we simply computed WER for the best fuzzy-matches from the TM, without any repairs).

5.3 Analysis

The NMT system performs best for FMR on matches and it also is more often successful at repairing segments. This raises two questions: Are the improvements solely or primarily due to successfully repairing more sentences? (Section 5.3.1) Why do the neural systems succeed in repairing more sentences? (Section 5.3.2) We focus on comparing SMT and NMT, due to their stronger performance over the RB system.

5.3.1 Direct Comparison

At the 60% FMT level, the SMT system successfully produced repairs for 788 segments, while the NMT system successfully produced repairs for 957 segments (out of a possible 1184 segments).[15] Since those are two distinct sets of segments, we cannot directly compare WER. We first examine the intersection of those sets (the subset of segments for which both systems successfully performed FMR).

A total of 754 segments were successfully repaired by both systems. There were 34 segments which the SMT system repaired and the NMT system did not, and 203 segments for which the opposite was true. Of the 754 segments repaired by both, 212 were repaired better by the NMT system, 139 were repaired better by the SMT system, and 403 were repaired equally well by the two MT systems (all in terms of WER). Computing the WER over this shared 754 segment set, we find that the WER of the SMT system (14.4%) is quite close to that of the NMT system (14.3%). This suggests that the NMT system's ability to patch more sentences plays a major role in its better FMR results.

The NMT system produced an average of 1.92 possible repaired segments per source segment (standard deviation: 1.29, maximum: 9). Using the SMT system, an average of 1.68 possible repaired segments were produced per source segment (standard deviation: 0.92, maximum: 7). In a real-world setting, the system would need to choose between more repaired options for the NMT system than the SMT system.

To see how important it is to select the best repaired segment, we compare the optimistic oracle approach to a pessimistic one, where for each of the 754 segments, we select the repaired segment with the highest WER (the *worst* possible outcome). For this set of segments, the TM baseline WER is 20.6%. When we choose the

---

[15]Professional translators typically use higher fuzzy-match thresholds, but we select 60% in this section to provide the greatest amount of data for direct comparison of repairs.

worst repaired segments produced by the NMT system, the WER is 20.5%, which is very close to the TM baseline. The WER for the SMT system appears slightly better, at 19.0%. Both represent a large drop from the optimistic oracle, but the drop is greater for the NMT system.

5.3.2 Analysis of Sub-Segment Translations

We examine the sub-segment translations produced by the NMT and SMT systems to gain insight about what allows that NMT system to repair more segments and produce more possible repaired versions per segment.

Without gold references for the sub-segment translations, we cannot evaluate them in terms of WER or BLEU, so we examine them quantitatively and qualitatively. First, we look at the lengths of the translations of the sub-segments. For both the SMT and NMT systems, the translations tend to be longer than the source sub-segments (64% of the time for the SMT system and 58% of the time for the NMT system). The NMT system produces translations that are shorter than the source 23% of the time, while the SMT system does so 18% of the time. They also differ in the range of lengths; the NMT system has more extreme values, sometimes producing no translation at all and even occasionally producing translations more than three times the length of the longest source segments. On average, the SMT translations are 2.37 tokens longer than the source sub-segments (SD.: 3.95). The NMT translations average 2.71 tokens longer than the source, with a much greater standard deviation of 10.26. The very long NMT translations may be more likely to be discarded (due to not matching), but the very short translations may be easier to find matches for in the TM target side, contributing to the larger number of sentences the NMT system patches.

We also note a qualitative difference: the SMT systems often add additional punctuation that was not included in the source, as well as determiners. These spurious tokens could make it harder to find matches in the TM target segments, resulting in fewer opportunities for fuzzy-match repair. This could be caused by the language model providing higher scores to the phrases that include those tokens.

5.4 Discussion

The sub-segments which need to be translated for fuzzy-match repair are not complete always segments, but often sub-segments which could be taken from any point in the original segment. Each sub-segment is then translated using the MT system, without full context (though Ortega et al. (2014) do note that the context provided by using "anchored" subsegments—those that have overlap with the matching subsegments—improves performance over non-anchored subsegments).[16] This poses a potential challenge for any MT system which is trained on full segments. In the case of the SMT system, the language model may prefer sub-segment translations that include, for example, determiners or additional punctuation, as we observed. NMT systems have been observed to do a poor job of handling data that differs from the original training data, often producing fluent-seeming text that has little to do with the source. While this mismatch does not seem to have had a strong negative impact on the overall results, it is possible that the results could still improve if the sub-segmental input were better matched to the training data. There would be several ways to do this. The first would be to produce parallel sub-segment data (using phrase alignments) and use this instead of the full sentences for domain adaptation. Another alternative (though it would require changes to the MT system, violating the goal of a black-box system) would be to always provide the MT system with access to the full context surrounding or preceding the segment to be translated, which it could use as a better starting state to generate the segment's translation.

6 Conclusions

We show that three very different types of machine translation can successfully be used in the black-box fuzzy-match repair approach described in Ortega et al. (2016). We find that despite lower BLEU scores on full-sentence translations, in the oracle evaluation, NMT systems outperform phrase-based SMT systems as sources of bilingual information for fuzzy-match repair (potentially surprising, given that the task requires translation of sub-segments). However, the greater variance in NMT results suggests a need for caution when deciding what type of MT system to use as a black-box, and underscores the need for work on quality estimation for real-world use in CAT tools.

Acknowledgments

This work was partially supported by a National Science Foundation Graduate Research Fellowship under Grant No. DGE-1232825 (to the first author) and by the Spanish government through the EFFORTUNE (TIN2015-69632-R) project (the second author). We thank the reviewers for their comments and suggestions, and Mikel Forcada and Felipe Martínez for useful comments on an early version of this work.

---

[16]We ran a brief set of experiments on the XML markup method described in Koehn and Senellart (2010), for which we omit detail due to space constraints. We found that on the sentences whose TM best-matches met or exceeded the 60% threshold, the XML method improved slightly over the TM baseline. This is in contrast to what Koehn and Senellart (2010) observed in their original work (namely, that the XML method only improved over the TM and MT output in terms of BLEU score for higher fuzzy-match thresholds).

References

Ondřej Bojar, Rajen Chatterjee, Christian Federmann, Yvette Graham, Barry Haddow, Shujian Huang, Matthias Huck, Philipp Koehn, Qun Liu, Varvara Logacheva, et al. 2017. Findings of the 2017 conference on machine translation (WMT17). In *Proceedings of the Second Conference on Machine Translation*, pages 169–214.

Ondřej Bojar, Rajen Chatterjee, Christian Federmann, Yvette Graham, Barry Haddow, Matthias Huck, Antonio Jimeno Yepes, Philipp Koehn, Varvara Logacheva, Christof Monz, Matteo Negri, Aurelie Neveol, Mariana Neves, Martin Popel, Matt Post, Raphael Rubino, Carolina Scarton, Lucia Specia, Marco Turchi, Karin Verspoor, and Marcos Zampieri. 2016. Findings of the 2016 conference on machine translation. In *Proceedings of the First Conference on Machine Translation*, pages 131–198, Berlin, Germany. Association for Computational Linguistics.

Lynne Bowker. 2002. *Computer-Aided Translation Technology: A Practical Introduction*. University of Ottawa Press.

Nadir Durrani, Hassan Sajjad, Shafiq Joty, Ahmed Abdelali, and Stephan Vogel. 2015. Using joint models for domain adaptation in statistical machine translation. *Proceedings of MT Summit XV*, page 117.

Miquel Esplà-Gomis, Felipe Sánchez-Martínez, and Mikel L. Forcada. 2015. Using machine translation to provide target-language edit hints in computer aided translation based on translation memories. *J. Artif. Int. Res.*, 53(1):169–222.

Mikel L. Forcada, Mireia Ginestí-Rosell, Jacob Nordfalk, Jim O'Regan, Sergio Ortiz-Rojas, Juan Antonio Pérez-Ortiz, Felipe Sánchez-Martínez, Gema Ramírez-Sánchez, and Francis M. Tyers. 2011. Apertium: a free/open-source platform for rule-based machine translation. *Machine Translation*, 25(2):127–144.

Mikel L Forcada and Felipe Sánchez-Martínez. 2015. A general framework for minimizing translation effort: towards a principled combination of translation technologies in computer-aided translation. In *Proceedings of the 18th Annual Conference of the European Association for Machine Translation*, pages 27–34.

Markus Freitag and Yaser Al-Onaizan. 2016. Fast domain adaptation for neural machine translation. *arXiv preprint arXiv:1612.06897*.

Y. He, Y. Ma, J. van Genabith, and A. Way. 2010. Bridging SMT and TM with translation recommendation. In *Proceedings of the 48th Annual Meeting of the Association for Computational Linguistics*, pages 622–630, Uppsala, Sweden.

Chris Hokamp. 2017. Ensembling factored neural machine translation models for automatic post-editing and quality estimation. In *Proceedings of the Second Conference on Machine Translation*, pages 647–654.

Marcin Junczys-Dowmunt, Tomasz Dwojak, and Hieu Hoang. 2016. Is neural machine translation ready for deployment? A case study on 30 translation directions. *CoRR*, abs/1610.01108.

Marcin Junczys-Dowmunt and Roman Grundkiewicz. 2016. Log-linear combinations of monolingual and bilingual neural machine translation models for automatic post-editing. In *Proceedings of the First Conference on Machine Translation*, pages 751–758, Berlin, Germany. Association for Computational Linguistics.

Rebecca Knowles and Philipp Koehn. 2016. Neural interactive translation prediction. In *Proceedings of the Conference of the Association for Machine Translation in the Americas (AMTA)*.

Philipp Koehn. 2005. Europarl: A parallel corpus for statistical machine translation. In *MT summit*, volume 5, pages 79–86.

Philipp Koehn. 2009. *Statistical machine translation*. Cambridge University Press.

Philipp Koehn, Hieu Hoang, Alexandra Birch, Chris Callison-Burch, Marcello Federico, Nicola Bertoldi, Brooke Cowan, Wade Shen, Christine Moran, Richard Zens, Chris Dyer, Ondřej Bojar, Alexandra Constantin, and Evan Herbst. 2007. Moses: Open source toolkit for statistical machine translation. In *Proceedings of the 45th Annual Meeting of the ACL on Interactive Poster and Demonstration Sessions*, ACL '07, pages 177–180, Stroudsburg, PA, USA. Association for Computational Linguistics.

Philipp Koehn and Rebecca Knowles. 2017. Six challenges for neural machine translation. In *Proceedings of the First Workshop on Neural Machine Translation*, pages 28–39, Vancouver. Association for Computational Linguistics.

Philipp Koehn and Jean Senellart. 2010. Convergence of translation memory and statistical machine translation. In *Proceedings of AMTA Workshop on MT Research and the Translation Industry*, pages 21–31.

Lambros Kranias and Anna Samiotou. 2004. Automatic translation memory fuzzy match post-editing: A step beyond traditional TM/MT integration. In *LREC*.

Minh-Thang Luong and Christopher D Manning. 2015. Stanford neural machine translation systems for spoken language domains. In *Proceedings of the International Workshop on Spoken Language Translation*.

Ângelo Mendonça, Daniel Jaquette, David Graff, and Denise DiPersio. 2011. Spanish gigaword third edition ldc2011t12. Web Download. Philadelphia: Linguistic Data Consortium.

John E Ortega, Felipe Sánchez-Martınez, and Mikel L Forcada. 2014. Using any machine translation source for fuzzy-match repair in a computer-aided translation setting. In *Proceedings of the 11th Biennial Conference of the Association for Machine Translation in the Americas (AMTA 2014*, volume 1, pages 42–53.

John E. Ortega, Felipe Sánchez-Martínez, and Mikel L. Forcada. 2016. Fuzzy-match repair using black-box machine translation systems: what can be expected? In *Proceedings of the 12th Biennial Conference of the Association for Machine Translation in the Americas (AMTA 2016, vol. 1: MT Researchers' Track)*, pages 27–39, Austin, TX, USA.

Santanu Pal, Sudip Kumar Naskar, Mihaela Vela, and Josef van Genabith. 2016. A neural network based approach to automatic post-editing. In *Proceedings of the 54th Annual Meeting of the Association for Computational Linguistics (Volume 2: Short Papers)*, pages 281–286, Berlin, Germany. Association for Computational Linguistics.

Rico Sennrich, Orhan Firat, Kyunghyun Cho, Alexandra Birch, Barry Haddow, Julian Hitschler, Marcin Junczys-Dowmunt, Samuel L"aubli, Antonio Valerio Miceli Barone, Jozef Mokry, and Maria Nadejde. 2017. Nematus: a Toolkit for Neural Machine Translation. In *Proceedings of the Demonstrations at the 15th Conference of the European Chapter of the Association for Computational Linguistics*, Valencia, Spain.

Rico Sennrich, Barry Haddow, and Alexandra Birch. 2016. Neural machine translation of rare words with subword units. In *Proceedings of the 54th Annual Meeting of the Association for Computational Linguistics (Volume 1: Long Papers)*, pages 1715–1725, Berlin, Germany. Association for Computational Linguistics.

Michel Simard and Pierre Isabelle. 2009. Phrase-based machine translation in a computer-assisted translation environment. *Proceeding of the Twelfth Machine Translation Summit (MT Summit XII)*, pages 120–127.

Ralf Steinberger, Andreas Eisele, Szymon Klocek, Spyridon Pilos, and Patrick Schlüter. 2012. DGT-TM: A freely available translation memory in 22 languages. In *Proceedings of the 8th International Conference on Language Resources and Evaluation (LREC'2012)*, Istanbul.

Antonio Toral and Víctor M. Sánchez-Cartagena. 2017. A multifaceted evaluation of neural versus phrase-based machine translation for 9 language directions. In *Proceedings of the 15th Conference of the European Chapter of the Association for Computational Linguistics: Volume 1, Long Papers*, pages 1063–1073, Valencia, Spain. Association for Computational Linguistics.

Robert A Wagner and Michael J Fischer. 1974. The string-to-string correction problem. *Journal of the ACM (JACM)*, 21(1):168–173.

Joern Wuebker, Spence Green, John DeNero, Sasa Hasan, and Minh-Thang Luong. 2016. Models and inference for prefix-constrained machine translation. In *Proceedings of the 54th Annual Meeting of the Association for Computational Linguistics (Volume 1: Long Papers)*, pages 66–75, Berlin, Germany. Association for Computational Linguistics.

Matthew D Zeiler. 2012. Adadelta: an adaptive learning rate method. *arXiv preprint arXiv:1212.5701*.